PLANNING
FOR
FAMILY BUSINESS SUCCESSION

PLANNING
FOR
FAMILY BUSINESS SUCCESSION

Niall Glynn

VARSITY

Planning for Family Business Succession
© 2011 Deloitte Ireland

First Published in 2011 by The Varsity Press
A CIP Catalogue record for this book is available from The British Library
ISBN: **978-1-908417-05-3**

Designed and typeset in Ireland by The Book Producers
Printed and bound in Ireland by The Varsity Press Group

www.thevarsitypress.com

CONTENTS

<

FOREWORDS

Running a "normal" business of any kind is complicated at the best of times. You have to coordinate your suppliers, your production, your sales, your IT systems, your accounts, your human resources, your customer relations, your marketing, and your public relations, not to mention tax. At the same time, you have to plan for the future by crystal ball gazing, in order to work out where your business is going to be in two or five years time. Then you have come up with a strategy, a plan to get there, and all that is just for a "normal" business.

Now take all the issues that affect any family, like parent child relationships, sibling relationships, marital relationships, not to mention illness, death, education, in-laws, family tradition and values – and overlay them on top of the "normal" business structure. What have you got? Probably the most complicated structure known to man: The Family Business.

And yet family businesses make up 70% of all business worldwide. They are the cornerstone of most economies and employ more people than any other type of business. It always amazes me that in that context, there is not more literature on family businesses. This book covers many aspects of family business that need to be covered, and I congratulate Niall Glynn, Deloitte and everyone else involved.

G. Alan Crosbie
Chairman Thomas Crosbie Holdings Limited
Author of *"Don't Leave it to the Children"*

Since its foundation in 1859, John Sisk & Son has evolved from being a small family construction business in Cork to become the large diversified international company – SISK Group today. Our business is now owned by the fifth generation of the Sisk family and their goal is to continue to grow the business for future generations. Looking back on that evolution brings into focus some of the factors that can allow family businesses to thrive through recessions, wars and other events that many other businesses do not survive.

The biggest factor in our longevity is undoubtedly the fact that being a family business enables us to take a long term view on strategy. A family business is focussed less on quarterly results and more on long-term value creation. So with a long history in the construction sector behind the business, the Sisk family felt in 2004 that the extraordinary success of the construction sector in Ireland was not necessarily a sustainable business model. They chose to diversify and expand, investing in the future and providing for security in the wake of a correction in Irish construction activity levels. This strategy was not necessarily new to the Group as we have a history of diversifying and travelling particularly in difficult economic times. We have strengthened the Group, reduced the risk associated with over reliance on one sector and geography and diversified to ensure we protected the business for future generations. It was the kind of long-term strategic decision that family businesses in general and this family business in particular, are good at taking.

Everyone working in the business knows who the Sisk family are and understands the company's and family's values. The family's values are reflected throughout the business from areas such as corporate social responsibility to staff retention – people stay with us for the long term and many families work with us for many generations. I can readily identify with many of the principles outlined in this book when they reflect on the ethos of family businesses and on how a family's vision can provide a unified corporate strategy for all stakeholders. Our vision is to create a diversified business built around our historic strengths and culture that delivers value for all stakeholders including family, staff and our clients.

The requirements of good corporate governance as detailed by Niall Glynn are reflected in our own business model with appropriate interaction between family and management. We have the experience of working with good family shareholders, the primary characteristic involving them playing an active, committed role, that is taken seriously and that makes a real contribution to the company but leaves freedom of action to the people empowered to deliver the day to day business and manage the strategic development of the Group.

Family businesses have been the subject of research the world over, based around what makes them so different from other businesses be it in the areas of corporate governance, performance, conflict resolution or compensation policies. This book details in a systematic way many of the issues that arise within family businesses irrespective of their scale. The importance of good planning comes through from many of the contributions. Many of these issues will arise in a succession situation. Long term family business's must ensure there is shrewd stewardship coupled with appropriate planning that the senior generation in a family business must engage in if it is to thrive and succeed for generations. Deloitte have produced a publication which will be of benefit to many family business owners as they come to terms with the steps needed to be taken in their business to ensure its continued success under the ownership of the next generation.

Liam Nagle
CEO SISK Group

As a firm, we have a significant history of dealing with family businesses. I have benefited from and enjoyed my interaction with many family business owners, each of whom in their own unique way, often with our assistance, negotiated many of the issues mentioned in this publication.

In the global economic environment, one might ask what the relevance of family businesses is. In both developed and emerging economies, they are a prime source of wealth creation and employment. The attraction of a family business career has improved in reaction to the lack of job security offered by large corporations, many individuals being attracted to the corporate values evident in many family controlled businesses. In addition, entrepreneurial activity is seen as an important contributor to domestic economic growth.

Family businesses have many positives for those who participate in them. Career options in family firms for both family and non-family professionals can be interesting. Even in larger businesses, the idea of family can be firmly rooted with all stakeholders, with a significant impact on culture and leadership styles. After having advised in this area for only a short time, I quickly realised that family businesses have certain unique qualities, challenges and problems. Issues that arise in a family business context are only magnified in a succession situation. Unfortunately, that tends to be the one time when practically all the issues that can impact on a family business can arise simultaneously.

As advisors, we tend to do what it says on the tin quite well. For years, the focus on family business planning centred on management succession and estate issues, and many advisors continue in that vein, seeking solutions based on what they have done well or implemented in the past. Family businesses are becoming more sophisticated, and such an approach is, in our view, far too narrow for the family business of today. Each family is different and can require unique solutions. Wider issues around the strategy supporting the business during any period of transition, appropriate corporate governance structures, wealth management, self fulfilment of family members and legacy, can interact with advice of a more traditional nature.

The most important aspect – the emotional aspect – is often not given the attention it deserves. Understanding family dynamics and the emotional interplay or undercurrents is crucial in ensuring the best outcome for all stakeholders in a family business. Potentially conflicted relationships are illustrated well in this publication, coupled with numerous case studies which provide insightful comparatisons as to what happens in other families when they get it right or wrong as the case may be.

Despite the negativity often associated with the emotional issues potentially arising in a family business situation, the family's emotional bonds can, with planning and appropriate communication, become a powerful uniting factor in building a significant business and a strategic advantage. Succession is one of those areas where emotions will play a greater than normal part. Managing them well can have a greater and more cohesive impact than all the other constituent elements of your plan combined.

With life-cycle transitions, families can face continuous change and renegotiation of relationships. As illustrated throughout this publication, such events can be anticipated in advance and planned for. Amazingly, large numbers of family business owners fail to do so. If this book achieves one purpose, I hope it is that having read it, a family business owner no longer prevaricates, and takes the first steps towards ensuring the continuity of their business.

Brendan Jennings
Managing Partner – Deloitte

PUBLICATION TEAM

The Deloitte practice in Ireland originates from the amalgamation of a number of smaller firms, and is the most recently formed of the "Big 4" firms. Deloitte has a long history of acting for many family owned businesses, which provides us and our clients with a unique insight and unparalleled experience in the family business area.

The information, experiences, and legal and commercial structures outlined in this book benefit from over 100 years of practical professional experience of the Deloitte publication team, and leverage different specialties within the Deloitte practice and the knowledge gained from advising many clients who face the same issues as those outlined in this book. The publication team includes professionals with significant experience of acting as lead succession planning consultant, and professionals with specialist knowledge and experience of family businesses.

Author: Niall Glynn
Editors: Padraig Cronin, David Deasy, Brendan Jennings, David O'Flanagan, Joanne Whelan.

LEAD CONSULTANTS:

David Deasy is a Fellow of the Institute of Chartered Accountants in Ireland and a member of the Irish Taxation Institute, the Insolvency Practitioners Association and the Chartered Institute of Arbitrators. He has been a partner in Deloitte for 25 years and has extensive experience in advising substantial domestic clients, both privately owned and publicly held, particularly in the area of strategy. He also handles a varied audit portfolio.

David is a member of the executive committee responsible for the management of the firm. He has served on the technical committees of a number of professional bodies and is currently a member of a global Deloitte Touche Tohmatsu research working party.

David O'Flanagan is a corporate finance partner for Deloitte in Ireland. He has over twenty-five years experience advising on corporate finance matters, conducting significant advisory and due diligence assignments for major corporate and private equity clients involving acquisitions, disposals, joint ventures, PPP and project finance engagements both in Ireland and internationally.

David has been the lead project partner on a number of significant assignments for public sector entities, including the Department of Health & Children, the Financial Regulator and the Department of Education & Science. David also leads the firm's forensic and dispute resolution practice. David is a Fellow of the Institute of Chartered Accountants in Ireland and holds a diploma in Corporate Finance from the Institute of Chartered Accountants in England and Wales.

Niall Glynn is a tax partner with Deloitte. He specialises in capital taxes, domestic corporate reorganizations and shareholder issues. He has 15 years experience in advising in the taxation area, primarily providing advice to private domestic businesses, private companies and high net worth individuals on property transactions, domestic corporate reconstructions, investment structuring and asset/wealth protection, estate planning, tax efficient structuring of wills and trusts, family business reorganisations, asset disposals, extraction of value from companies, offshore structures and niche executive share schemes.

Niall is a practicing solicitor, a member of the Law Society of Ireland, a member of the Irish branch of the Society of Trust and Estate Practitioners, and an associate of the Irish Taxation Institute. He is a former examiner and lecturer for the Irish Taxation Institute and has also lectured and tutored on taxation issues for the Association of Chartered

Certified Accountants, the Institute of Incorporated Public Accountants, the Law Society's Law School, and joint courses run by the Society of Trust and Estate Practitioners and the Law Society. He is a former member of the taxation committee of the Law Society of Ireland.

SPECIALIST CONSULTANTS:

Pádraig Cronin is a tax partner and leads the Deloitte tax practice in Ireland. He specialises in advising multinationals, high growth Irish companies and private equity houses on mergers and acquisitions and general corporate tax matters. Pádraig has over 20 years corporate tax experience advising on a wide range of global tax issues including structuring of Irish operations for multinational corporations, foreign acquisition and disposal planning and mobile income planning. He is an expert in the areas of international tax, group reorganisations/joint ventures, property taxation and related incentives and outward investment by domestic groups.

Pádraig is an honours law graduate of National University of Ireland, Cork. He is a member of the Irish Taxation Institute and a Fellow of the Institute of Chartered Accountants in Ireland. He was named in the list of top tax advisors in Ireland in the International Tax Review Survey. Pádraig has written various articles for the Irish Taxation Review and the International Tax Review.

Brendan Jennings is the managing partner of Deloitte in Ireland. He previously served as the national partner in charge of audit services for the Irish firm. He has led the delivery of professional services to a broad range of national and multinational clients, and has been responsible for the provision of accounting advisory services to a number of Ireland's largest and most complex organisations. Brendan has worked with clients across a wide range of industryin a number of sectors and has assisted many growth organisations, with particular expertise in the consumer and retail sector. He has worked on client teams delivering many projects for these clients including, audit, risk services, acquisition support and fund raising, systems development and tax planning.

Brendan has a Bachelor of Commerce Degree, University College Galway and is a Fellow of the Institute of Chartered Accountants in Ireland. He is a member of the quality review committee of the Chartered Accountants Regulatory Body.

Joanne Whelan is a tax partner and is responsible for managing the firm's Private Client Service Line. Joanne also leads the Corporate and Legal department of the firm. She has extensive experience advising high net worth individuals and private individuals on tax and legal related issues. She has particular experience in relation to advising clients on transfers of wealth, succession and estate planning issues and tax efficient structuring of wills and trusts. Joanne is a practicing solicitor, a member of the Law Society of Ireland, a member of the Irish branch of the Society of Trust and Estate Practitioners and an associate of the Irish Taxation Institute.

Joanne has lectured on capital tax and estate planning matters. She has contributed to a number of professional publications including the Irish chapter of Estate Planning for UK Individuals Residing or Investing Abroad, and the capital tax chapter of Taxation in the Republic of Ireland, both published by Tolley Tax Intelligence. Joanne currently sits on the committee of the Irish branch of the Society of Trust and Estate Practitioners.

ABOUT DELOITTE

Deloitte refers to one or more of Deloitte Touche Tohmatsu Limited, a private company limited by guarantee, and its network of member firms, each of which is a legally separate and independent entity. Please see **www.deloitte.com/ie/about** for a detailed description of the legal structure of Deloitte Touche Tohmatsu Limited and its member firms.

Deloitte's 1,100 people in Dublin, Cork and Limerick provide audit, tax, consulting, and corporate finance to public and private clients spanning multiple industries. With a globally connected network of member firms in more than 150 countries, Deloitte brings world class capabilities and deep local expertise to help clients succeed wherever they operate. Deloitte's approximately 170,000 professionals are committed to becoming the standard of excellence.

This publication contains general information only, and none of Deloitte Touche Tohmatsu Limited, Deloitte Global Services Limited, Deloitte Global Services Holdings Limited, the Deloitte Touche Tohmatsu Verein, any of their member firms, or any of the foregoing's affiliates (collectively the "Deloitte Network") are, by means of this publication, rendering accounting, business, financial, investment, legal, tax, or other professional advice or services. This publication is not a substitute for such professional advice or services, nor should it be used as a basis for any decision or action that may affect your finances or your business. Before making any decision or taking any action that may affect your finances or your business, you should consult a qualified professional adviser. No entity in the Deloitte Network shall be responsible for any loss whatsoever sustained by any person who relies on this publication.

Deloitte Ireland is a world-class firm of expert business advisors, serving senior business leaders who are seeking to protect and create value in a complex, dynamic environment. Our objective is to help our clients succeed by anticipating tomorrow's agenda with focused, insightful and fresh thinking borne out of our multidisciplinary strengths. We draw upon our specialist skills in audit, tax, consulting and financial advisory both within Ireland and across the Deloitte worldwide network.

Deloitte is differentiated by its people, who focus on building long-term relationships and are determined to deliver measurable value for our clients' business. Deloitte's 1,152 people in Dublin, Cork and Limerick provide audit, tax, consulting, and corporate finance services to public and private clients spanning multiple industries. With a globally connected network of member firms in over 140 locations, Deloitte brings world-class capabilities and deep local expertise to help clients succeed wherever they operate.

Our multidisciplinary capability ensures that we have access to professionals with the right expertise and experience to provide a range of integrated audit, tax, consulting, and corporate finance services across all industry sectors. We have implemented a focused strategy to grow our market presence and this in turn has yielded considerable success, both in terms of marketplace recognition and client wins. For the ninth consecutive year, Deloitte was recognised as one of the 40 Best Workplaces in Ireland 2011.

Deloitte's global network of 169,000 professionals is committed to becoming the standard of excellence. Deloitte's professionals are unified by a collaborative culture that fosters integrity, outstanding value to markets and clients, commitment to each other, and strength from diversity. They enjoy an environment of continuous learning, challenging experiences, and enriching career opportunities. Deloitte's professionals are dedicated to strengthening corporate responsibility, building public trust, and making a positive impact in their communities.

Deloitte.

INTRODUCTION

The vast majority of family businesses do not plan adequately for succession. Family owned firms make up 90% of the indigenous business sector in Ireland and provide approximately 50% of all employment. According to a survey carried out by the Small Firms Association and Ulster Bank in 2008, 67% of owner-managers have no succession plan in place. Other studies show that only 27% of family businesses successfully pass to the second generation, and 13% to the third generation. Since such a significant portion of start-up businesses are owner managed or family owned, this is a worrying statistic. These statistics accord with Deloitte's own experience, and represent an accurate reflection of the general marketplace. These figures also seem to reflect the situation in other countries. This is by no means solely an Irish problem.

As most of the wealth generated in Ireland in recent years has primarily accrued at an entrepreneurial level, most of the wealth is first generational. Unlike the US and continental Europe, Ireland has not yet developed as sophisticated strategies for managing wealth and planning succession in a business context. Transferring the management or ownership of a business is a complex process, regardless of its size or scale. There are a myriad of financial, legal, commercial, tax and business issues to consider. Within a family owned business, there is the added emotional and personal complication of dealing with family members throughout the process.

Not having a succession plan in place creates several difficulties. The business may pass to family members who are unsuitable. The business may pass to family members who have the abilities to operate the business, but may not be the intended beneficiary of the business. The business may pass to a number of family members without any framework to resolve disputes among them, and without any framework to acknowledge the different roles they may take in the business. Some family members may be actively involved, while others are only shareholders. Not having a succession plan in place may result in tax liabilities being significantly higher than they need to be, placing a financing constraint on beneficiaries and invariably on the business. The beneficiaries may have no choice but to raise finance through the business, thus burdening the business with their tax liability.

The high level of first generational wealth in Ireland means that substantial wealth transfers can be anticipated in the next ten years. After successfully running businesses for many years, it is surprising how many owners of family-held businesses fail to effect a smooth transition of ownership and management of the business to the next generation. Surprising, but understandable, given the complexities involved. While many business owners will ultimately consider a sale of the business, too many of them will not consider steps needed to prepare the business for such sale, nor will they consider an appropriate retirement plan. Even in the case where business owners plan never to retire, a certain amount of planning is required to effect any ownership transfer under their will, and to protect the value of the business for the next generation. In all situations, it is critical that the next generation of management is identified and groomed to ensure the operational continuity of the business. While shares or ownership of the business may pass to family members, management may devolve to others who are more suited for that role.

Due to the complexities of succession planning, this book does not attempt to cover every conceivable scenario. It provides a broad analysis of issues that business owners should generally be aware of and take into account when considering an orderly transition. Although many of the principles discussed here concern the transition or succession to a family business, they also cover situations where the family no longer has any direct business involvement. For example, the family may have sold their previous business, but may still wish to continue holding assets through the historic corporate structure to deal with their accumulated wealth.

Many of the principles apply not just to the transition of a business, but also to the general transfer of wealth in the broader sense, and to the management of the relationship in that context.

STARTING THE PROCESS

In starting the process, there are a number of questions you need to consider:

— Have you identified your successor?

— Is he/she in place?

— Do they need managerial development or other talent development?

— Do you have a contingency plan in place should you become disabled?

— Do you have a shareholder agreement in place?

— Are you aware of the value of your business?

— Have you considered your overall corporate structure and how ownership will devolve as part of your overall succession goals?

— Have you determined your own personal goals and aspirations for the transfer of ownership and management?

— Do you have an appropriate retirement plan in place? When was the last time you assessed this?

— Will you completely end your involvement in the business, or will you have some other type of involvement in the future?

— Have you considered family involvement in the leadership and ownership of the company going forward?

–   Have you assessed your tax position and potential planning opportunities to minimise your taxes?

–   Are you dependent on the business to meet your income requirements in retirement?

–   Have you generated wealth outside of the business to avoid a forced sale of your business to meet your retirement needs?

If you have not yet considered some of these questions, or if your answer is in the negative, there are opportunities and benefits to be gained from undertaking a more focused and comprehensive strategic planning process. This will hopefully start you thinking about what you need to do in your own business to ensure its efficient transition to either family or to a third party on sale or otherwise. Since the reason many thriving family businesses fail to succeed from one generation to the next is a simple failure of planning adequately for succession, hopefully reading this book will push you to take some action. There is no substitute for having a plan and obtaining appropriate advice where necessary. The sooner you put a plan in place, the greater certainty you will have in respect of an orderly transition of the business. You will also find it easier to let go if you know that sound structures are in place to facilitate the future continuation of the business.

CHAPTER 1

ELEMENTS OF SUCCESSION PLANNING AND THE ROLE OF ADVISORS

OUTLINE:

By the end of this chapter, you will have an understanding of:

– The various components of your succession plan.

– Particular considerations for family operated businesses.

– How to adopt a multi-pronged approach to succession planning.

– Starting your succession plan, including:

  – Articulating goals and communicating the goals to key stake-holders/family members.

  – Understanding the critical issues.

  – The overall goal setting process.

– The role of the succession planning advisor.

– The role of the lead consultant.

– The considerations in selecting the right advisor for you.

An effective business succession plan requires a multidisciplinary process, encompassing a number of different areas. This process presents business owners with a deliberately considered and integrated approach to transitioning the management and ownership of their business over a defined time frame, incorporating the needs of the family and personal goals into the overall succession plan.

Succession planning is critical if the ownership and control of a family business is going to continue for more than one generation. A properly executed succession planning process can give the family business a means of dealing with critical strategic decisions in the future. It also provides a platform for family to discuss and manage potential external threats to the family business, including taxation, divorce and individual bankruptcy of key family members/shareholders. Succession planning can be described as the process by which the transition of ownership and control of the family business from generation to generation is discussed, planned, facilitated and implemented.

The willingness or otherwise of family business owners to plan for the succession process is often the decisive factor in determining whether the business will survive into the next generation or fall by the wayside. International studies show that only around one third of family businesses successfully transfer from one generation to the next. Some commentators believe that family businesses should never be put in the hands of the next generation, on the grounds that successors are rarely as talented as their predecessors. As first-generation entrepreneurial businesses are driven by the energy and determination of the founder.

Worldwide, most businesses are family owned. In Ireland, there are plenty of examples of profitable and well-run family businesses that have transitioned from one generation to the next and remained in family ownership for a number of generations. One reason for their success is that the leaders of the business have been able to manage the complex issue of succession to the next generation, and to cope with family emotions which add a further layer of complexity. The focus of any family business succession exercise is two-fold: to transfer the management and to transfer the ownership of the business. These may not happen at the same time, and may not necessarily involve the same individuals. Parents are often willing to hand over the burden of management before they are willing to transfer ownership and control.

When companies are founded, they are rarely conceived of as a family business. Typically, they are the product of an entrepreneur's drive, need for achievement and self determination. The founders view the business or company as "my business" or "my company". This is usually apparent when the business operates through a company, and the owners reflect on the constituent parts of the business as being theirs, totally ignoring the corporate legal structure. While the family may be fully supportive, they often remain in the background. The business is regarded as the achievement of the founding entrepreneur.

Yet at any stage in a business life cycle, whether operated by the first generation, second generation or subsequent generations, there comes a time when the current generation needs to examine transition of the business, and to consider how to deliver value to the family for the input they have put into the business over the years. This usually occurs by selling the business (or taking it public and divesting a large share of it); or by transferring ownership to the family. The current generation's interest in family succession may first be stimulated when their young children start asking questions about the business. As teenagers, the children may go on to work part time in the business outside of school hours. The option of family involvement can then become a real alternative. As the founding generation matures, alternatives such as selling the business, or obtaining a Stock Exchange listing, may be considered risky and may threaten their role, as against the abilities of the next generation to potentially carry on the business.

Keeping the business within the family has benefits. From a control perspective, the current generation can keep their hand in the business. It provides the possibility of furthering family relationships, and there is the economic advantage of the family still controlling their own destiny. Many business owners believe that the business benefits the family. They consider that their children, in entering the business, could enjoy the same financial freedom that the business provided them with, and that further opportunities may arise for the business to grow. Involvement of the next generation means the family's tradition being maintained, the business is viewed as providing a structure to facilitate keeping the family together, and wealth being generated. Involving the next generation may also assist in the overall retirement plan, providing for financial security of the existing retiring generation.

Conversely, it may not be in the interest of the business to continue in the family. There are numerous issues that either singularly or together may make it unwise for the family to carry on the existing business to-gether. If there is a long history of conflicted family relationships, work-ing together may not be easily facilitated. Sometimes, a family member's life and career interests will not involve the business, no matter what other family members expect of them. Finally, there may be an unwill-ingness to make commitments to support the business's long-term growth, whether at a personal level, or at a financial level in financing the business.

Many business owners, however, may be reluctant to give up control or to live without the business. It is their identity. This often results in them ignoring the potential to either sell the business or to consider the issues involved in transferring it to the next generation. Doing nothing, how-ever, is often disastrous for a family run business. We are all mortal. To safeguard the continued successful operation of the business and to pro-tect its future viability, business owners should view planning for suc-cession as one of their principal responsibilities. Consciously formulating and devising an appropriate succession plan is one of the most important business decisions a business owner can make.

There are three problematic issues in family business situations:

1. Personality – when another family member is impossible or illogi-cal, irrational, unreasonable.

2. Structural – a particular aspect of how the family relates to the busi-ness is not operating correctly. This will create difficulty with deci-sion making and impact negatively on the family dynamic.

3. Business problems – which usually relate to financial and commer-cial issues associated with the performance of the business.

The issue of succession is a primary example of a structural issue facing the business.

However, structural issues are quite predictable in family businesses. Given the flexible nature of a family business (compared with the more formal structures of a public entity), there is an opportunity to resolve such problems before they occur. Family members, particularly those employed in the business, should not have to wait until the reading of the business owner's will to resolve issues, such as who will now manage the business or who will inherit the shareholdings in the business. Such issues should easily be addressed ahead of time in a calm and collected manner by way of a predetermined process agreed by all stakeholders, thus reducing the potentially damaging impact of events such as the death or incapacity of existing owners/managers within the business.

The benefits to business owners who plan properly include:

– Survival and growth of the business

– Preserving family harmony

– Facilitating the type of retirement the business owner aspires to

– Opportunity to consider other financial considerations, such as tax issues that may arise

A MULTI-PRONGED APPROACH

Business owners who are considering succession to their business may well be daunted by the number of issues that need to be addressed. However, approaching succession from one facet only, such as tax planning or addressing ownership transition, means that various other areas of the business may suffer. Ultimately, the efforts involved will have been futile due to certain issues not having been appropriately addressed. A multi-disciplined approach is a powerful basis for business owners to achieve and implement a broad-based, all-encompassing succession plan. Most business owners will not be able to draw on the depth of relevant experience, since implementing a succession plan is likely to be a one-off event. Further attempts at creating a succession plan or revising a succession plan usually only arise if the first plan was inadequate, and did not sufficiently take into consideration all the issues involved, or where there has been a change in circumstances meriting a revision of the original plan.

Adopting a multidisciplinary approach allows the business owner to draw on the experiences and expertise of several advisors working to-

33

gether as a team to assist the business owner and other key stakeholders in defining and meeting the overall succession goal, and in determining how this interacts with the overall strategy for the business. The key issues for consideration are outlined in the chart below.

Setting personal and business goals	Business strategy assessment	Corporate structuring
Shareholders agreement	Family information and communication	Current business valuation
Disability and contingency planning	Managing managerial talent	Compensation planning
Having a retirement plan	Investment strategies	Life insurance analysis
Corporate finance	Estate planning	Share transfer considerations

By considering all these issues, the business owner is assured of an informed view of the possibilities involved and can address them in light of what is suitable. The key issues are:

— *Establishing Goals*
    This should be examined on a dual basis: personal goals (which may include family goals); and the goals of the business. What size would you expect the business to grow? Do you plan to keep it within the family? Who will continue to lead the business once you exit? Do you propose grooming the business for a sale? Personal goals would include a time frame over which you may reduce your involvement in managing the business, and your personal lifestyle ambitions for retirement.

— *Business Strategy Assessment*
    Ensuring a clear strategy and business plan which will drive value for stakeholders in order to facilitate either a sale or succession. In the case of the latter, to provide a framework under which management can be transitioned.

— *Managing Talent*
    Identifying suitable candidates within the management ranks of the business, including assessments of their development requirements,

having a definite strategy around their development, and/or recruiting external management where required.

— *Family Information and Communication*
Possibly the most important issue is the distribution of relevant information to family members in order to keep them fully informed in relation to the business.

— *Estate Planning*
Ensuring that an appropriate plan is in place, covering what should or should not happen in the event of the owner's death.

— *Corporate Finance*
Assessing the value of the business, its financing requirements and implications for acquisitions of other businesses or disposals of existing businesses.

— *Investment Strategies*
Considering how wealth should be generated or held, either within the business or outside of the business.

— *Corporate Structuring*
Assessing the overall legal structure of the organisation, and whether restructuring it would make it more effective from a commercial and tax perspective.

— *Shareholders Agreements*
Ensuring that there are appropriate terms and conditions, outlining how shareholders interact and governing issues around future exit from the business.

— *Retirement Planning*
Having an eventual plan for transitioning from managing the business to retirement, and ensuring that financially you can fund your desired lifestyle in retirement.

— *Life Insurance Analysis*
Examining requirements for the business and business owners in the event of the untimely death of a key employee or the owner.

– *Compensation Issues*
Examining remuneration issues for business owners and employees, particularly where some family members are involved in the business while others are not, while they all remain shareholders in the business. Compensation paid to business owners and employees should be commercially based. Family who work in the business should be appropriately remunerated to reflect their role and time investment. In addition, the compensation of key employees and their incentives should be considered.

– *Ownership Transfer*
This involves assessing the various ways in which ownership of the business may be transferred between the existing owners and either the next generation or third parties.

CHALLENGES IN FAMILY BUSINESS SUCCESSION

Two primary issues arise for the owners of closely held businesses:

1. The complexity of the planning issues facing them, which is significantly greater when compared to that of other individuals of similar net worth who do not own their own business.

2. Balancing family's needs as against the business's demands.

Complexity

Succession planning is not just about preserving and maintaining family wealth through succession and estate strategies, assessing investment alternatives, investment structuring and insurance needs. There are also a myriad other issues related to the continued success of the business, including:

– Building a long-term business strategy so that key stakeholders are fully informed about the direction the business is taking.

– Developing a formal talent management structure in order to groom successors for management.

- Addressing compensation planning issues for key executives and potential successors in order to decrease the likelihood of losing key individuals, and to reduce the potential for disputes at any later stage.

- Examining and establishing contingency plans for the business in the event of unforeseen circumstances that would interfere with the performance of key individuals.

- Considering shareholders' agreements.

- Evaluating corporate finance and structuring alternatives for the business.

- Considering issues around share valuation.

- Examining various ownership configurations and transfer mechanisms in passing shares to the next generation and the basis under which this can be achieved tax effectively.

Family issues

Although numerous challenging complexities arise on a business level, the added complication involving family, including interpersonal dynamics, various personalities, issues around legacy or entitlement and the communication amongst family members, further exacerbates the difficulties on a personal level. What can appear to be a relatively straightforward succession plan proposition can be much more complex when family interests or individual family members are involved. When emotions enter the picture, families focus inwards and generally resist change. Business systems must take the opposite approach if they are to survive. Their focus is outwards towards the external environment as they look for ways to exploit change.

In examining the contrast between a business system and a family system, family needs are neglected when the business system is pre-eminent. Against this, families can over-emphasise home matters to the detriment of the business. Families who give equal importance to family and business requirements create a positive environment where the family thrives and the business performs. This mindset is particularly important in a succession context. Clear communication and a predetermined or pre-established process for entering the family business and obtaining share ownership in the family business, assists in minimising the potential for family conflict, and ensures that family issues do not impact on business issues.

Lastly, as the business owner, you may not wish to retire from all aspects of the business you have helped create or develop. You may wish to remain involved, but on a less active level. You may wish to hand over issues you no longer wish to deal with, while at the same time benefiting from some of the mental and/or physical challenges of continuing to work and being involved in the business. If this is the case, it is important that your role and involvement in the business is redefined as part of the overall succession process. It is equally important that this does not impede transfer of ownership, and ensures that the broader succession issues are dealt with appropriately. Different options may be considered to facilitate continued involvement in the business, while allowing new managers or owners to progress with the day-to-day running of the business.

Delaying Succession Planning

Business owners delay succession planning for many reasons, including:

–   Fear of death – few people find it easy to come to terms with their own mortality.

–   Reluctance to relinquish control.

–   Owners are generally doers rather than planners. They often perceive formal planning as bureaucratic and restrictive.

–   Owners worry about being fair to all potential successors. An unwillingness to choose amongst children often works against succession planning. Family values often dictate that children should not be subjected to a selection process, but should be treated equally.

- They fear the possibility of straining their interpersonal relationships.

- They are concerned with how to acknowledge key personnel who are on the management team and need to be retained, but who are not in line for ownership.

- They may not wish to retire. They may have very few interests that could be developed in retirement. Consequently, they may focus on negative considerations, such as expected loss of self esteem, and the risks of entrusting the business to an unproven successor.

- They assert that because successors are not ready to assume control, nothing can be done.

- They may have difficulty in disconnecting from the day-to-day operation of the business in order to focus on long-term planning.

- The founder's spouse may be reluctant to encourage a partner's move into retirement.

- They have difficulty discussing financial matters and personal goals with others because they regard this as too private.

- They avoid the difficulty of discussing financial matters with children, and the family's future in the event of the parents' death.

- The key stakeholders may not be sure who exactly to turn to for help and how to start the process.

- They may perceive succession planning as a cost to be incurred with no immediate benefits.

- The entire process may seem too daunting.

With all these perceived obstacles, it is no surprise that most businesses do not have an achievable and well thought through succession plan in place. In practice, it is our experience that most business owners either do nothing, or focus on one or a small number of elements of the overall succession planning process. They often ignore equally important issues. In the end, this can lead to a poor result for everyone with an interest in the business.

STARTING YOUR SUCCESSION PLAN

A holistic approach to succession planning can substantially increase the possibility of a desirable outcome for you and your family. Critical issues for initial consideration include:

– Articulating and compiling your goals as a business owner.

– Identifying and consulting with key stakeholders regarding their goals.

– Developing a shared vision with key stakeholders.

– Identifying and prioritising critical issues.

Articulating your goals as the business owner and communicating these goals to other key stakeholders

Issues lurking in the background which no one ever thought fit to address can present the biggest obstacle to the successful transition of the business between generations. Existing shareholders in the business may have different views on its future transition. Some may wish to sell the business, while others may wish to pass it to their family. Without open communication and understanding of their respective positions, the possibility of some unexpected event could lead to conflict between both parties. Lack of a uniform vision, accompanied by different expectations among owners and/or stakeholders, can lead to interpersonal difficulties and lack of an overall coherent plan for the future continuation of the business. The first step in any succession plan should therefore involve you as owner considering your own goals and vision for the future of the business. Consider what you want or aspire to, write it down, reflect on it, change your goals if necessary, and when you are ready, communicate those goals to the other key stakeholders.

You should also assess the goals of the other key stakeholders, and understand the individuals who will be affected by the succession plan, whether they are senior employees, family members employed in the business, those with an expectation of joining the business, or other shareholders. By including all interested parties in the overall goal setting process for the business, the owners and anyone else in the business with decision making capability can then have access to relevant and important information which will help them reflect on their own goals and expectations. Formulation of these goals provides a framework for the succession planning process, the expectations for the business, the issues that will arise for the business in light of the succession planning process, and the position of all those individuals likely to be affected by the succession planning process. One of the overriding objectives in undertaking any succession process is the desire to ensure a smooth transition of the business and the wealth it represents from one generation to another, while maintaining harmony within the family and ensuring that the business continues successfully into the future. That's why the succession plan should not resemble a decree from the senior generation. A plan is far more likely to be successful where borne out of agreement and discussion with those who are to be affected by it. An authoritarian approach is unlikely to be fruitful in the long term.

Communication of goals and expectations between owners and other stakeholders is likely to result in "buy in" into the process. Their involvement is likely to give them a sense of ownership and input into a process that may have significant implications for them, greatly improving the likelihood of the ultimate success of the succession plan and reducing the possibility of later animosity between any of the parties. None of the decision-making authority of the business owners is diluted by stakeholders, as ultimately authority will rest with those shareholders who have voting rights as owners of the company. The purpose is to ensure that everyone with an interest in the business has a formal process through which they can express their goals and expectations, while providing the ultimate decision makers with a framework for making good and informed decisions. A succession plan implemented without proper communication or without cognisance of issues that may be important to key stakeholders, will usually encounter problems and may prove a waste of time and money. Even where technical aspects of a succession plan have been excellently prepared, such as the founder or owner's will and/or appropriate shareholders agreements, these can fall apart and result in problems if based on assumptions about the needs, expectations or desires of others. This is particularly the case when those individuals have not been presented with an opportunity to outline their personal requirements or ambitions for the business.

THE GOAL SETTING PROCESS

Developing a shared vision

Every business, large, small, family owned or a non-family business, must define and establish a road map. Often referred to as a vision, this road map is an image of the future state of the organisation, and indicates where you see the business many years from now. The overall vision, its longevity and the aspirations included within it, will be fed by issues like the size of the business involved, whether or not it is incorporated, the stage it is at, whether it is still an owner-managed business, an entrepreneurial business still run by its founder, or is being run by second or third generation family members. The vision will provide a framework for establishing the goals. If the vision is a road map, then individual goals are the individual towns and villages you aspire to reach and visit on your journey. Smaller companies may only develop a relatively short-term vision. Larger businesses, particularly where operated in a second or third generation family context, need a clearer vision to ensure a uniform framework within which the family can interact and both ownership and development of the company can be outlined. Every family business begins with the founder's particular vision of success. It is that original passion and strength of the vision, driven by the dreams of the entrepreneur, that are responsible for the initial success of the business. The power of that original vision often comes from its singular and undiluted focus, and forms the fundamental core of an entrepreneurial business and the basis around which their family and life might also revolve.

Ironically, when it is time to transition the business to the next generation, it is often the existing generation's vision that paralyses the family and prevents the business moving forward. The historical founding vision may no longer be as relevant as it once was. If beliefs and attitudes remain static and entrenched in the past, this can lead to a disconnect between generations. A shared family vision can cure any potential disenfranchisement or dissent that many families face in transitioning the business from one generation to the next. This can often be a difficult process. Questioning the original founder's principles can be met with: "If they were good enough for your parents to build their business on, why aren't they good enough for you?" However, dreams change. In order for a family business to thrive and successfully pass to the next generation, the initial founding vision must be transformed from a singular and personal idea driven by the ambitions of one person, into an inclusive and current version, which reflects present family circumstances and the needs of all key stakeholders.

At this stage, the business is no longer bound solely by one person's values and dreams, but by the values of the wider family. While the succession process is not the only occasion on which a family will encounter the review and revision of the family business vision, it is definitely the most opportune time to engage in this task.

It may very well be a period of uncertainty for key stakeholders in the business. In this context, before positions and policies are firmly re-established, the consideration of new ideas and different ways of doing things should be promoted and encouraged. Clearly, elements of the original vision will at all times remain fundamental to the core values of the business and family. In addition, some areas of the original vision will require scrutiny. Its scope and focus, which were previously based on the founder's singular vision, may change in light of an expansion of the family, and of needs and perspectives that may differ from the goals of the senior generation. An expanded family involvement has an impact on the original relationship between the family and the business. These changed circumstances require an expanded vision which acknowledges and reflects the current circumstances of the family. The potential for conflict is accentuated in a vacuum, as there is no uniting vision binding the family together. Such conflicts arise from unmanaged or unanticipated expectations, inaccurate perceptions and assumptions that are simply wrong. A shared family vision is the ultimate resolution to such problems. At best, such a vision revitalises the sense of connection between family members and the organisational mission, providing a way to unite family. Even when this optimistic scenario is not played out, such a vision provides a structure for individual, family and overall organisational behaviour and can act as a catalyst for change.

A vision is more than just an outline of aspirations or a dream. It must include a commitment from multiple stakeholders to make such a vision reality. A vision that is appropriate for the business, and is well articulated and communicated, will assist in building consensus amongst the key stakeholders. Naturally, the vision must be ambitious and must establish standards of excellence that all parties must strive to attain. Envisioning the future requires honesty and an understanding of the present. The opinions and options that are explored at this juncture, and the changes made, will determine the direction of the business and the relationship between the business and the family for years to come.

Goal Setting

Performing the tasks of creating, revising or establishing a vision is not enough to constitute a valid succession plan. Following creation of a vision, the bite sized chunks required to realise such a vision, must be established. In other words, goals must be set. The goal-setting process should start with a desired end result. The goals should all support the vision, and be consistent with it. While it can be a time-consuming process, establishing goals is essential. As the Cheshire cat said to Alice, unless you know where you are going, you're always going to take the wrong path. As an owner of a family run business, the goals must not only centre round the business. They must reflect personal and family goals. They must incorporate an overall plan that encompasses your retirement goals, your exit strategy and personal ambitions. Holding brainstorming sessions with relevant or key decision makers in the business and with family will assist in determining goals. Many questions should be addressed during the goal-setting phase:

– Does the business need to remain family owned? If so, why?

– Should I sell the business?

– What would happen if I dropped dead tomorrow?

– Who would take over the family business and what would be the impact on it?

– Will selecting a new leader create relationship issues within the family?

- What steps can I take to enhance the value of the business in the short term should I wish to sell it?

- Is the current business operating strategy maximising value for shareholders?

Consider when the goals should be accomplished and how they are to be accomplished. By benchmarking goals against a certain time frame, it is easier to prioritise them. Unrealistic goals should be set aside and priority given to goals that are more realistic and achievable. Only a clearly established preordained, definable, specific and measurable set of goals will provide you with the mechanism to identify and review objectives for management. It will also assist in clarifying the overall strategies for continuity and success of the business in the context of the overall business succession. The goals are not just about business succession. The goals are to ensure the future success of the business. The succession process is only one important chapter in the overall history of the business, but this succession chapter can produce difficulties that have a detrimental effect on the business. A well thought-out, well articulated process with challenging, measurable but achievable goals will assist in successful delivery of the succession plan.

The Role of the Advisor

Despite the numerous advantages of implementing a comprehensive succession plan, most business owners will not proactively engage in such a process. Some will go it alone and adopt a DIY approach based on a need to retain control or a perception of potentially escalating costs if a team of advisors is engaged. In some situations, the process may be commenced with a non-unified team of advisors, with no one lead consultant pulling the advice together into a coherent manageable, recognisable plan. The result for the business owner is confusion and frustration. In addition to all this, the business owner must still focus on the day-to-day management of the business. In effect, given difficulties in discussing emotions or dealing with family relationships, there is never one ideal time to develop a succession plan. Yet this is a matter that should simply be faced into at an early stage. Where a business is not relatively complex, the DIY approach may well work. In most cases, however, it will be necessary and wise to seek the help of an appropriate advisor. This is particularly the case where your business has any degree of complexity. The involvement of an advisor will provide you with the opportunity to continue with the day-to-day business management, while they address some of the issues and act as a buffer on your behalf in collating and providing some of the necessary information to assist you in the process.

When selected appropriately, outside professional advisors and consultants can offer a different perspective. They can bring an additional dimension of competence, experience and objectivity to issues affecting the business and facing the family.

Key Attributes of an Advisor

Historically, advisors and consultants have worked in one of three systems of a family business: the general business advice area; the general area of advising the family; or advising on the overall ownership/governance structure. This is best illustrated by the following diagram:

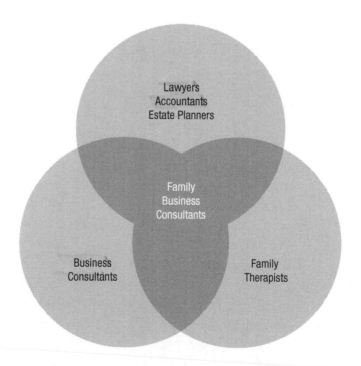

Advisors often operate as if the systems were totally separate, but ideally, an advisor with experience in more than one of the two areas will have a better understanding of the issues facing the family business. They will have the skills, training and experience that would be relevant in ensuring that most of the important issues are covered as part of your succession plan.

Regardless of the size of your business, the key ability of any advisor is to listen. Good communication skills are critical, particularly good listening skills. Advisors must be able to interact effectively with business owners and stakeholders by communicating various concepts involved in the succession plan. In return, it is essential that they understand and probe the information provided. A unilaterally imposed solution to accomplish one aspect of an overall succession plan, without allowing enough time to understand family wishes, goals and expectations, will have the long-term consequence that some aspects of the succession plan will be overlooked, with all the problems that this entails.

Advisor Selection

Succession planning is usually a one-off event. By definition, it is a process which few business owners will have prior experience of. Getting it right the first time will, in the long run, save both time and money. If your business operation is particularly complex, the advisor can help identify potential problems that might otherwise be missed. The advisor should have the right level of experience, insight and resources to suit your requirements. Advisors must acquaint themselves with how any particular family business operates. You should assess whether they are taking the time to maximise their understanding of your particular family dynamics, such as why are the family members in business together, what motivates the family, and where the family want to take the business. This will help the advisor better understand their role and what is expected of them. Their advice will then be not only accurate but will properly reflect the overall family requirements, and not just the requirements of the business. When selecting advisors for your business, your overall goals will influence your decision as to who may or not be appropriate for the job.

Your advisor must have the right mix of skills, experience and knowledge in order to make the overall process less onerous for you, your family and other key stakeholders. The three most important skills for your advisor are communication, ability to build trust, and facilitation. Discussing family issues is often sensitive and potentially distressing. Your advisor must have the communication skills required to assess the various undercurrents of what is being said. Your advisor must be an excellent listener. What is unsaid can often provide an insight into how key stakeholders are feeling, as opposed to what they directly say. The advisor needs to be able to build trust within the family. The parties must understand that the advisor is engaged by the business and the family as a whole, and not for any one particular individual or group at the expense of others. As the overall emotional component can take a toll on personal relationships, your advisor must use professional discretion to facilitate the overall discussions, particularly during the goal-setting process. Your advisor must be able to discuss difficult issues and deal with them in a subtle and sensitive way, minimising the possibility of a confrontation amongst family members.

A facilitator should be able to assist the family discussing issues in an informed and logical manner, guiding them towards a consensus and managing the different viewpoints. The advisor should also assist the family in making compromises in order to arrive at a shared vision for the future. When selecting advisors, you are entitled to ask for their track record and their credentials. The successful candidate will be playing a key role in the transition of your business and its success into the future. You need to be sure that you can develop a close working relationship with them, since you will be spending a significant amount of time with them discussing the overall business transition.

If you engage existing advisors to assist you in the succession process, be careful to avoid any potential conflicts of interest. Carefully define at the outset for whom the advisor is acting in respect of what matters. Define the nature and extent of their responsibilities, and to whom they owe a duty of care. Particularly in family situations, the advisor must be seen to be acting on behalf of the business, and not on behalf of any one group or branch of the family. If, as often happens, one of the owners or directors of the company has particularly close ties with the advisor, it is important that the advisor be perceived by everyone else at the company, as being neutral. Any perception that they are sympathetic to the views and outlook of one particular stakeholder may compromise their position, and it may be impossible for them to facilitate overall agreement on a succession plan with all key stakeholders. In such a situation, it is recommended that your advisor step aside, and arrange to be replaced by a colleague who has no historic links with your business.

Selecting Advisors in a Team Context

Where you anticipate retaining more than one advisor, it is important that you select advisors who can work together. When individuals with different specialities come together to work in a team environment, it may take some time before they function efficiently as a team. It is difficult to create a functionally cohesive advisory team where there are competing egos and relationships that need to be managed among the advisors. The advisors are there to assist you in managing your relationships with the key stakeholders. You should not have to manage their relationships with one another. An advisory team that gels together professionally is a team that will be able to communicate freely and offer direct and non-contradictory analysis and assessment.

The need for cooperation amongst advisors means that it is up to the family to choose their advisors carefully. It may be appropriate to hold an interview or "beauty contest," rather than depending solely on recommendation. You may even consider hiring advisors on a probationary basis. With larger businesses, a succession planning project can often prove too complex without expert professional assistance, in which case it is likely that you will need a large team of advisors. You will usually require the assistance of professionals with different areas of expertise, such as tax specialists, corporate finance advisors, lawyers, management consultants, insurance professionals, financial planners, and compensation and benefit specialists. The extent to which you would need them all depends very much on the size of the business and the issues involved. Some professionals may be able to fill more than one area of expertise. Members of an advisory team could include the following:

— *Family Business Advisor:*
   The sole role of the family business advisor is to retain the appropriate links between the business and the family that owns the busi-

ness. Typically, this role is to help family businesses negotiate transitions, ownership or management. A family business advisor will often help with the creation of family and corporate governance systems, processes and structures, and will help families achieve their aims at several stages of the life cycle of the family business. A family business advisor will help organise, negotiate and improve family dialogue in meetings, and will encourage family communication and cooperation. The engagement of a family business advisor will usually be more relationship-based than technical-based.

— *Corporate Finance Specialist:*
This requires a broad strategic advisory role. In specific situations, this involvement is usually concerned with the sale of a business or examining appropriate funding mechanisms to bring about succession planning. If an IPO (initial public offering) is being sought to create liquidity, the corporate finance specialist provides assistance in relation to the commercial and legal requirements to float/list the company.

— *Tax Specialist:*
The tax specialist usually deals with both the tax compliance and tax consulting needs of the business, as well as for shareholders at an individual level, in ensuring a tax efficient transition of ownership to the next generation.

— *Accountant:*
Accountants usually provide general business, financial and management advice. They can also help with the training of successors. Often, accountants have additional skill sets, such as tax specialist or general family business advisor. They may be in a position to assist with business transfer succession and estate planning issues around retirement and personal financial planning.

— *Management Consultant:*
The management consultant's involvement may include undertaking a strategic review of the management and operation of the organisation, as well as assessing management capabilities within the organisation to ascertain whether they are adequate for succession,

or whether new management capabilities need to be sourced outside the business.

– *Lawyer:*
Lawyers assist in determining the form of business ownership and capital structure. They assist in drafting wills and other shareholding documents such as shareholder agreements. They also examine issues such as prenuptial agreements and employment agreements for family members.

– *Compensation and Benefits Specialist:*
This role assesses the various forms of compensation or benefits to be provided to employees, particularly key employees and family members.

– *Financial/Investment Advisor:*
Financial/investment advisors assess investments undertaken by both the business and the key stakeholders at a personal level. They may also provide investment advice from an overall retirement perspective.

– *Insurance Specialist:*
Insurance professionals help business owners protect themselves against large unpredictable demands for cash to pay taxes, or to convert the cash into securities on death or disability.

– *Valuer:*
This is an expert who is competent in establishing a true market value on the business in order to establish a buying or selling price or a value for tax purposes, when transferring interest in the business to the next generation.

Role of the Lead Consultant

While consultant teams offer more comprehensive advice, they also pose challenges. That is why the most crucial member of the team is the lead planning consultant, even though all the different specialists in a succession planning service team are also important. Without a single clear leading consultant, the advisory team members will have to answer the following questions:

— Who will direct the team's activities?

— Who will see that the work is coordinated?

— How will the costs of the succession plan be managed?

— Who will coordinate and resolve differences of opinion between advisors?

— Who will ultimately liaise with the business owner and pull all the constituent strands of the plan together?

— Who will manage the relative merits of different recommendations and benchmark them or assess them in the context of presentation to the business owner?

Having a lead consultant means that key stakeholders and owners will work directly with one individual throughout the overall succession planning process, rather than having to hold countless meetings with different advisors. The lead consultant must have an overall understanding of the process and how the different constituent pieces of the jigsaw fit together. Although a lead consultant will not possess all of the required specialist technical skills, he or she should have sufficient competency in the various elements of succession planning, and must be able to immediately access a network of specialists when necessary. Ideally, the lead consultant will; be highly experienced in this role, and will bring a broad understanding of all the issues involved.

The lead consultant should have a background in dealing with privately owned businesses, as well as excellent communication and facilitation skills. The lead consultant may very well possess some of the constituent specialist technical skills. In addition to general business acumen and experience, the lead consultant must have extensive experience in dealing with interpersonal relationships and family situations and the emotions that accompany this process. While many advisors may claim to have the overall succession planning experience of the lead consultant, in reality they may only be specialised in one aspect of designing a comprehensive succession plan.

For a large business, the ideal situation is to utilise the services of a large professional services firm that employs all the required expertise in-house, that has a focused professional commitment to succession planning, and that can put in place a tried and trusted consulting process for such projects. The lead consultant can access advisors in a time effective way. They have a proven relationship with working together, all the specialities are situated under one roof, and any potential for conflict or difficulties arising among advisors is removed. Too often, advisors who do not have a regular working relationship with one another, struggle to integrate and coordinate elements of the succession plan on a timely basis. This leads to inefficiencies, cost overruns and conflicting advice that will impede implementation of solutions and ultimately delay the overall process. Members of a single coordinated succession planning team are more likely to devise a coherent, logical, effective and appropriately structured plan at a reasonable cost, relative to the complexity involved.

The succession planning process is one of the more important events in the life cycle of your family business. The decisions made will impact not only on your business and its future continuation, but will affect the people you care about for generations to come. It is important that it is taken seriously and that you take the time to address the issues involved and do it right. For that reason alone, it is important that you find the right advisor for your needs. This is a one-off event. You need to get it right the first time round.

CHAPTER 1 – ACTIONS

– Confirm the vision for your business.

– Start discussions with key stakeholders on their visions and goals for the business.

– Articulate your own goals to the other relevant parties.

– Develop a list of overall goals for the succession planning process.

– Look at any critical issues you may need to address.

– Consider whom you should get advice from and the scale or level of involvement required from different advisors.

– Ensure there is an agreed understanding of your goals and what the advisor needs to achieve.

CHAPTER 2

FAMILY BUSINESS DYNAMICS

OUTLINE:

By the end of this chapter you will have understanding of:

- The different requirements of family and business

- The interaction and potential for conflict between family and business

- The different categories of people involved in a family business

- Attitudes of different individuals to the business

- How interpersonal relationships may impact on the business

- The life cycle of the family business

Family businesses are different. This difference derives from the mixing of family chemistry, family priorities and challenges with business imperatives and business opportunities. The dynamics affect the way the business is organised, and the people who participate in the family business, particularly in an ownership context. The dynamics are part of why family firms become more complex once they have passed through a number of generations. The dynamics that impact on the operation of a family business and its interaction with the family, and its effects on interaction among family members, incorporates many different perspectives:

- The requirements of the business vs. the requirements of the family.

- The additional requirements of owners/shareholders of the business who may or not be family members.

- The life cycle of the business. Is it still controlled/owned by the founding (first) generation, the second generation (a sibling partnership) or held in the third generation or beyond, which is usually a collection of cousins and possibly others (a cousin consortium).

- Specific individual relationship-based dynamics central to personality types and potentially conflicted relationships:

  - Attitude of the founder to future succession.

  - Different male/female roles or perspectives.

  - The potential for father/son conflict.

  - Sibling rivalry.

  - Involvement/inclusion of in-laws.

The "business family" clearly encompasses a wider range of individuals than just those family members directly involved in the business and their immediate relatives. The family may involve a number of generations and spouses of family members who will not be related to the original founder by blood. All these relationships can play a key role, not only in the general operation of the business and its management, but in particular in the context of implementing and devising a succession plan.

For large publicly run companies, or even private businesses that are not operated by families, the primary objective is maximisation of shareholder return. In a family context, the family may initially wish to primarily achieve a financial return from their enterprises. However, as the business grows and develops, the family is more likely to want the business to provide other non-financial benefits as part of the family's wider vision. The one significant advantage in a family business is that decisions can be taken with a much longer-term perspective, compared with the short-term purpose of shareholder return. Decisions can be made in light of transition of the business to the future generation and what is important for the business 20 or 30 years hence. There is therefore a trade off between shareholder return and other priorities of the family in operating the business. Business decisions taken without considering the requirements of the family can impact on relationships. Conversely, decisions taken for personal or family reasons are sometimes not in the best economic interests of the business. In effect, two conflicting systems interact within the overall family business system.

CHARTING THE FAMILY BUSINESS SYSTEM

The primary differentiation of a family firm is that many of those involved in it share a family relationship and have the same values and behaviour patterns. By virtue of their involvement, these are carried over into the business and the work environment. Families means emotions. This can be both positive and negative. The focus of families tends to be inward, looking out for the needs of family members. The family system focuses on stability, which produces a conservative structure. A major drawback of this is resistance to change, and a wish to maintain the status quo among family members. Business systems usually take the opposite approach to survive. They are primarily focused on the accomplishment of tasks. They focus outward on the external environment. They are built around contractual arrangements, where courses of action or behaviour are consciously planned. Performance and results are analysed. The external marketplace is taken into consideration, and the business system operates to exploit change and maximise opportunities.

FAMILY   BUSINESS

1. Emotional Concerns   1. Business performance

2. Family needs   2. Business demands

3. Maintaining stability   3. Managing change

Control

Careers

Capital

Conflict

Culture

The family business dilemma
Source: Carlock, Randel and John Ward, *Strategic Planning for the Family Business* (Macmillan, 2001)

Since there are two totally different systems, should matters be examined from a family or business perspective? Different results will materialise, particularly in a succession context. How should control be transferred? When and how should ownership be transferred? What about the involvement of family members who are employees?

A family wish for all the children to be treated equally may be reflected in the current generation transferring ownership in equal proportions, regardless of the involvement of different family members in the business, and regardless of the potential for conflict. Similarly, family members may be permitted to join the business regardless of whether they possess the relevant skill sets, educational qualifications, experience or abilities. Sometimes, once they have joined, all family members are paid equally, regardless of their abilities, and regardless of how much they contribute to the overall business success. In effect, the family principle that all members be treated equally can result in some family members being treated unequally, especially if they believe their contribution to be higher.

Conversely, when the business system overrides the family system, there is potential for negative feeling. Its influence is all-encompassing and can determine or pervade all aspects of the lives of the family members. The owner of the business can become preoccupied with business success, thus ignoring broader family issues. At family gatherings and events, family members not involved in the business may feel marginalised. They might resent every family meeting turning into a business discussion on business issues and recent business wins or disappointments. Obviously, in the event of a dispute between family members in a business situation, problems may spill over into family life outside of business hours. This is less likely with a non-family business, where the participants may not interact socially.

The most desirable situation is to have a balanced approach, where family and business systems are given equal importance in order to create a positive environment in which both the family can thrive and the business can perform. A balanced approach should incorporate a simple plan or strategy to guide and coordinate both family and company/business issues. This provides the possibility of recognising, analysing and addressing family and business issues in a way that ensures an appropriate balance. In a succession context, the primary lessons to be learned are:

1. Be proactive.
    Many of the problems that arise in a family business context can be anticipated well in advance. Clear and open communication can resolve many issues and can manage expectations. This includes having a family constitution and holding formal family meetings.

2. Managing change.
    Change, particularly in a family context, can cause concern. Apart from changes in the wider business environment, the complex issue of transfer of the business from one generation to the next can be of huge importance.

3. Control.

    Control can be both financial and a function of the ability to make decisions. The person who has the final say in operating the business, or who has control in respect of its finances, can exert a major impact on the future of the business.

4. Run the business professionally.

    A considered strategic plan is important in managing expectations. It assists in removing subjective and often emotional family considerations that can obscure appropriate business judgment.

In any business involving more than one person, there are two primary categories of people to be taken into account in business decisions and planning: the owners of the business, and those running the business. In family businesses, ownership and family were often one and the same. However, as businesses progress through generations, the reality is that there can be three different categories of people involved:

1. Those who own the business and work in it.

2. Those who work in the business but do not own any part of it.

3. Those who own the business but do not work in it.

The three circle model outlined in the diagram below identifies the range of different interests present in a family business situation by outlining the three separate but overlapping systems of ownership, management and family. The different perspectives, expectations, ambitions and behaviour of individuals in each category helps to demonstrate why there is potential for conflict in a family business situation. Obviously there is a finite level of resources. The constituent stakeholders have different needs and different perspectives. People will want different things. Financially, they have different expectations based on their needs. Assessing the interests of different members within the system can assist in managing the resulting complexity and conflicts. This can also help manage a successful and smooth transition of the business from one generation to the next, and ensure its continued unhindered operation into the future.

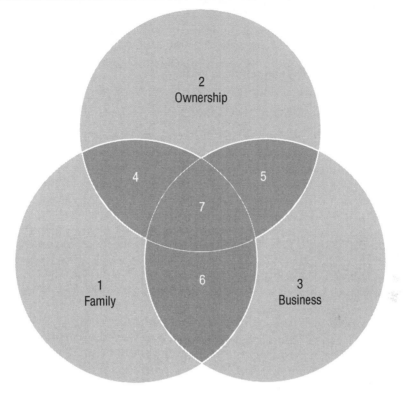

The three circle model
Source: Tagiuri and Davis (1982) *'Bivalent attributes of the family firm'*.

Everyone involved in the family business falls into one of the following seven segments:

Segment 1: Family.
Even if they do not own a share of the business or work in it, every member of a business family will have some attachment to the business. There may be a future expectation of owning a share in the business or working within it. From a lifestyle perspective, they may be interested in the wealth generated by the business that is transitioned through the owners of the business to the wider family.

Segment 2: Owners.
Those who own part of the business but do not work in it and are not family members will be principally concerned with return on their investment and liquidity. This could include private shareholders, venture

capitalists, and others. They would have an expectation of business decisions being separate from family dynamics.

Segment 3: People employed in the business.
Whether they are at management level or a more junior level, they will primarily be concerned with career prospects and job security. If a business operates on a family first basis, it may be difficult to recruit good managers and employees, since they would be wary of favour afforded to family members when promotions, salary increases etc. are being considered.

Segment 4: Family members who have shares in the business but are not employees.
When a business passes from one generation to the next, some of the new shareholders may not work in the business. Their expectations may centre around whether their shareholding is their primary source of wealth on which they rely for dividend income, or whether the overall family values include a responsibility to transition those shares to future generations. Ownership may be tempered by family responsibilities. Some of those family members may ultimately aspire to future employment within the business.

Segment 5: Non-family working owners.
This usually arises where equity incentives have been given to non-family managers or employees as part of incentive arrangement in recruiting them. They will be concerned with the financial return on their equity allocation via dividend income, and with capital return on disposal and provision of an exit mechanism for them realising their equity holding in the future.

Segment 6: Family employees.
There is potential for conflict between the efforts of a family employee who may not feel financially rewarded, unlike family members who may own shares but are not employed in the business. Family employees will also be concerned with career development, and they may have expectations around future ownership.

Segment 7: Those inhabiting all three circles – family member employees of the business with a shareholding. They will have interests in all the various segments, and may therefore face many conflicting choices, particularly in a succession situation.

Sources of tension and conflict will arise in issues such as: Who should lead the business? Who should be employed in it? How should they be paid? Who should own shares either now or in the future? With dividend payments, family members who work in the business will often take a different view from those who own shares but are not employed in the business. Structurally, a family business is a complex mix. The three circles model outlines the range of views and opinions that can exist in any family business, and the conflicts that can inevitably arise depending on the roles of the individuals and the potential for different perspectives. Recognising the perspectives of the different categories of individuals within your family business will help you form a considered view of the concerns of various stakeholders as part of any succession plan.

Personal Attitudes and Relationships

The three circle model helps explain the family business system, and provides an objective outline of likely perspectives of individuals in the different categories. However, inter-family relationships and attitudes also play an important part in determining who should be involved, at what level and how conflict should be managed. This will also determine the nature of any transition of ownership, or management during any such transition, or in managing relationships after such transition.

The legendary Gucci brothers feud represents a pattern of escalating sibling rivalry and failure to unite as one family. Guccio Gucci had three sons, Aldo, Vasco and Rodolfo. Each worked in the business. When Guccio died, he left the company equally among his sons. Each had different roles in the business. They were highly competitive, but managed to contain their rivalry. One brother, Vasco, died. This left the two remaining brothers owning the business equally. Aldo became the driving force in the second generation. His three sons joined the business, as did Rodolfo's son. Resentment grew between Rodolfo and Aldo as Aldo took increasing control of the business. Rodolfo felt slighted by his older brother. Aldo, who had planned to give each of his sons one third of his shares, simply felt that his brother's contributions did not equal his 50% ownership in the company. Aldo therefore began to direct more profits into one of the family company's other businesses where Rodolfo had a lesser stake. In the absence of their middle brother to balance things, it all boiled over. Friction developed when one of Aldo's sons, Paolo, grew discontented at not having more of a say in the company. When he initiated steps to start a business of his own, his father Aldo fired him. Fighting also erupted between Aldo and Rodolfo when the latter sought a larger stake in those businesses to which Aldo was channelling profits, and in which Aldo had a larger share. With control very diluted among several entities, board meetings turned into family battles. One board meeting erupted into a well-publicised physical fight. When Rodolfo died in 1983, his son Maurizio inherited a 50% stake in the Gucci empire. Shortly afterwards, he and his cousin Paolo, who had been fired from the company, made a secret pact whereby Maurizio would buy Paolo's shares and gain control of the company. The agreement eventually fell apart, but not until after Maurizio became chairman and Aldo was effectively sidelined. Shortly afterwards Aldo went to prison in the US for tax evasion, after his son Paolo disclosed information to the tax authorities about his father. Ultimately the fashion empire was hobbled by the conflict and eventually sold.

Attitude of the Founder

In a first generational business, the personality, attitude, drive and behaviour of the founder will impact throughout the family enterprise. Their visions, ideals and goals will often continue to influence the business well into the future, long after their involvement with the business has ceased. Because of their all-encompassing influence, their attitudes are central to the future development of the next generation of management and ownership of the business.

Founders can have difficulty in being accountable to others. This is often the reason why they start their own business in the first place: to escape the authority and rivalry of other individuals. An inability to take on board others' opinions or engage with others can however be detrimental to the succession process. Often, founders continue to view the business as "their" business. This can make it extremely difficult for them to let go. So although many entrepreneurs build an organisation to significant proportions, they are often characterised by the one dominant feature of having great difficulty in establishing succession. Their competitive and possessive streak often conflicts with the development of appropriate successors.

For an entrepreneur, the business is essentially an extension of themselves. At a paternalistic level, it provides them with an opportunity to enhance their self-image. Family members may be pushed to enter the business on grounds of loyalty, yet would tend to be submissive in the face of the founder's dominant behaviour. This can obviously sow the seeds for future conflict. However, not all entrepreneurs necessarily portray such dominant traits. Many will encourage their children to join the business and provide them with genuine opportunities to develop. Many are willing to give real control over areas of the business, and may encourage family members to join the business to preserve a sense of family harmony.

In these situations, consideration must be given to who ultimately will control the business. If a founder has allowed a number of family members to be employed or involved at a management level, it is important that the founder puts in place a clear plan. Failure to make such provision and failure to openly discuss succession and communicate it to all family members, will lead to disharmony, especially where a number of family members have expectations to take the role of CEO. The founder's attitude here is of paramount importance. Any deferring or dithering around succession decisions can lead to family disharmony.

In some businesses, the founder has established and driven the business forward thanks to creative talent or technical knowledge. The business is built around their skill sets. No one family member may have a similar level of technical knowledge. When children join the business, the founder may feel that they are not appropriate successors, since they do not share the founder's technical aptitude. That is why it is imperative for the founder to realise the different abilities of the children and to harness their skills so that they can perform in other areas of the company. Simultaneously, the founder must pass on knowledge of the core processes of the company to others, and coordinate this as part of an overall succession plan.

It is important that a founder has the self-awareness to assess the likely impact on the transition phase of any succession process.

Steinberg's Supermarket chain was founded in 1917 as a small local grocery store in Montreal, and grew into one of the leading family businesses in Canada. Sam Steinberg, second son of the founder, was responsible for transforming the business into the sizeable chain it became. By the time he was ready to retire in 1969, the chain had approximately 180 stores. However, Sam naively believed that the business should welcome any family member who wanted to join. This meant finding a place for four of his brothers, one sister, his mother, assorted aunts, uncles, cousins, nieces and nephews, and even sons-in-law and grandchildren. Although all these family members were admitted, Sam continued to make all major business decisions himself. Because he had old-fashioned attitudes about female involvement in the business, he isolated his four daughters from the complications of the business. He had no sons. So when it came to naming a successor, he chose his most capable son-in-law who was married to his second daughter. However, the oldest daughter objected. To pacify her, Sam named her husband as CEO instead of his first choice. This CEO was poorly qualified to head the business. When Sam died, his four daughters inherited all the voting stock, and his oldest daughter and her husband assumed control of the company. Under their control, the company declined. The board of directors ultimately recommended selling the company. But the voting stock was held in a trust jointly owned by all four sisters, and some of them refused to vote for a sale. The matter eventually ended up in court. The company was ultimately sold, but family relationships had been irrevocably damaged. The company failed a few years after it was sold. Although Sam Steinberg had meant to do the right thing, and had wanted all of his family to participate in the business, he made the error of giving the voting stock to his daughters who were not in the business. He allowed his personal feelings to dictate the choice of successor, instead of choosing the individual most competent to run his business.

Male/Female Involvement in the Business

More women than ever before are now business owners. They bring a different, and some would say more positive, all-inclusive, influence to a family operated business. It will be interesting to see over the coming years as to how they manage the transitions in their businesses. In a traditional business, where the husband may have been the spouse primarily involved in the family enterprise, wives often act as a sounding board for their partners, playing behind the scenes roles as a business advisor and confidante. Their focus was on maintaining family unity. When conflict arose between the father and children employed in the business, it was often the role of the wife to mediate and resolve the situation and maintain family harmony. Women are good communicators, and they are very good at dealing with issues of character and human perception. They can be a powerful force within a family in fostering teamwork and in striving for unity between family members.

In a succession situation, the historically prevailing chauvinistic attitude meant that daughters were not usually part of their father's thinking in the context of family succession. Usually the family business passed to one of the sons, typically the eldest. When daughters do join a family business, they generally find working with their father far easier than when a son joins the business, which usually has greater potential for conflict. Daughters will usually have a more respectful disposition towards their father, which engenders a better working relationship. Unlike the potential disposition in sons to regard entry to the family business as an entitlement, daughters rarely adopt this view.

Father/Son Conflict

Problems can arise in father/son relationships. Naturally, there are many positive father/son relationships, where mutual respect fosters a positive working relationship. Working together is a natural process, and they form an effective and formidable business partnership. However, sometimes, a father/son working relationship is a cause of tension. Entrepreneurs take great pride in their business. It is an extension of them and a measure of their personal achievement. Those who work for these entrepreneurs are their instruments in the process of shaping the organisation. That is why entrepreneurs often have great difficulty delegating authority. They also refuse to retire, despite repeated promises to do so. While they may wish their sons to participate in the business and ultimately to pass the business to them, subconsciously this involves losing part of themselves. They unconsciously feel they need to demonstrate their own competence. Transfer of the business would be a loss of masculinity. They need to show that they are stronger than their sons. They worry that they will become marginalised if their sons take over. They may feel that they alone are competent to make "their" company succeed. Unconsciously, if the son is successful and takes the reins, he is seen as displacing the father from the top position. While wanting to pass the business to his son on the one hand, these contradictory feelings result in erratic behaviour, represented by conflicting actions, such as admitting the son to the business yet not allowing him any responsibility.

In many situations, sons may be left on the sidelines for years, way beyond the stage where others of similar ability and experience in other organisations have taken over. Often, the father has not yet retired despite repeated promises that this is ultimately what he wishes to do. This contradictory stance can frustrate the son. Consequently, the father and son can both be significantly emotionally frustrated, as the father looks on the son as ungrateful and unappreciative, whereas the son is hostile, feeling he is a victim of emotional blackmail. The son in such circumstances obviously seeks clarity, yet the father relies on ambiguity to maintain his position, thus increasing the son's frustration.

However, when the son does eventually get to take control, the organisation may have grown beyond the founder's capability to control it effectively. The founder's drive, vision and energy may be impossible to duplicate and there very may well be a lack of other appropriate experience at a managerial level. Consequently, the son may well be taking over a much weaker organisation. For this reason, many businesses decline or are sold when the founder is no longer involved. If a son joins a business in such circumstances, and acts to repair weaknesses left within the organisation, he will be subject to criticism by those who are waiting to illustrate his inadequacies and failures. They are of the view that he is not as good as his father. Consequently, if his performance is not similar to that of his parent, regardless of any unfavourable commercial circumstances, he is criticised as having wasted an opportunity that others could have successfully converted. In effect, the son cannot win. If he takes over a successful business and develops it further, expands it, makes it more profitable such that it is a much more successful organisation, he will still be subject to comments of "Look what you started with. What did we expect?"

Ideally when a son joins his father in a family business, both should rethink their relationship. Hitherto, the relationship was based on their interaction within the family context, not a business environment. The son may well have no experience of what his father is like in a business context. He may not have worked elsewhere, and has no other context within which to frame his father's behaviour. However, in the experience of most succession professionals, even when entrepreneurial fathers understand the processes that are at work, they are not good at addressing the problem. Yet as the more mature of the two, it should be up to the father to take on the responsibility of attempting to ensure the relationship operates effectively. However, the entrepreneurial founder's fears of losing control mitigates against them taking any action. As a result it often falls at the son's doorstep to address the conflict that may arise.

Where a son has been pressurised by a father to join the family business, this may further exacerbate problems that may arise at some future stage.

Feelings of rivalry or anger on the son's part will automatically lead to defensive measures by the father and entrenched positions being taken by both. That is why communication is crucial and the benefit of external counselling or coaching sessions may be advantageous. Where possible, one alternative is for the son to operate a new venture within the family business or an existing separate division, in order to provide them with an opportunity to have their own space and branch out and mature. The son has his own degree of autonomy, running his own separate aspect of the business, yet is still supporting his father and avoiding the possibility of having to leave and work elsewhere. The son must ultimately respect what his father has achieved, and his aptitude and abilities in bringing the business to its current level. The son should recognise the psychological intertwining of his father's identity with the business and its importance to him, and not necessarily expect him to be rational about his relationship with the business. If all fails, it may help to invite an outside consultant to hold a number of meetings between the father and son to discuss their concerns, with a view to them making compromises so as to foster a healthier working relationship. Such an approach usually requires continued effort on both sides with the relevant professional, in order to resolve the differences involved. As the son matures, it may provide time for any divisions to heal. Ultimately if the situation cannot be resolved, the son is either faced with leaving the business to pursue other opportunities, or learns to accept and tolerate the situation until it changes in the future.

Sibling Rivalry

The root cause of sibling rivalry is as children, individuals vie for the attention of their parents. In childhood, sibling rivalry can stimulate healthy development in children as they learn that they will not necessarily always get their own way. At a basic level, this can be illustrated by the jealousy of a first-born child when a second child arrives in the family. Even if there is sibling rivalry in childhood, there is an expectation that as adults, the children will pursue separate careers and have their own families. The opportunity for rivalry thus diminishes. In the context of a family business, this process is reversed. Childhood rivalry may well be perpetuated in adult life through the day-to-day contacts in the business context. This can have a very negative impact on the operation of the enterprise, and be further exacerbated if the founding parent tries to play one sibling off against the other, or has decided that one child should succeed to his position.

The problem is further complicated when the siblings' mother and their spouses are also directly or indirectly involved in the business. Regardless of what they say, mothers often have their favourite children, and a spouse will always argue and defend the position of their husband/wife who is involved in the business. It is quite common that the eldest sibling – often the eldest son – succeeds their parent in the business. This custom obviously reaffirms the belief of younger siblings that the oldest is indeed the favourite. By virtue of his age, the oldest child is physically stronger and more knowledgeable and competent than younger siblings. By the time they reach adulthood, the relationship is established where the oldest sibling has difficulty regarding younger siblings as adequate or competent, even though younger siblings in childhood have not had the opportunity to match the skills, competence or experience of the elder sibling.

Since the eldest child, as the first born, is in longer contact with the parents, in a family context their control efforts will fall more heavily on them. As a result, the older children drive themselves harder, control themselves more rigidly than younger ones, expect more of themselves and develop stronger consciences. In establishing high standards for themselves, older children are likely to be a harsh judge of their younger siblings. For a younger sibling, the effect of the childhood relationship and the efforts of an elder sibling to control them is for them to strive to carve out their own niche or identity, separate from that of their other siblings. In effect, younger siblings demonstrate their own competence and their own area of expertise.

Such psychological factors can colour management decisions. Where both children have an equal share and an equal say in the business, they can argue from equally strong positions. This works in the context of a company where there are external board members to mitigate any rivalries. If siblings continually adopt conflicting views in a situation where each has a commensurate level of control, the result is organisational paralysis. Even where siblings hold similar positions at board level, if one is subservient to another in the day-to-day operation of the business, they can find it extremely difficult to deal with this. In families where parents have fostered a competitive spirit amongst siblings, the latter should be careful not to not allow themselves to be played off against one another. This only serves to magnify any rivalry that might already exist. If parents wish to ensure the future continued success of the business, they should allocate separate niche roles to each child, so that they can operate relatively independently. Siblings in situations of potential conflict should discuss their differences and consider how to divide tasks in the organisation, so that each has a chance to acquire and demonstrate competence, and they can both work in a complementary relationship. Where siblings cannot resolve conflicts, it becomes necessary to seek professional advice. If the situation still does not improve, they may have to consider working in separate businesses. One would have to leave, or the business would have to be split between them. When the family principle of treating all children equally is applied to the distribution of interests or shareholdings in a family business, this can cement into place the potential for rivalries between siblings into the future.

Cesare Mondavi was a first-generation wine maker in the early days of the developing Californian wine industry. When he passed on his wine-making business to his two sons Peter and Robert, he gave them divided responsibility over the family winery. Peter ran the vineyard while Robert focused on sales and marketing. After Cesare died, differences between the brothers developed into a battle for control of the company. Ultimately, Robert left the business and started court proceedings which forced the company to buy out his 20% share in cash. Robert acquired further land holdings and established a new and bold high quality wine venture in Napa Valley. Under his stewardship, this new business became the foundation of a hugely successful winery. In his role of founding father of his own company, Robert wanted to develop his sons to become the future leaders of the family business. However, the skills of business visionary and family steward do not necessarily go hand in hand. Part of the problem was that Robert, like his father, wanted to see both his sons involved in the family business. By placing his two sons in open competition with each other, he was unwittingly reproducing his own past. This drove a wedge between the brothers, commencing when Robert named both his sons as co-CEOs of the Mondavi Corporation in 1990. From the start, the brothers fought constantly over the company's direction. Robert had been afraid that if he chose one son for the CEO role, the other would leave the company, but his decision to appoint both only muddied the waters. Finally in 1994, the brothers asked their father to name one of them CEO. Robert chose his eldest son Michael. This ended the fighting, and the company continued with a management team comprising the two brothers and seven other executives. All plans were subject to approval by an outside board of directors. Robert was lucky that his sons realised that they needed one brother as CEO and the other serving under him. The winery went public in 1993. The initial public offering, which was designed to help the business finance growth, marked the opening of the final chapter for the family business. Michael's reign as CEO was unsuccessful. In 2001, after a relatively short period at the helm, he stepped down. With the board of directors firmly in non-family hands, the decision to sell the business after an offer from a large competitor went through unopposed. By the time the company lost its independence in 2004, both brothers had left the business.

This illustrates the issues that may arise when parents force siblings into the same business. Rivalry is likely to flourish instead of cooperation. In the case of the Mondavis, the error did not only occur at first generational level. It was repeated when the business was passed to the second generation. A clear and distinct separation of roles between family members involved in a business would have helped. But ultimately, if the children are not competent, it will only serve to delay the inevitable decline.

In-Laws

When a child or family member marries, the family must consider how the spouse will fit in, and whether they should eventually have any claim to ownership of the business, particularly on the death of the family member they married. Apart from ownership considerations, other issues include entitlement in the future to be employed in the business, and access to financial information on the business. In some families, spouses are treated just like all other family members. They are given the same access to financial information, and similar opportunities to participate in governance or even management of the business, just like

their spouse and their spouse's relatives. In other situations, the involvement of in-laws is restricted. They may be allowed some partial opportunity to participate, with access to a limited amount of information.
They do not get to vote, and they have no say in any of the business
dealings. In other words, they are trusted, but only up to a point. In
many situations, in-laws are excluded from any conversations regarding
ownership and financial matters relating to the business. The extent to
which in-laws are trusted is affected by a number of factors, including
the family's history with divorce or separation, the quality of marital relationships of other members within the family, the overall family's values, its religious/ethnic background, and the financial independence of
the in-law.

Business families share common goals and a passion for their business.
New family members with no prior experience with the business, may
feel excluded or under pressure to conform to the family's beliefs and
attitudes. In some families, children's spouses are actively encouraged to
work in the family business. This can be a poisoned chalice, since non-
family employees may believe the in-laws got the job solely because they
married into the family. Other family members may treat the in-laws as
outsiders. As a result, any inadequacies or weaknesses in their business
performance become the focus of attention. If they are to prove themselves and be accepted, they must be quite competent. In this respect, it
can be helpful if they have had outside business experience prior to joining the firm. Ideally, the family should have a policy to cover all even-
tualities in dealing with new in-laws. There must be no ambiguity if the
potential for dispute is to be avoided. In some business families, it is a
requirement that all family members enter into a prenuptial agreement
when they marry, to ensure that the interests in the business or shares
in the family company remain exclusively within the family. The marital
status of family members and the relationship of the family with part-
ners/spouses will colour any succession plan and entitlements around
ownership, management, corporate governance, and the drafting of
wills, trusts and shareholders agreements.

FAMILY BUSINESS LIFE CYCLE

We have considered the structural form of family enterprise as part of
the three circle model, and we have considered potential difficulties with
relationships. Family dynamics are also a function of the relative stage

of the business from an ownership perspective, and whether it is transitioned from the first to the second or third generations. Where sons carry on a business and one of them dies, the surviving sons may find themselves working alongside nephews and nieces or a sister-in-law. Over time, family relationships may become more distant. Ownership can become more fragmented when it passes through a number of generations. There are three primary stages of evolution:

First generation – Owner-managed business

This is the starting point for entrepreneurial owner-managed businesses. They may become family businesses when more family members are recruited into management, or are allocated ownership interests. These are typically businesses where one individual has voting control and makes all key decisions. Sometimes, a husband and wife team run the business together. In these situations, governance is not an issue. The owner/manager may be relying on the children to join the business to ensure its continued operation. The alternative is to sell the business or to consider transferring ownership to the children, bringing in professional management to run the business on their behalf. The primary challenge here is to choose the right ownership structure for the next generation. This decision must take account of the people who would be involved in the management of the business, the people who would be owning the business, and protecting the wealth of the business for the family as a whole. This gives rise to a number of questions:

– Who should I leave my shareholding in the business to?

– Do family members who join the business have sufficient ability or qualifications to operate the business?

– How should they be remunerated?

– How will their performance be evaluated?

– Will their employment impact on long-standing employees?

– What part of the business should they be employed in?

–   When a number of children join the business, how can it be struc-
    tured so as to minimise the potential for future conflict between
    them?

–   To whom should I ultimately leave control of the business?

Second generation – Sibling Partnership

If ownership of the business passes to more than one child, it becomes
a sibling partnership. Power and control are now shared by a group of
relatives rather than being centralised in the hands of one individual.
Some of them may not necessarily be employed in the business. Developing processes for sharing power and control among siblings and avoiding sibling rivalry are the challenges that face family firms at this point.
It is essential that good communication and governance structures are
in place to manage the relationship between those family shareholders
employed in the business and those family shareholders not employed
in the business. If non-working shareholders are investing their inheritance in the business under their sibling's leadership, it is important that
they are kept appraised of all financial matters impacting on the business. If siblings wish to exit, there must be formal structures to govern
their departure, since shareholding interests may be passing amongst a
much wider group of individuals. Those involved may wish to seek out
roles for their children. The different and varying abilities and ages of
sibling's children can result in siblings holding conflicting views on the
future involvement of their families in the business.

Third generation and beyond – Cousin consortium

With increasing levels of fractional ownership, at this stage family businesses can be at their most complex at the ownership and governance
level. By now, interests in the business can be held by many cousins from
different branches of the family. Often, no single family or shareholder
will have a controlling interest. Some of the family members will work
in the business, others will not. Different family members will have alternate views on the value and security of their investment and the extent to which they feel connected to the business. If the complexity
arising from the diversity of ownership is not properly controlled and

managed, there remains huge potential for dispute and contention among shareholders. Unlike siblings who have been reared in the same family, cousins may have little in common. The powerful "family" connection that cemented business relationships in the first and second generation may be much weaker in the third generation and beyond. It is therefore vital that the right organising mechanisms are in place to manage the expectations of family ownership and other key stakeholder groups. Appropriate governance structures should be in place and each situation will require different tailored solutions specific to the particular family's needs.

These changes and transitions may occur over a very long period of time. This will feed into the overall organisational structure and ethos of the business. Different considerations and issues need to be absorbed and remembered at each stage in the context of the overall succession planning process. The level and stage of your business, and the relative positioning of all key stakeholders and their individual family units, will feed into the overall ownership and governance structures. When managed correctly, this will optimise the opportunity for the future continuity and success of the business.

CHAPTER 2 – ACTION

- Consider who the key stakeholders are and what their concerns and expectations might be.

- Consider family relationships and how different family members work together.

- Reflect on the areas that are likely to cause conflict between family members.

CHAPTER 3

BUSINESS STRATEGIES – GETTING THE BUSINESS INTO SHAPE

OUTLINE:

By the end of this chapter you will have an understanding of:

–   Developing a strategic plan for your business.

–   How to document a strategic succession plan.

–   The various structural alternatives for your business.

An effective succession plan will enable a company to examine and integrate a wide range of business planning elements into one overall co-ordinated plan. Issues such as transition of ownership, the potential of family members in a management capacity, how family members will interact in running the business and the wider financial commitments family may place on the business, should all be examined as part of the overall strategic plan for the business. Creating a strategic plan is a key component of planning for growth. This will help you prepare a realistic vision for the future of your business. By doing this, you can maximise your business's potential for growth, and ensure that it is in the best possible condition for passing to the next generation.

The key foundations for a good business are a sound and clear business strategy, an efficient and well-working corporate structure, and knowledge of how much the business is actually worth. It is important that all of these elements exist to achieve the goals of the company's stakeholders. Any oversights may result in the business suffering while a succession plan is being implemented. This could lead to conflict with staff or family members, and ultimately jeopardise the overall succession plan.

Business strategy assessment

Succession issues must be commensurate and appropriate to the overall strategic direction of the company. Unfortunately, this is a matter which many private business owners leave to chance. While some individuals may have developed a written business plan, it is often not up to date or relevant in the context of the future running of the business by other family members or the existing family management team. While nothing can replace the existing family management's business experience, a more structured approach based on formalised planning improves the consistency and quality of the plans and decisions as the business grows in size and scope.

What is strategic planning?

Strategic planning provides analysis of the business and its environment in order to create a formal programme for guiding its development and success into the future. A strategic plan is not to be confused with a business plan, which is about setting short or midterm goals and defining the steps necessary to achieve them. A strategic plan typically focuses on a business's mid to long term goals and explains the strategies for achieving them. The purpose of strategic planning is to set your overall goals for your business. It involves stepping back from your day-to-day operations, asking where a business is headed, and asking what its priorities should be.

Three key elements of strategic planning

Developing a strategy for business growth requires an in-depth understanding of the way your business works and its position relative to other businesses in your market. A simple starting point is to ask the following questions:

–   **Where is your business now?**
    This involves understanding as much as possible about your business, including how it operates internally, what drives profitability

and how it compares to your competitors. Your review should be separate from your day–to-day tasks. It should be realistic, detached and critical in holistically assessing how your business operates.

– **Where do you want to take it?**
You need to set out your core objectives. Work out your vision, mission, objectives, values, goals and methodology for achieving them. Where do you see your business in 5 or 10 years? What should be the focus of your business and your source of competitive advantage over competitors in your market?

– **What do you need to do to get there?**
What changes will you need to make in order to deliver on your strategic objectives? What is the best way of implementing those changes? What changes to the structure and financing of your business will be required? What goals and deadlines will you need to set for yourself and others in the business and in this process? In considering the business as a whole, what issues arise in the areas of acquisition plans, organic growth, diversification, as well as any other functional matters in key areas?

How is strategic planning done?
Strategic plans are unique to the individual business involved, and there are many methods for arriving at the end result. The basic steps you should consider in the context of an entrepreneurial business are:

– Diagnosis of the business situation. Examining where the business is in the current environment.

– Developing a mission statement, where the business is heading.

– Developing short – and long-term goals for the business. The short term goals should feed into the overall long-term goals from an operational perspective.

– Defining strategies. How you see these goals being met.

– An impact assessment on the business.

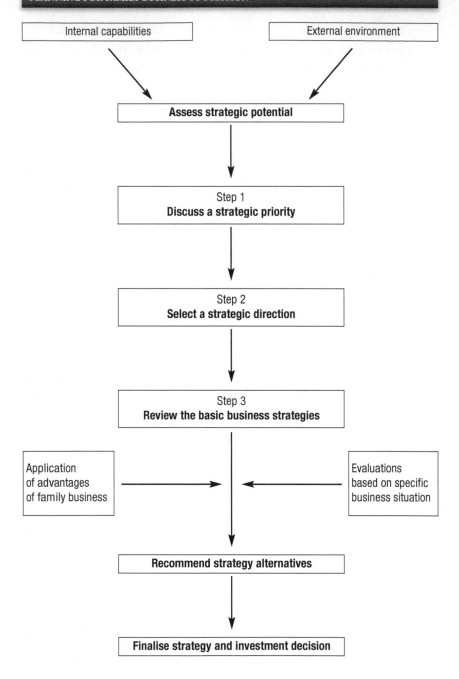

Once you decide to take action, you should consider the following steps:

1. **Formation of a strategic team**
    Basically, this means: who do you involve? Look for people who
    show the kind of analytical skills that strategic planning depends

upon. Ideally, you need a mix of creative thinkers and people with a solid grasp of operational detail. This step includes bringing together all the people you need to move forward with, in developing a succession plan.

2. Business Diagnosis

Strategic planning positions your business as effectively as possible in the marketplace by taking a critical look at the business and the environment in which it operates. There is a choice of strategic models that you can use to help structure your analysis. These models provide a simplified and abstract picture of the business environment.

One of the best known models is a SWOT (Strengths, Weaknesses, Opportunities and Threats) analysis, which is used by both smaller and bigger businesses, both in the profit and not-for-profit sectors.

A SWOT analysis assists in identifying the strategic issues confronting the business and the subsequent decisions that are required. At the conclusion of the strategic diagnosis, the management team should agree on the most critical issues, and spell out the means to address them as part of the overall strategic plan.

SWOT Matrix Model

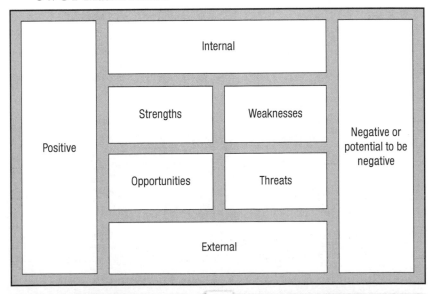

SWOT Analysis

— Strengths. Positive features of the organisation and factors that differentiate the business from its competition.

— Weaknesses. Deficiencies of the organisation and other areas of competitive disadvantage.

— Opportunities. Positive conditions such as new market openings and demographic changes that present new potential for the business. Changes in technology and market conditions can generate opportunities.

— Threats. Negative conditions such as government regulations, increased competition, market segment decline, a changing economic climate, and anything that constitutes a challenge to the business.

Below is an example of areas that a SWOT analysis can cover:

Strengths and Weaknesses Internal Factors	Opportunities and Threats External Factors
— What advantages does your company have? — What do you do better than anyone else? — What unique or lowest-cost resources do you have access to? — What do people in your market see as your strengths? — What factors help you "get the sale"? — What could you improve? — What should you avoid? — What are people in your market likely to perceive as weaknesses? — What factors lose you sales? — What are the advantages/disadvantages of your proposition? — What are your capabilities/gaps? — Competitive advantages? — USPs (unique selling points)/Reputation? — Resources, Assets, People? — Experience, Knowledge, Data?	— Where are the good opportunities facing you? — What are the interesting trends you are aware of? Useful opportunities can come from such things as: — Changes in technology and markets on both a broad and narrow scale — Changes in government policy related to your field — Changes in social patterns, population profiles, lifestyle changes, etc — Local events — Market developments — Competitors' vulnerabilities — Industry or lifestyle trends — Technology development and innovation — Global influences — New markets, vertical, horizontal — Niche target markets — Geographical, export, import

Strengths and Weaknesses Internal Factors	Opportunities and Threats External Factors
– Financial reserves, likely returns? – Marketing – reach, distribution, awareness? – Innovative aspects? – Location and geographical? – Price, Value, Quality? – Accreditations, Qualifications, Certifications? – Processes, Systems, IT, Communications? – Cultural, Attitudinal, Behavioural? – Management cover, Succession? Other factors may include: – Resources: Financial, Intellectual, Location – Cost advantages from proprietary know-how – Creativity/ability to develop new products – Valuable intangible assets: intellectual capital – Competitive capabilities	– New USPs – Tactics – surprise, major contracts, etc – Business and product development – Information and research – Partnerships, agencies, distribution – Volumes, production, economies – Seasonal, weather, fashion influences – What obstacles do you face? – What is your competition doing that you should be worried about? – Are the required specifications for your job, products or services changing? – Is changing technology threatening your position? – Do you have bad debt or cash-flow problems? – Could any of your weaknesses seriously threaten your business? – Political effects – Legislative effects – Environmental effects – IT developments – Competitor intentions – various – Market demand – New technologies, services, ideas – Vital contracts and partners – Sustaining internal capabilities – Obstacles faced – Insurmountable weaknesses – Loss of key staff – Sustainable financial backing – Economy – home, abroad – Seasonality, weather effects Other factors may include: – Takeovers – Market Trends – Economic Condition – Mergers – Joint Ventures – Strategic Alliances – Expectations of Stakeholders – Technology – Public Expectations – Competitors and Competitive Actions – Poor Public Relations Development – Editorial Criticism – Global Markets – Environmental Conditions

In a family business, the internal aspect of a SWOT analysis may highlight family related issues in which family influence may have a positive or negative effect. These include company culture, company image, key staff, their position or level of experience, the financial resources made available to the business by the family, how family relationships impact on operational capacity or efficiencies, and how the interaction of family members affects the overall organisational structure.

In addition to SWOT, other strategic models include:

- A PESTLE (Political, Economic, Social, Technological, Legal and Environmental factors) analysis.

- Porter's Five Forces (competitive rivalry within the industry, threat of new entrants, threat of substitutes, bargaining power of customers, bargaining power of suppliers), which look at the industry within which an organisation operates, and specifically competition within it.

- The 7S model (which examines Structure, Systems, Skills, Style, Staff, Shared Values and Strategy).

3. **Mission formulation**

As part of the company's self examination, management should develop a vision statement of what the business mission will be over the next number of years. This is the basic expression and communication of where the business intends to be. Its importance cannot be over-emphasised. A mission statement should answer the following questions:

- Why are we in business? Is it to provide for family members, to make a profit or to provide for secure employment to others, both family and non family members employed in the business?

- Who are our customers now, and who will our customers be in the future?

- How do we want to be known by our customers? Do we want to be known for the quality of our service, the efficiency of our systems or the cost of our product?

- What is our existing business? Will we remain in this business in the future?

4. **Goal definition**
    The findings of the strategic diagnosis, whether arrived at via a SWOT analysis or other model, should feed into setting strategic goals for the business – the major goals you need to achieve in order to realise your vision for the business. The team should set a goal for each critical issue area highlighted during the SWOT analysis. Each goal should be written as a measurable and precise statement in order to explain the specific execution and timeframes required. Clearly indicate how the goal is to be accomplished and the specifics of successful and measurable performance. Goals might include attracting a new type of customer, developing new products and services, or securing new sources of finance. These are the questions you should ask when formulating each goal:

    - What quantity is to be achieved?

    - What quality is to be realised?

    - How much will it cost?

    - Within what timeframe?

5. **Strategic business options**
    This involves setting out the key actions needed to attain your top level objectives, including:

    - Action steps to be taken

    - The individuals responsible for completing the steps

    - Timeframe for performance

- Resources or assistance required to take the steps.

Resourcing

This final step involves a summary of the implications of your proposed strategy for the resources your business needs. Use your newly defined mission goals and strategies to assess the demands they will place or the effect they will have on the business. This is a reality check to see what resources are available to determine the overall goals and strategies achievable. Where appropriate, you may need to revise goals and expectations. Unrealistic goals will make the overall strategic planning process redundant. Areas to be considered include:

- Financing requirements. What is the total implementation cost of the strategic plan?

- Staffing levels:

    - Are human resources adequate?

    - Will additional staff have to be hired?

    - Will staff need to be developed, re-trained or replaced?

- Premises and equipment:

    - Is the production capability sufficient?

    - What changes will be necessary?

- Organisational structure:

    - Is the business appropriately organised?

What form should the strategic plan take?

It is not essential for a strategic plan to be presented as a written document, especially with a small-scale business where the overall shared vision of the future can easily be communicated to stakeholders. Illustrative charts, tables or diagrams can often communicate the necessary information simply and effectively. As businesses increase in size and more people are involved, more people have to buy into the concept and implementation of any overall strategic plan for the business. In this scenario, a written document becomes an essential tool for all stakeholders. A written document often becomes a statement of intent, outlining the seriousness of the overall planning effort as well as presenting a tangible reference point from which progress and future efforts may be evaluated. Once a strategic plan is in place, it should not simply remain a written document. It must become a framework for management decisions in order to achieve the overall vision of stakeholders for the business. The strategic plan should be used regularly so that its stated goals are met and future business decisions made in light of the plan's requirements.

6. **Integrating action plans**

   Once an action plan has been determined, it must be integrated with any other business plans, including marketing arrangements, contingency plans and remuneration structures, making sure that the action plan does not conflict with any of the existing plans. If such conflict arises, you will need to ascertain the overriding action in relation to the overall goal of your business as a whole.

7. **Implementation**

   Implementing any strategic plan will very much depend on how your business operates. Different businesses have different ways of implementing what they feel is appropriate for them. The main steps owners should take to ensure effective implementation include:

   – Communicating the plan to everyone involved in implementing it.

   – Evaluating progress in respect of implementation of the plan.

   – Appointing individuals within the organisation to be accountable for areas of the plan for which they are responsible.

- Rewarding successful performance in light of meeting targets under the plan.

- Using the plan as a reference tool when taking important decisions.

- Reviewing and annually updating the plan to ensure it remains relevant.

Important strategic planning issues to consider

Growing a business can pose personal challenges for the owner or manager whose role could change dramatically, particularly when examined in the context of an overall succession plan. Effective strategic planning involves considering options that challenge the way business has been conducted hitherto. Decision making in some areas may be handed to others, as processes which have worked well in the past may no longer fit with future plans and may require change. It can be tempting for owners or managers to overlook alternatives that are uncomfortable for them personally. However, disregarding your options on the grounds of discomfort can seriously compromise your strategic plan. Ultimately you could compromise the growth of the business and its future continued successful operation under future family members as part of the overall succession process. Here are some examples of issues that tend to get overlooked:

- *The future role of the owner:*
  It may be in the best interests of the business for the owner to focus on a smaller number of responsibilities, or to hand over day-to-day control to someone with greater, or different type, of experience.

- *Location of the business:*
  Most small businesses are located close to where the owner lives. As a business grows, it may make sense to re-locate the business closer to customers or logistical infrastructure, in order to facilitate ease of access to customers. Relocation could be a response to changes in the marketplace, or to be closer to employees with certain skills.

- *Ownership structure:*
  Growing businesses in particular must get this right. The more a business grows, the more sophisticated it needs to be about meeting

its financing needs. The best option is often for the owner to give up a share of the business in return for equity finance, but this can be enormously difficult. It might also be appropriate to allocate equity to key management in order to ensure their retention by the business and their ongoing motivation. In an owner managed family business, the owner can often find this unpalatable.

In the final analysis, it is the owner of the business who decides the strategic plan. An honest assessment of the options allows for any decisions made to be as informed as possible.

Structuring your business for the future

Considering the entity you currently operate is another part of getting your business in order before you commence any succession planning exercise. A business owner may choose to change from one type of legal structure to another for a number of reasons, including growth, introduction of new business partners, tax efficiencies in repaying debt obligations, creditor protection or sub-division into different units.

Entity structure

The type of entity through which the family business is held can hugely impact the way and extent that a family's goals and aspirations for the transition of the business interests between generations can be achieved. Existing structures and possible future structures need to be considered, in addition to any other aspects that may impact on the overall structure. These include residency status of family members and any other international aspects of the family business that may affect how family wealth and its overall business interests should be held. Structures can often involve more than one type of entity, and can often be tiered. Any succession planning process may involve a review of each constituent part or component of the overall family holding structure. Commonly, a family trust may own a family trading company which in turn may own a number of subsidiaries. The focus of wealth and allocation of wealth may have more relevance with the trust structure. The focus of family involvement in management and operation of the business needs to be considered at the corporate level. Owners of larger public companies have little or no alternative in how their ownership is ultimately determined. However, owners of closely held businesses may have a number of alternatives:

– Sole trade/proprietorships

– Partnerships

– Private companies

– Trusts

There are many tax related and non tax related issues that owners of closely held businesses must consider when structuring or restructuring if they want to achieve their goals. The right choice of entity is crucial, as the financial transactions of a closely held business may have a large immediate and direct impact on the owner's personal finances, cash flow, tax bill and the overall wealth of the business family. Consideration must be given to the financial impact of any decisions on all key stakeholders. It is undesirable to devise a restructuring plan that accomplishes the goals of one at the expense of the other. This is best illustrated in the situation of a member of the elder generation and a member of the younger generation in a family business. One is concerned with exit strategies and achieving value on retirement. The other is concerned about growing the business from a long term perspective. Clearly, both goals are not mutually exclusive. Any structuring would need to involve some compromise, depending on resources available in the circumstances.

Sole Trade

The major disadvantages for sole trade are unlimited liability and high marginal rates of taxation. The primary advantage is lower compliance costs. Unlike a company, there are no annual filings or publicly available information on your business in the companies office, which means you gain a greater degree of privacy. Once any business goes beyond a certain size, unless there is a specific regulatory prohibition on incorporation, it rarely makes sense to continue to operate as a sole trader.

Partnerships

The advantages of a partnership structure include:

– It allows individual family members to be treated differently by virtue of the nature of their rights governing their partnership interest or partnership share. At the same time, it provides some benefit to all the family members who are partners in the partnership. For example, in many family investment partnerships, the partnership controlling interests may be held by the parents or by a family trust separately from the shares providing economic benefits, which may be distributed amongst all of the family.

–   The ability to incorporate a wide spectrum of rights or obligations by conferring different entitlements to capital and income and separating management from enjoyment of the assets through different classes of partner. In particular, in many family partnerships, income may be more heavily weighted in favour of the older generation while the current generation are still young.

–   It may be possible to obtain a degree of limited liability through having a limited liability partnership, where the general partner is a limited liability company.

–   Where ownership is fragmented, it may be possible to justify a discount in valuing the interest for tax purposes.

However, the primary disadvantages of a partnership structure are:

–   The majority of trading partnerships are general partnerships, so there is no liability protection for the personal assets of the partners.

–   Partnerships are tax transparent. Accordingly, profits are taxable on the partners at their marginal rate of taxation (currently 55% when income tax, PRSI and the universal social charge are accounted for.)

–   It can be difficult to distribute profits to one partner to the exclusion of another partner of the same class. Pro rata payment out of profits is the usual course of action. From an overall family management and succession planning perspective, this can be a deterrent if it is intended that those family members who work in the business are rewarded to a greater extent than those who do not directly participate.

– The greater number of partners, the greater degree of complexity. Difficulties arise on the death of a partner, requiring an overall integration of new partners and management of the exit of retiring partners.

Private Companies

This is the most common form of business structure. Obvious benefits include:

– The availability of limited liability for shareholders. This helps to protect the wider family wealth from third parties in the event of a business failure.

– The ability to include pre-emption rights and similar devolution clauses in the Articles of Association, thus ensuring that the company shares remain within the family. These clauses serve to restrict whom shares may be transferred to.

– The level of flexibility that can be incorporated through having different classes of shares carrying different rights to suit different generations. For example, voting control can be separated from having an entitlement to dividends or assets on a winding up. Alternatively, shares can be designed such that over time value may flow into them, which could facilitate an efficient transfer of value from one generation to the next.

– The ability to fragment value through minority holdings and/or different classification of shares, potentially attracting valuation discounts for tax purposes.

– Companies are suitable vehicles for equity raising, and can take advantage of any research and development grants or tax reliefs that may be available.

– Profits generated by trading activities are liable to corporation tax at 12.5%.

– Potential for the company as employer to make contributions to an employer sponsored pension scheme.

There are also disadvantages:

—   Lack of privacy, as all limited liability companies must file annual accounts with the Companies Registration Office.

—   Directors face personal liability and assume fiduciary duties on the acceptance of the office.

—   There is a potential double charge to tax at both company and shareholder level on the extraction of profits, which is a consideration where any succession plan may anticipate a future sale of the family business.

—   Unless the shares in the company are in turn owned by a trust, there is only a limited level of protection in the event of a divorce. The divorcing spouse can potentially seek recourse to the shareholding held by the family member as part of any financial provision made as a result of the marital break-up.

The table below outlines some of the comparative advantages/disadvantages between a corporate structure and other forms of ownership.

	Discretionary trust	Company	Individual	Partnership
Exposure to liability	Limited – subject to trust deed	Limited	Unlimited	Unlimited, and joint and several
Control over assets	Uncertain	Separated	Absolute	Joint
Accommodation of general wealth creation	High level of asset protection	Company wealth at risk	Wealth at risk	Wealth at risk
Ability to obtain finance	Reasonable	Good	Good	Good

	Discretionary trust	Company	Individual	Partnership
Disclosure of results	None	Disclosure under Companies Acts	None	None – other than between partners
Compliance costs	Medium	Medium – high	Low	Low
Exposure to family disharmony	Moderate	Low	Moderate to high	Moderate to high
Ability to restructure	High	Moderate	Low	Low
Rates of tax on income	40% on income, including surcharge	12.5% on trading profits, 25% on investment income	55% – top marginal income tax rate	55% – top marginal income tax rate
CAT business relief	Yes where conditions met (potential for discretionary trust tax)	Yes where conditions met	Yes where conditions met	Yes where conditions met
CGT retirement relief	No	Yes where conditions met	Yes where conditions met	Yes where conditions met

Trusts

Trusts may be used for a variety of purposes. The flexibility of trusts is perhaps the major reason they are so widely used in tax planning. Trusts can be created by funding them during one's lifetime (inter vivos trust) or they can be created by the terms of a will (testamentary trust). The terms of the trust may allow it to be changed or even revoked. The terms of the trust may be fixed or irrevocable at the date of creation. Primary purposes for using trusts in both financial planning and for holding family businesses for more than one generation include:

–   They facilitate the retention of control of the business by the senior generation (as trustees) while allowing for its economic value to accrue for the benefit of the next generation (as beneficiaries).

–   Asset protection. In certain situations, a properly drafted trust can protect assets in the trust from the creditors of a beneficiary. This is particularly useful with a discretionary trust where the beneficiaries have no automatic or specific entitlement to receive income or capital of the trust. Additionally, they may potentially offer at least some protection in a divorce situation.

–   They protect the family's privacy, since there is no requirement to publish trust accounts in the same way as private companies have to.

–   They may be used to avoid the probate process. The assets that are held in the trust, created and funded during the settlor's lifetime, are controlled by the terms of the trust. This can be useful, particularly if family members contest a deceased's estate.

–   Trusts can be created for the benefit of multiple beneficiaries and can allow the trustees discretion in making distributions in a tax effective manner.

–   The trusts can allow individual family beneficiaries to be treated differently. This is particularly important in providing for beneficiaries that may have special needs relating to education, health and more.

–   A trust can help fragment ownership and thereby potentially secure valuation discounts for taxation purposes.

–   By contrast, a trust can also be used to preserve the power of block voting for shares in a family company.

–   Trusts can be long term in nature. While they may not exist as long as a corporate vehicle, they can last longer than most partnerships, without the requirement for being substantially altered in form.

There are also disadvantages to holding assets or a business through a trust structure:

–   If a trust is not sufficiently flexible and changes are required, an application to court may be necessary to achieve the desired result. This can be a costly exercise.

–   Beneficiaries' rights are limited, making it critical to select suitable and appropriate trustees to administer a trust.

–   With discretionary trusts, an initial 6% tax charge and an annual one-off charge of 1% may arise.

–   From a governance perspective, trustees' decisions are usually taken on a unanimous basis. Practically speaking, each trustee has an effective veto on any potential decision. In the context of a family business where there is a need to act quickly in response to prevailing economic circumstances, the potentially unwieldy nature of a trust's management structure may not be advantageous.

–   Trustees have fiduciary obligations and can be held personally liable for breaches of trust. Family members thinking of taking up the position of trustee should consider carefully before accepting such a role.

Privacy and confidentiality

A family may wish that information relating on its asset holdings and wealth is not easily accessible to the public, journalists or other parties. The names of shareholders in a company can easily be obtained from a search in the Companies Office where limited companies must file accounts. This provides information on asset holdings, trading position and accumulated wealth held by the company. Similarly, details of the registered owner of a particular property or properties can be obtained through a search of the Land Registry or Registry of Deeds.

Trusts

However, utilisation of certain trust or corporate structures can limit publicly available information. If the trust is the owner of an asset, whether property or shares, the names of the trustees or the corporate trustee company will appear in the share register or on the property title deeds as owner of the property. This provides a degree of confidentiality from anyone wishing to pry into your affairs.

Company filing

In relation to information on company asset holdings, there is a divergence in the level of detail that needs to be submitted to the Companies Office for limited and unlimited companies. Obviously, you would not wish to avail of a more favourable disclosure regime if you lose the benefit of limited liability.

Non filing structure

An unlimited company does not have to file accounts if it has at least:

– One individual who is a shareholder, or

– One non-EU company with unlimited liability which is a shareholder.

Accordingly, if your existing limited liability holding company was converted into an unlimited company, since you are an individual shareholder this requirement would be met. As it would be generally imprudent to encourage any individual to hold shares in an unlimited company that is actually trading, then to achieve the effect of not having to file accounts while preserving limited liability, a non-EU limited company would be incorporated as part of the overall group structure as illustrated in the diagram below.

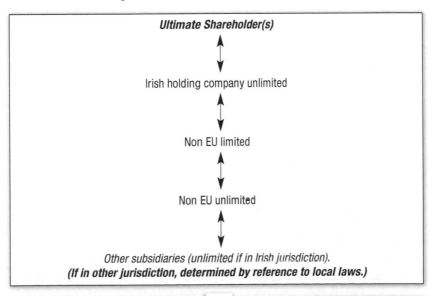

Ultimate Shareholder(s)

Irish holding company unlimited

Non EU limited

Non EU unlimited

Other subsidiaries (unlimited if in Irish jurisdiction).
(If in other jurisdiction, determined by reference to local laws.)

The use of limited company shareholders for the non-EU unlimited company is to create a backstop on liability rising higher in the group or for you personally. All other Irish subsidiaries that are limited still have an accounts filing requirement.

Business valuation

Having an accurate valuation of your business will feed into many of the decisions to be taken in the context of your overall succession plan. The value of your business can impact on many succession planning issues:

– *CAT and CGT*
  What is the tax cost and benefit of transferring the shares in the business to your family now as opposed to in the future?

– *Shareholders Agreements*
  What value should be included in a shareholders agreement for transfers and buyouts? What is the nature of the valuation formula? What is an appropriate valuation formula, given minority shareholdings? Will the agreement provide for the appointment of a valuer, or will there be an arbitration clause governing who the valuer should be in the event of a dispute?

– *Retirement*
  How much will the sale of the business provide for retirement? Will it be enough to support an enjoyable retirement?

– *Life Insurance*
  Is life insurance adequate given the value of the business and other financial commitments? Does your life cover need to be reviewed and updated?

– *Corporate Finance*
  Should you need to raise equity or debt, how much value is in the business from a leverage perspective? Is an IPO a viable option? The actual valuation of a business will be shaped by the price that willing buyers are prepared to pay for the company. For tax purposes, even though a buyer is not imminent, it still needs to be valued on a

market value basis. A business valuation can obviously vary, depending on who does it. An independent expert valuer is the best person to carry out such a task.

— Even though valuing a company is not an exact science, the following key factors can determine a company's value:

    — The company's historic and projected financial performance.

    — The size of the company.

    — The strength of its management team.

    — The company's asset base.

    — The attractiveness of the sector in which the company operates and the strength of its market position.

    The usual methods for valuing a company may be based on one of the following:

    — Assets based valuation.

    — Multiple of normalised earnings (typically a weighted average over the last number of years).

    — Discounted cash flows.

In anything other than a sale situation, a company valuation is a theoretical exercise. There is usually no widespread market for closely held business interests, and usually very few comparable sales for an appraiser to use in carrying out a valuation. That is why the valuation of closely held businesses can be more complex and more subjective than for other kinds of assets. However, it will give you an overall indication of potential tax liabilities and potential value as represented by the business, and this will have a bearing on your overall thought process in determining how you wish to proceed.

CHAPTER 3 – ACTIONS

–   Follow the various steps in assessing and drafting a strategic plan suitable for your business.

–   Examine the best overall holding structure for your business going forward.

–   Obtain a professional valuation of your business. This will impact on many of your choices in a succession planning context.

CHAPTER 4

MANAGEMENT TRANSITION

While many family business owners hope that the next generation will take over ownership and leadership of the business, it is surprising that a successful development and formal training programme for family members is largely ignored, or at best implemented on an ad hoc basis. If the business is to continue to thrive, it is vital that competent, capable management, family or non-family, continue to run the business, and that they are equipped with skills, knowledge and experience to face future challenges. Not all children will be interested in managing the family business. For those that are, preparing them for management and leadership roles is a formidable exercise. Most families wish for meaningful careers for the next generation, so it appropriate that they get the right level of support to assist them in whatever career path they choose. However, family members can be an important source of talent for the business. Implementing training and development activities to support those family members who wish to become involved in the business, and preparing for this earlier on in their careers, will ultimately assist in generating capable leaders to support the family legacy.

All key stakeholders will want to know how the business will continue into the future. To ensure the success of successor selection and development, a clear process is required. Responsibility for grooming the next generation lies with the senior business owners. They will decide who will be the next CEO of the company. The level of effort and seriousness with which they take this responsibility is hugely important in the continued future success of the business during a pivotal time in the life cycle of the business.

INFLUENCE OF THE LIFE CYCLE ON FAMILY BUSINESS CAREERS

Where management talent is harnessed primarily from family members, the family life cycle will impact on future potential family business careers. Every child born is a future potential employee. For senior members of the family, retirement and/or death trigger an event for management succession. Difficulties arise where these events are not planned for. The senior generation is facing the uncertainties of retirement, their children are entering middle life, and the grandchildren are entering young adulthood. All three generations are struggling with a big question: "Who am I and what does the family business mean in my life?" In family businesses, the CEO retains the role for much longer than in a similar position in a public company. Family members being groomed for succession can therefore play a significant role and exert significant influence on the family business's (and the family's) fortunes over an extended period of time. Given the family life cycle, the attitudes and beliefs of different generations may be a potential source of conflict. In addition, the fact that the successive/next generation's involvement in the business is at a separate stage from that of the senior generations, can give rise to potential conflict. Ideally, each phase of a generation's involvement in the business should be along the lines of planning the strategy, growing the business, mentoring the successor, letting go of control and supporting the transition. If the next generation is to be mentored, while the current generation is not prepared to let go of control and support a transition, there is clear potential for conflict.

FAMILY BUSINESS AS A CAREER

Most parents who own a business want to pass it on to their offspring. Many family members would happily prefer to work in a family business rather than in a non-family owned business. There is no guarantee that children will actually enter into a career in the family business. Parents may be emotionally conflicted in encouraging their children to do so. On the one hand, they may wish to pass the fruit of their endeavours on to their children. On the other, they do they wish to trap them or make them feel there is any onus on them to join, as opposed to pursuing their own path. Parents also consider issues around conflicts between children and themselves. They ask themselves whether bringing children into the business will de-motivate valuable non family managers.

Important attitudes towards work and the family business are formed during childhood. Children become conscious of their parent's behaviour, attitudes to the business and the family's values in a business context, long before they receive any formal request to join the business. Children learn by example. They look to their parents and grandparents as role models. A family culture that encourages independence and competitiveness helps build an entrepreneurial disposition. In addition, many children of wealthy parents claim that one of the best things their parents did to motivate them was not make their life too easy. Parents should set limits for their children and lead by example. As children get older, they will learn about the structures in the family business. They may get an opportunity to attend family meetings where business issues are discussed. Time spent working in the family business during school and university vacations can give next generation family members valuable work experience. It will give children valuable insights into the culture and relationships of the family business before they eventually join the business or decide that this is not for them and pursue roles elsewhere. Open communication and exposure to the family business provides children with an opportunity to make an informed decision as to whether or not to join the business when the time comes. This can only be to everyone's benefit.

Although a family culture that encourages independence and competitiveness helps builds entrepreneurship, it may not be for everyone. Rich Products, an international food products company, is one of the largest private companies in the United States. It was founded in 1945 by Robert Rich Sr. According to one of Robert's grandsons, his aggressive genes run in the family. It was impossible to work for this family and not feel the importance of competition. But competition needs to be positive, and can impact on each family member differently. Robert Sr fostered competition between his two sons. He would wake them every morning at 5 a.m. and make them do push ups. At their holiday home, he would have them do morning sprints until they could do no more. He made them compete against one another in a range of sports. One son was a natural athlete and thrived under these conditions. The other son was not and did not. The natural athlete joined the family business and succeeded his father as chairman. The second son chose to become an Anglican priest rather than join the family business. This illustrates that while the entrepreneurial culture of the family can influence the next generation, its impact varies for each family member.

DECIDING WHEN TO RETIRE

Fear of retirement can be a powerful factor. Owners of family firms identify with the business. They view any impending retirement as a loss of self esteem, which is why they often prevaricate and put off the succession process. Sometimes, the founder's spouse is reluctant to encourage a partner's move into retirement. The culture of a family may discourage open inter-generational discussion about the family's future in the event of the death of one of the parents. Owners must prepare themselves for a phase of their lives that does not revolve solely around the family business. Financially, they need to make provision for themselves and their spouse. Emotionally, the process can be easier to engage in if other activities have been planned for retirement, and if some involvement in the business remains. The family connection with the business makes it impossible to sever ties entirely. The existing/retiring generation should consider how best to realign their involvement in the business going forward. The vast experience of the founders remains a huge resource to a business. New roles leveraging that experience can benefit the transition process and ensure continued involvement by the current (senior) generation, albeit with a reduced time involvement.

Ideally, you should have a clear retirement date in mind. Communicate this date to all key stakeholders. In larger-scale family businesses, clear and explicit management criteria should be drawn up on HR issues, including addressing the CEO's retirement age. Whether or not formal policies are in place, problems can still arise when founders are reluctant to step down from the day-to-day operation of the business. Succession will proceed much more smoothly if founders step down when they are still in full command of their abilities and are in a position to provide guidance to succeeding management. Holding on into your 70s and 80s affects the lives of next generation successors, who are probably in midlife and are anxious for the recognition, opportunities and independence that leadership affords. In short, decide when to retire and stick to that decision. This does not involve having to stop all involvement in the business. It does mean that any new role is not directly related to the day-to-day operations of the business.

UNDERSTANDING FUTURE BUSINESS MANAGEMENT NEEDS

Once you have decided on an appropriate retirement date, any process involving selection of successors must consider the future management needs of the business and the existing state of the business. The progression of the family firm from generation to generation, the growth of the family, and the ever-increasing complexity and dynamism in the wider commercial marketplace, create new demands on future family leaders. The family business is likely to be very different in 15 years time, just as the existing business is very different from the business that operated 15 or 20 years ago. Management skills and styles that may have served well historically may be less effective today, due to changed markets, increased use in technology and greater competition. On the other hand, today there is greater focus on human resources, which is beneficial. Families tend to be inward-focusing. Family businesses often replicate skills and practices that have served them well in the past, while remaining aware of the changes in the wider environment. Ideally family businesses should identify what management tasks the business will need to emphasise in the future. When considering required future management competencies and the next generation's capabilities, it is important for the successor generation to be viewed in light of the overall strategic plan for the business. This will also feed into any personal development plan being devised for the successor generation, so that it is not simply a replica of existing management practices and experience. This is a useful exercise for larger family businesses, where there are a number of successors. It can assist in identifying those individuals with the correct skill sets for roles within the organisation, and match them accordingly.

Before considering actual candidates, you should review the current state of your business. Look at the vision for the business, the mission statement, the strategic plan, the market position and the company culture. Where appropriate, engage with key stakeholders in examining these as part of potential future management transition and training programmes for candidates. It also helps to compare your business with your competitors or other identical businesses, and with standards within your industry. An up-to-date understanding of the company's current position, direction and strategy within your market will feed into the appropriate criteria when selecting management candidates. Your review should examine the external job market, and ascertain the company's standing in the market. This allows you to benchmark roles within the company and the individuals filling these roles against current practise. This is a useful exercise even if no family management candidates are immediately appropriate, and where recruitment of suitable external management must be considered.

The Murugappa Group, founded in 1900, is an Indian conglomerate, where family management transitioned to professionally managed executives in the late 1990s. In 1990, an external group chairman was brought in, with the family taking on advisory roles. The family remain involved as cultural ambassadors throughout the companies, and spent a lot of time with non-family CEOs and executives, providing support, assuring succession, and representing the family on the boards of all the subsidiaries. When the external professional chairman retired, another family member assumed the lead role, but the overriding criterion is competence rather than being a family member. Next generation family members considering a career in the family business are encouraged to first obtain outside experience. If they do join the business, advancement is based purely on merit. Professional management competencies, whether the executives are family or not, are regarded as key to management transition.

DEFINE KEY LEADERSHIP POSITIONS

The existing management team and board of directors should define the future key leadership positions of the company, identify the related core competencies for each position, and compile a list of the skills and behaviours required by a relevant candidate to perform the job. If required, bring in outside management consultants for this exercise. You need to know what executive positions are needed over the next few years, and what criteria that candidates should possess in order to be considered for the roles.

IDENTIFY CANDIDATES

Create a pool of potential successors, and review candidates using core competencies as a framework. Examine these in light of their current roles and responsibilities, previous work history, education, abilities, professionalism, years of experience, particular talents, people skills, inherent positive or negative personality traits, and other relevant job related criteria. Explore the professional and personal expectations of each candidate, in order to obtain a better understanding of the capacity to perform within the context of the company.

MATCH CANDIDATES

Once you have documented the future leadership needs of the business and assessed potential leaders, senior management should analyse and match the criteria for each candidate against positions that are suitable for them. Independent management consultants can assist with this process, using interviews and other tools to assess behavioural traits, core competencies and any other talents that candidates may possess. Independent consultants can bring a fresh and different perspective, and may shed new light on the traits and abilities of existing employees. If a successor is readily apparent within the family, a grooming programme should be developed to train the successor appropriately. If family members do not necessarily have the skills or talents to undertake a leadership role, you will have to examine successors outside the family. If an appropriate successor is not currently employed in the business, you will have to consider recruiting external candidates. You will also have manage the expectations of existing members of the leadership team, and help them plan their own exit strategy. You will have to sensitively manage expectations of family members and key staff in this situation.

Once you have identified a successor, or a number of potential successors, and you have assessed their existing level of preparedness, you need to match their existing skill sets with the required job core competencies.

Any areas of weakness must be identified and the required skills or experience developed. The overall process must at all times take account of and acknowledge the successor's personal career goals and expectations, since there is a presumption that the individual will remain in a role for a long time.

HR ISSUES

To preserve family harmony and to ensure sound decision making, owners of family businesses must successfully separate family issues and business issues when deciding on the next business leader. There is often a conflict between what is right for the business and what is right for the family, such as deciding to employ a family member when an external candidate would do a better job. Ways have to be found of assessing the performance of family members involved in the business, and deciding at what rate they should be paid. It helps to have clear policies in the areas of recruitment, training, mentoring, remuneration, performance appraisal and promotion. Below are some potential HR issues that can arise when family members are involved in an employment or management role within the business.

Recruitment

Business principles require that only the most competent individuals suited for the job should be employed. Recruitment policies based on family relationship, or the need to take care of a family member, can of course conflict directly with what may be best for the business. Family principles are often concerned with providing for family members and ensuring their financial security. That is why family members are sometimes employed regardless of their ability to perform the role assigned to them. There is often an expectation by owner managers that family members will join the business, even if they do not possess the right competencies. The hiring of individuals simply because they are family presents a threat to the overall effectiveness of the management unit within the business. When family business owners contemplate the long term welfare of the business, they sometimes have to choose between employing someone from the family not capable of doing the job, or facing family fallout if they choose to employ a non-family member. An attempt to compromise between what is good for the family and what is good for the business often results in decisions that are not good for the business.

That is why you should establish clear and explicit management criteria. Procedures should be developed to identify and manage the conflicting requirements between what is good for the business and what is good for the family. Ideally, there should be a clear separation between management and ownership, with management criteria governed by business principles, and ownership governed by family criteria. This allows for family members to be provided for through ownership stakes in the business, while only those individuals suitable to run the business would be admitted to employment roles. Confusion about who can and cannot join the company can damage family relationships. Draw up a clear set of guidelines, specifying in what circumstances family members may join the business. Prepare a predetermined set of criteria, such as experience acquired elsewhere and formal education and training, to provide guidelines that family members can adhere to and that avoid ambiguity. If family members are aware from the outset that they need to fulfil certain criteria before being admitted to the family business, they are under no illusion as to what is required. Their expectations can also be managed better.

Transparent selection criteria could include:

—   A minimum requirement of further education.

—   Outside work experience.

—   The availability of a legitimate vacancy, so that jobs are not "created" for family members.

—   Selection based on objective criteria. It must be clear that family members are only considered if their skills, qualifications and experience are appropriate.

—   In addition to any recruitment process, there must be a training and promotion policy.

Training and Development

Family members admitted to the business will need appropriate training. Roles allocated should offer clear responsibility and accountability. The job should be one that the organisation needs, not a job specifically created to provide a family member with employment. If the successor's job description is clear, both the next generation family member and the seniors can be comfortable with their respective roles. Clarity of the family member's role allows other managers and non-family employees to recognise how they will fit into the business. Founders must not invest the company's resources to provide their children with an opportunity for promoting their wellbeing and development, unless this is also in the best interests of the business.

At all times, the training and development of family members should be based on and be consistent with the business's needs. If family members' employment ambitions are inconsistent with the family firm's requirements, it might be better for them to seek employment elsewhere. It is worth considering whether any skills or training of family members should focus on areas where existing management is not strong, thus filling in gaps within the management structure. This would involve appropriate use of the next generation's talents and abilities where it fits in with their own career aspirations, and would also help a family member create an independent niche within the business. If family members have developed the relevant skills and experience to perform all the task-based roles within the business, the next stage of their development is to enhance their skill set by providing them with genuine management and leadership opportunities. When a family successor is committed to his or her career, incremental increases in responsibility will allow them to gain the trust of key stakeholders and gain the respect of the employees.

Mentoring

A well-chosen mentor with broad business experience from outside the family can support young adults as they learn how to run the business. A mentor can be invaluable in helping a family member achieve his or her potential. The mentor could be a trusted, long-serving member of management within the business, who is responsible for core business activities. If an honest and effective teacher-coach relationship is to be achieved, the mentor should be so secure in their job that they do not view the family member as a threat. The mentor should be willing to share their expertise with the junior family member, and promote their self-development. The mentor will help the successor grow into an executive and leadership role, and will coach the successor on how to exercise good business judgment, how to relate to other staff members and how to assess risks within the business. Given the dynamics of parent/child relationships, a non-family mentor may be more successful in developing the knowledge of the family employee.

Remuneration

Family principles might dictate that all family members be treated equally. If a number of siblings join a family business, they are all remunerated on a similar basis. In a business context, however, salary and benefits should be based on the individual's performance and contribution to the overall success of the business. Problems in family businesses arise over business and personal monies, and where remuneration is viewed as a means of extracting value from the business for the benefit of family members. This leads to confusion as to whether the payments made are by virtue of the individual's status as a family member or for the role and job they are performing. Pay scales sometimes vary significantly within family businesses. Some companies pay family members less than the market rate on the basis that the business will ultimately be theirs. Other companies pay family members in excess of the market rate. When all family members are paid the same, top performing family members are actually being underpaid, while incompetent and underperforming family members are being overpaid. This sows the seeds for disharmony, and could prompt more competent family members to consider employment elsewhere. This is another argument for making sure that family HR policies specifically recognise totally separate roles of management and ownership. Based on management principles, family members would be paid the same as all other employees on the basis of what is best for the business and what is a market rate remuneration package relative to the role they are performing, their skill set and their overall level of competence.

Performance appraisal and promotion

Each individual is ultimately responsible for their own career and personal development. This is why most employees want to know what is required or expected of them, and why they welcome constructive feedback on their performance. Establishing performance indicators helps management provide criteria against which both the successors and management can ensure that long term goals will eventually be met. Performance indicators assess the progress of potential successors within the business, and allows them to assess their own development. Any performance appraisal system should obviously indicate areas that need improvement and areas where the employee performs well, so that their strengths can be leveraged.

Most modern businesses have objective performance appraisal criteria whereby individuals are judged on their overall contribution to the business and its organisational goals annually or more frequently. In a family context, this can be more tricky. When a parent has to review the performance of a child, it can be extremely stressful. Impartiality is very difficult, and family members often receive unfair or inappropriate feedback. Where there is a clear family history or culture within the organisation of a distinction between ownership and management, family members employed in the business must be subject to the same evaluation criteria as all other employees. As with any modern appraisal process, the feedback and overall collation of information must be objective, with the same criteria applying to all individuals throughout the organisation. An appropriate framework would involve a standardised annual performance appraisal form, regular employee meetings with management to establish their goals and ambitions, a development plan for the next year, review points for this plan, and the establishment of new objectives and development criteria. Management feedback to the employee must be based on the opinions of a number of individuals throughout the organisation, so as to obtain a comprehensive view of the employee's performance. It may sometimes be necessary for performance feedback to be anonymous, to avoid staff providing inaccurate feedback to cover up the inadequacies of family employees.

Ultimately, determining the appropriateness of family members to lead the business as part of any performance and appraisal process, is not restricted to their performance within the business context. It also depends on how they relate to family outside of the business, particularly in an ownership context, and how they relate to family members who may be owners but are not employed in the business. Genuine management prospects are not enough. They must possess leadership skills. They must have people skills. They must be able to liaise with all key stakeholders. They must safeguard family harmony and minimise disruption to the business.

Any performance appraisal process must feed into the promotion processes within the organisation. A formal policy, with clear criteria and standards for both the family and non-family employees, and with no ambiguity or potential for favouritism, is critical. This also reduces the potential for conflict between family members striving for the same leadership/management role, or family members and non-family members competing for positions/promotions within the organisation. A formal appraisal process which feeds into the overall promotion process creates a much more transparent professional managerial system, and minimises the potential for conflict.

Importance of outside experience

Work experience outside the family business has advantages for both the business and the individual. When family members gain experience away from the family, they can develop confidence and self esteem. They learn to stand on their own two feet, and they learn to have their performance evaluated in an objective way, with no family influence. Family members are likely to receive more constructive criticism and to be more open to coaching when the coach is not a family member.

When a family members learns how other companies work, this brings benefits to the family business. Working in a business which is different from the family business may expose family members to new concepts and ideas. Working in a business in the same sector or industry may provide insight into competitive practices in other organisations. It is not mandatory, but obtaining experience in a larger, more professionally organised company certainly enhances the overall experience perspective. New ideas can be brought back and applied within the context of the family business. Moving into the family business straight after school or college increases the potential of the naturally inward looking focus of the family to be more prevalent in the business context. Outside experience makes it more likely that the family member will explore new ways of doing things in the family business. Outside experience is also very beneficial when dealing with employees. It makes it easier to gain respect on the basis of their ability and not of their name. The benefits for family members who gain outside experience include:

– They have the opportunity to be evaluated and promoted on their own merits.

– They will get honest feedback from their employer.

– They will learn management skills and different ways of running a business.

– They will learn what their value is in the terms of salary and benefits.

– It provides them with an opportunity to make mistakes, which are valuable as part of any learning experience, away from the eyes of future colleagues.

– They have an opportunity to assess the advantages or disadvantages of being involved in business outside or inside the family firm.

– They avoid the perception of having taken the easy option of moving to the family business without ever having worked anywhere else.

– Next generation family members get to expand their personal network, meeting people who may later be important business contacts.

– They broaden their view in a business context, enabling them to identify new business opportunities which can prove advantageous to the family business if they ever become employed in it at a later stage.

SELECTING THE RIGHT SUCCESSOR

When making decisions about the ongoing management of your company, what is best for the business often needs to be put ahead of what is best for individual family members. In many family businesses, policies are in place to shape successor's expectations of when, how and under what conditions they will be offered a position in the family business. So long as pay and performance standards, the selection process, and other factors are communicated clearly and early, it is possible to manage the expectations of family members considering joining the business and of the senior generation selecting them. In drawing up transparent selection criteria for selecting a successor, the following questions should be considered:

– Do the candidates have the ability to move the business forward?

– Do they have leadership skills and the requisite determination, focus and motivation to enable them to make hard decisions while motivating others within the organisation?

– How committed are they to the family business?

– Do they exercise good judgment?

Beyond specific job performance criteria, other behaviours or characteristics can determine an individual candidate's potential for a senior
leadership role. It is unlikely for any one successor candidate to possess
all of the ideal behaviours and characteristics. It is family and management's responsibility to prioritise what they wish to see in the next leader
of the business. It is their responsibility to configure their selection criteria based on the overall business situation and the family's values. For
example, a family that gives priority to placing trust in relationships may
choose a more trusted successor over a slightly more competent family
member who lacks the family's complete trust. A clear set of selection
criteria that is part of the overall HR selection process enables potential
successors to accept and support the outcome of the selection process.
An important question is: Who should make the selection decision? Is
it the existing owner/manager, should it be others within the business,
or should outside assistance be sought? Naturally, having other individuals involved will provide an objective element of assessment against
which the existing family leader may benchmark their decisions.

Considering succession candidates within the family can raise difficult
issues. If you are lucky, the choice of successor is straightforward. There
is one clear logical choice. The candidate will have the necessary capabilities, is committed to the family business, and will grow into that
role. This could be the eldest child. Competence, however, must be the
overriding criteria. If there are two or more competent candidates, it
may be appropriate to consider a dual leadership role, even if this can
be a less realistic option. Co-leaders must have the requisite skills to foster collaboration, maintain teamwork and be able to arrive at a consensus from a decision making perspective.

While the senior generation or founder may have possessed excellent
business acumen, entrepreneurial abilities, and managerial and leadership skills, there may be no obvious successor in the next generation. It
would be to the detriment of the business to force family members into
a senior leadership role where they do not have the abilities to perform
to the level required. Even if there are potential successors, possible rivalries would make it inappropriate to position particular family members as leaders of the business where they would not be accepted by other
members of their generation. The only appropriate outcome may be to

sell the business rather than force an unsuccessful succession that would diminish the overall wealth generated by the family through its endeavours. With a sale, the wealth generated may be distributed amongst the family in due course. If a large family business has several different divisions or enterprises, it may be possible to reconstruct them into separate business units, and for different family members to succeed to different businesses, which can then continue separately. Such a decision, of course, must still be commercially viable. If the companies cannot operate successfully as individual enterprises, this may not be an alternative.

When the next generation of management is simply too young or has insufficient experience to commence running the business, an outside managing director or senior non-family employee could be appointed to run the business until the transition within the family takes place. A professional manager could also act as mentor to the next generation, training them and developing them to succeed to the leadership role in the business following the retirement of the professional manager. If there is no capable or appropriate next generation leadership within the family, it is highly advisable to employ a professional non-family manager who would be appropriately remunerated. This situation is particularly apt where family businesses reach the third generation and beyond, with numerous family members holding ownership stakes within the business. Introducing professional management may be the only real alternative that ensures the continued success of the business. If a clear successor is not apparent, this should be addressed. Promoting a family member who does not have the ability to run the business does no one any favours: not the individual, and not the business. This is where third party advice can be hugely valuable, helping decide how best leadership roles can be fulfilled as part of the overall business transition, and whether non-family management should be appointed on either a temporary or permanent basis to the most senior roles.

DEVELOPING SUCCESSORS

Senior generations should try to establish a balance that ensures that family members are fully aware of the business, its positives and negatives, while being under no undue pressure to join the business. Family members should be encouraged to obtain outside experience and education, and to pursue their own career. If their career ambitions include involvement in the family business, this decision should be freely made with the full understanding of what is expected. Often, family members who join the business start at the lowest level, working their way up from line employee, to supervisor, to middle management and finally to upper management positions. Rightfully, this process takes years. Learning every job on the way up can be very valuable. The successor should be brought along and gradually afforded more and more responsibilities. Training must be appropriate to the overall career development strategy. Where mistakes are made, appropriate sanctions should be in place. Some of the most valuable business lessons are learned from mistakes.

The move of a successor into an executive position is a highly critical time. Even though they may have worked in the business for years, they may still require additional development to step up to what is required at upper management level. A mentor relationship with a senior individual within the organisation will assist in growing into a future executive leadership position. Objectives should be set and feedback given on a timely basis. At management level, an entirely new set of skills will be required that will forge an understanding of strategic and financial planning, accounting fundamentals, relevant industry specific issues, crisis management, sales and marketing, leadership, communication and all important interpersonal skills. The adequate development of the various skill sets may necessitate working outside the family business for a while, taking appropriate management courses, and finding an internal mentor. Knowledge transfer to the next generation should at all times be facilitated by hands-on experience, developing capabilities and strengths, and encouraging and promoting team development. Interpersonal skills are critical, and will help deal with individuals throughout the organisation and in any conflict situations.

As part of any long term management development programme, adequate consideration should be given to providing for interim management while the successor is developing. Plans do not always follow a desired timetable, and interim leaders may need to lead the company in times of crisis, especially if the founder/owner manager/leader becomes ill or disabled. An undeveloped successor candidate should not be forced into a leadership role. Instead, a more experienced, interim leader should assume command until either the founder/owner is able to return, or until the successor development programme is complete and the next generation family leader assumes control. The existence of a plan is paramount. It may contain a provisions that cover the situation where family companies require that successors have worked outside of the family for a period of time. It may also address the need to improve their understanding of company operations by rotating them through a series of responsibilities in different divisions, or by participating in large proposals or special strategic projects. Typically, a development plan should include:

– On-site specialist projects within the family business.

– Community projects or participation in a wider business context.

– Self-development initiatives.

– Formal training initiatives.

– Shadowing a senior individual.

Any plan should include compensation strategies for successors that reward achievements within the overall management development plan. Motivational short term incentives can be provided for the successor, tied in to their overall performance and appraisal process and linked into training, educational and development goals. A longer term incentive package is helpful to retain the successor through the life of the development plan and beyond.

Once a plan is designed and implemented, it is critical to monitor the development of the candidate and the validity of the recruitment programme. The successor's progress should be compared with the development plan, and potential areas of difficulty identified and examined. The plan can be then be refined or redesigned as required to meet the individual requirements of the proposed successor, taking account of changes in the business and wider commercial environment. Soft skills and behavioural traits should also be examined to ensure that the future leader has good people and team management skills, so that they can interact appropriately with a wide variety of individuals in a wide variety of situations. Selecting and evaluating development candidates for leadership positions within the company is an ongoing process. The next generation should not be expected to gain necessary executive skills exclusively through ongoing involvement in the family business. Programmes need to be developed to assist new leaders and ensure their development.

The Bechtel family is an example of a successful family business that has passed on the entrepreneurial drive to the fourth generation. Bechtel is an engineering giant that started as a small road building business, and today is one of America's largest private companies. Reilly Bechtel is the fourth generation head of the company. Growing up, he did various jobs at Bechtel. He was an oiler, mechanic's helper, labourer and front end loader operator. He went to law school, briefly practised law, then rejoined the company. He took on various strategic assignments, working from the bottom up to fill the various gaps in knowledge he had in relation to the company and how it operated. He undertook a number of assignments overseas in various roles. As he successfully completed each assignment, he moved further up the ranks of the company, eventually reaching the CEO position. Today, as Reilly Bechtel says, members of the fifth Bechtel generation are working in the company, learning the basics, earning their pay and building their following. Whether individuals gain experience inside or outside a company, it is important that they gain the right experience, and that the criteria for employment and advancement are the same as those applied to non-family employees.

CONTINUING ROLE OF THE FOUNDER

It can be difficult planning an orderly transition of responsibility from the founding generation to the succeeding generation. Founders can find it hard letting go, and may wish to remain active in company management. It can be unreasonable to expect the founder to have zero involvement in the business once it has passed to the management of others. Founders will often be emotionally attached to the business, and may want some kind of ongoing involvement. In fact, a semi-retired founder with a continuing role in the business can be of huge assistance to a successor. This works when an appropriate role is engineered for the retiring founder, a role that utilises their experience and industry insight in assisting the successor without potential for conflict.

Here are some of the roles the founder may continue to play in the company after passing day-to-day responsibility to the successor generation:

– Maintaining long established relationships with important clients and other key business contacts which might otherwise deteriorate if the founder was completely removed from the business. This enables the goodwill they have developed to gradually transition to the successor.

– Assisting in handling customer complaints and problems.

– Providing guidance in forming long-term strategic plans.

– Providing ongoing mentoring and assisting the next generation management team to develop.

– Assisting with special projects or expansion plans.

The founder can serve as an outside consultant, play a role on the company's board of directors, or be involved in special project teams. Any of these roles can help ensure the smooth transition of the business, enabling the next generation management to develop while leveraging the retiring generation's skill sets. It is also helpful if the ongoing role of the founder/retiring generation is documented. This defines their involvement, and ensures that there is no duplication of responsibilities between the retiring generation and successor generation. Such a document could address the following terms and conditions:

– Availability of the founder for certain projects.

– Availability of the founder for a defined transition period.

– Description of the founder's other specific roles within the organisation.

– Founder's right to use company property and resources.

– A basis for the founder's communication to individuals within the company.

– Fees and expenses for the founder.

Within an overall management context, careful thought and attention must be given to all these issues during this transition period, when both the founder's role and successor's roles are evolving and transitioning. Business owners often overlook the need to develop mechanics and formalities to help them through what can be a challenging transition period.

CHAPTER 4 – ACTIONS

– Consider the management needs of your business.

– Think about the potential successors at management level.

– Consider how the skill sets of next generation management candidates may be developed.

– Develop a training programme for them.

– Consider the transition period and what your future involvement in the business might be.

CHAPTER 5

NON-FAMILY INVOLVEMENT

OUTLINE:

By the end of this chapter you will have understanding of:

— The roles of non-family management.

— Considerations in appointing non executive directors.

— Balancing the board of directors.

As a company grows and becomes more complex, a more structured co-ordinated approach is required, in contrast to the more centralised approach of an entrepreneur and their family. Families tend to look inwards for help and skills. This makes it significantly more difficult for a family business to branch out and leverage other resources available, than for a non-family business. To be successful, the family business needs the right people. Although a family's pool of talent can be an excellent resource, if there is nobody with the right experience, it is a mistake to restrict the candidates to family, and to ignore candidates in the wider marketplace.

As a business grows and develops, the family may not be able to run all aspects of the business themselves. The board will need to ask itself whether the family members in the business have the right skills. This is particularly important in relation to directors, since the Companies

Act requires them to act with the general knowledge, skill and experience that may reasonably be expected of a person carrying out the functions of a director. Situations where outside talent can be useful to the business include:

–   If the business is diversifying into areas where there are not enough individuals at director level or management level with the relevant experience.

–   If there are actual or potential conflicts between family members, where an outsider can bring a neutral, measured and professional approach.

–   Where the family wishes to sell part or all of the business, it can be very helpful to have an outside manager with experience in grooming a business for sale and knowledge of the sales process.

–   Where the family wishes to pursue a strategy of growth through acquisition of other businesses, it can be very helpful to have a manager with appropriate experience to gear the business up for such acquisitions, and who can assist with their integration into the existing family business.

–   A separation between family issues and business issues when deciding on matters such as selecting the next business leader, in order to preserve family harmony and promote sound business decisions.

The latter could be achieved in a variety of ways. The company may appoint an outside unrelated advisory board to consider various candidates, monitor their progress and appraise the owner of their development and their potential to act as a future CEO. Another option is to use an impartial outside consultant to develop and monitor management grooming and incentive compensation plans.

Effective use of outside talent can counter the tendency to introversion in family businesses. Outside talent can be divided into three broad categories:

–   Advisors and consultants (see Chapter 1).

– Non-family managers.

– Non-executive directors.

NON-FAMILY MANAGERS

All the issues covered in Chapter 4 concerning grooming, developing, retaining, rewarding and managing talent of family managers apply equally to non-family managers, except that the latter, in addition to their day-to-day work, will also need to deal with the politics and emotional cross currents that arise in a family owned business. They may perceive that they have only limited opportunities for advancement. Talented managers often resign because they feel they have run out of opportunities. Family companies can therefore face a recruitment problem when seeking talented outsiders. If family companies succeed in hiring non-family managers, it can be a challenge to retain and motivate them. The concerns of non-family managers include:

– Is there a coordinated and integrated talent management process?

– Will they have a fair chance against family employees?

– Is their salary and overall compensation commensurate with that in a non-family business?

– To what extent will their decisions be overruled by family members?

– Will they ever be able to acquire an ownership stake?

– How will family tensions affect the business, and will this impact on their ability to perform their role?

– Are the vision and strategy for the business clear enough for non-family management to have a clear view of the future? Non-family management may be unsure about job security in the absence of an overall management succession plan. If the family's children are not in a position to run the business, the business may be sold, especially if the owner has not indicated to the non-family management that he wants them to continue to operate the business on behalf of the family.

- In a smaller business, the management style of the owner can impact on the development of non-family managers. A more open management style is more likely in a larger organisation.

- What level of involvement will non-family management have? Will they be excluded from key planning decisions or operational information?

- Will the non-family manager be used as a go-between by family members? This can waste valuable time, where the issues should have been discussed directly between the family members.

For non-family managers, there are advantages of being employed in a family business:

- A strong organisational culture. Family businesses typically exude a camaraderie that extends to non-family members. There is the informality of working in a close-knit team.

- Personal relationship with the owner and perhaps their family.

- The long-term investment view taken by family businesses can feed into areas such as job security.

- Operating within a flexible organisation. By nature, family businesses are informal and more flexible compared to larger corporates with their greater bureaucracy.

Non-family managers can fulfil a number of important roles within the organisation on behalf of the family, including providing leadership and being a counsellor or mentor to the next generation. Where there is no successor in the family to lead the business, they may be asked to head the management team. Sometimes they are asked to operate the company until the next generation is ready to take on a management role. Non-family managers can thus perform a number of important leadership roles in the family business. As a family business progresses beyond the first and second generations, the operational requirements will differ significantly from that of a first generation entrepreneurial enterprise. Due to the size of a third or fourth generation business, there may be a greater dependence on external senior executives as the best means of ensuring continuity. This is either because of a lack of appropriate family members at a management level (particularly with larger organisations), or because of the impact of the separation between ownership and management, where ownership has become much more fragmented, and is no longer necessarily interlinked with the management of the business.

When seeking to attract and retain a non-family member, remember that the outsider will not always share the same aspirations and values as the family. Many family businesses have a strongly defined culture that may be difficult for a non-family manager to absorb. For this reason, it may be helpful if non-family managers have previous experience working in other family businesses. The existing management team needs to establish the competencies and behaviours required of non-family management. When recruiting non-family management, ensure that the overall package of salary and benefits is competitive and that there is simultaneously a sufficient deterrent in place to make leaving the family business unattractive. In addition to remuneration, senior executives joining the family business will be concerned about how much decision-making capacity they have and about career development. They will need to be reassured about the range of decisions they can take in the business without unnecessary family involvement. Their career development should be charted on the basis of a performance culture that will result in promotion where merited, regardless of the whether the individual is a family member or not. When non-family employees have a clear career path, feel they will be given a fair chance, believe that the company is professionally managed, and see clear policies defining their role, the overall result can be that taking a role in a family business can be an attractive career path for the right individual.

It is important to present the appointment of non-family management carefully to family members, especially those already employed in the business or those planning to join the business in the future. Some family members may feel threatened. Hopefully, they will eventually realise that such an appointment is a commitment to enhance the business and drive it forward. The owner should put in place a management succession plan that is explained to both family and non-family managers. This avoids any potential for conflict caused by uncertainty over the future roles or opportunities available to those involved in the business.

Katherine Graham, in her book *Personal History*, gave credit to the Washington Post's outside board of directors for some of that paper's success. Graham's father bought the Post at auction in 1933 at a time when the Washington market was dominated by the Washington Star, another family-owned paper. When Katherine took over in 1964 as a second-generation family owner, she shared leadership with a professional manager, Richard Simmons, at a time when the Washington Star was still the leading paper in Washington. Since 1964, the Washington Post company has grown phenomenally. Both its annual compound earnings rate and its annual return on equity averaged in excess of 20% for the first thirty years after Graham took over. She attributed much of this transformation to her shared stewardship with Richard Simmons, and compares it to the fate of the Washington Star, which no longer exists partly, she says, because too many family members were involved with the management. The Washington Post is currently led by a third-generation member of the Graham family and a team of professional managers. It is an illustration of a family business that has been able to grow with professional guidance and has managed to stay family controlled.

INCENTIVE ARRANGEMENTS

It is advisable to have a detailed employment agreement, particularly for directors and senior individuals. This agreement should include provision for confidentiality and restrictive covenants: a non-compete clause in respect of the business, not to deal with business customers or clients, not to entice customers or clients away from the business, and not to poach the business's employees. This covenant would on balance be enforceable for a period of about six months after the individual has ceased employment with the business. Apart from the basic contractual arrangements, there is the issue of the division between cash and non cash incentives.

The incentive strategy should be linked to the overall strategy of the business. For example, if an Irish corporate or plc is seeking to grow aggressively, a lower base salary is appropriate, with most of their remuneration linked to growth performance. In this case, growth performance could be met by way of stock awards. In a more risk-averse family business, where usually a much longer-term view is taken, the remuneration package should try and reflect steady growth over a prolonged period. The fixed salary element may accordingly be higher, with a lower performance-related variable. Having the right performance measures will help non-family executives focus on demonstrating behaviours that will support the family's business, values and strategy.

Interestingly, the 2009 Walker Report in the UK on the governance of financial institutions, made no fewer than 12 recommendations (out of 39) in the area of pay and performance. Many of the report's principles do not just apply to financial institutions. The report raised concerns that in the recent past, performance objectives and associated remuneration outcomes have in practice been unduly weighted to the short-term. With the exception of pension provision, the practice in many companies incorporates basic salary, short-term bonus and long-term incentives. There is no conclusion regarding the optimum overall balance between basic salary and the variable remuneration components, which depend on a business's particular circumstances. Whatever sum is treated as variable remuneration, a key issue is the scale of deferment that will ensure sufficient executive focus and dependency on company performance over the long term. In other words, deferral of incentive payments should provide the primary risk adjustment mechanism for aligning rewards with sustainable performance. The report recommends that short term bonus awards are paid over a three year period, with not more than one third paid in the first year. At least half of variable remuneration for any one year should be in the form of longer term incentives, half of which should not vest for three years, with the remainder after five years.

For many family businesses, the question of whether rewards should be met by way of cash/bonuses or by way of equity can be problematic. Often, there is no wish to extend share ownership to outsiders. An outsider will not share the same aspirations and values as the family. One way of getting non-family members to "buy into" the family's goals is to allocate them a share in the company. From a motivational perspective, any increase in value of the company enhances the value of their shareholding. The advantages of share-based awards include the possibility of locking the manager in for a period of time, usually 3-5 years. Any prior departure results in forfeiture of some of the shares or options.

Equity can also be efficient, as from a cash perspective, there is no expenditure on the company's behalf, since the cost is met by the other shareholders through a dilution of their shareholdings. Accounting standards require that the cost of share-based awards to employees is assessed and recorded as an expense in the company's accounts.

Other considerations when awarding shares to executives, particularly non-family executives, include:

–   *Pre-Emption Rights:* This ensures that individuals cannot sell their shares to outsiders without offering first refusal to the other (family) shareholders. Usually, either the other shareholders or the company acquire the shares.

–   *Drag Along Rights:* This ensures that if the family wishes to sell the entire share capital of the business, it can force any minority shareholder to join in the sale.

–   *Tag Along Rights:* This ensures that if the family sells their shareholding, the minority (executive) shareholders can force the purchaser to buy up their shareholdings.

–   *Non-Voting Shares:* To limit potential loss of family control, it may be possible to create a class of non-voting shares with the same overall economic rights as the family shares. The separate class of non-voting shares can be allocated to non-family employees.

–   *Forfeiture Provisions:* The Articles of Association or any shareholders agreement or contract which the non-family executive enters into on acquiring the shares should provide that, on their departure, they offer to transfer their shares to the other shareholders. A distinction is commonly made between so-called "good leavers" and so-called "bad leavers". The departure of a good leaver is usually prompted by retirement, redundancy or ill health. A bad leaver may be categorised as an employee who departs because of poor performance or dismissal, or who leaves to work with a competitor. Bad leavers are usually denied the full value of their shares. The shares are either forfeited, or the employer has the right to reacquire them at a reduced or nominal value. In addition, funding the purchase of a departing manager's shares should be structured such that the purchase price is paid over a number of years. This avoids any upfront cash-flow issue for the company.

—   *Vesting:* Another way of ensuring a degree of retention or incentivising the non-family member to remain in the employ of the family business is to potentially defer the moment they can acquire equity or share options in the company. The vesting period may either be time related or linked to specific performance related goals.

—   *Liquidity:* Liquidity is often achieved upon a sale or flotation of a family business. In the absence of a trade sale or flotation, niche arrangements may need to be made to facilitate any disposal of shares by a departing non-family executive.

Chapter 10 outlines the tax implications of allocating shares, or the various types of share awards, to management. In brief, it may sometimes be advantageous to structure the increase in value of the share awards so that it is subject to capital gains tax rather than to income tax. Types of share award include:

—   *Free shares:* Where shares are awarded to an executive for nil consideration, e.g. as a bonus payment.

—   *Stock options:* An option to acquire shares in the employer company, with either an exercise price equal to market value, or less than market value. When granted at market value, the employee effectively participates in any uplift in the underlying value of the business. If they exercise their option, they pay a price for the shares equal to the market value when the option was granted. Since the option might not be exercised for a number of years, there is potential for waiting to see whether there is any benefit in exercising the option. When granted at less than market value, there is an immediate benefit to the employee, subject to potential upfront tax charges. These can usually be avoided when the options must be exercised within 7 years of grant.

- *Restricted shares:* These shares usually have voting or transfer restrictions. If all other conditions are satisfied, there are certain tax advantages to restricted shares.

- *Share options over restricted shares:* A combination of stock options and restricted shares.

- *Forfeitable shares:* Shares are granted up-front to an executive. When he/she leaves the company, they forfeit any equity rights they had.

- *Convertible shares:* Shares that have limited rights initially. The shares are either converted to ordinary shares in due course, or additional rights are added at a later date, giving an uplift in value.

- *Growth shares:* A class of shares that may have no value initially, but to which future value can accrue. For example, if a company has a value of €10 million and re-designates its existing issued shares as A shares to which the first full €10 million in value accrues, then any value in excess of €10 million is attributable under the arrangement to a new class of B shares. Most of these B shares are allocated to existing shareholders, but some may be allocated to non-family management, allowing them to participate in the future growth of the business.

- *Phantom share scheme:* In reality, this is a bonus scheme linked to shares. The executive is allocated a "notional" number of shares in the family company. As the business grows in the future, the value of those shares grows. The increase in value is provided by way of cash bonuses to the executive. Since most family businesses have no regular market for their shares, a key issue with a phantom share scheme is the valuation of the shares. It is critical to have a clear valuation mechanism from the outset.

These are the more common types of share plans for rewarding executives. There are a number of Revenue-approved plans, including approved profit sharing schemes, save as you earn schemes, approved share option plans, and employee share ownership trusts. However, all these require Revenue approval, and must be available to all employees. They are of little use when a business wishes to reward one or two key individuals.

NON-EXECUTIVE DIRECTORS

There are distinct advantages in appointing one or more non-executive directors from outside the family. A right candidate with experience of the wider business world can be very beneficial to the business, bringing a new dimension of experience and independent objectivity that is often lacking among family members or employees. Family business often have lower staff turnover. One result is less exposure to the new and innovative ideas and processes that an outsider can bring. Typically, non-executive directors have made their careers in large businesses and no longer want full-time involvement. They might also be people who have run their own business in the past and sold it. Non-executives may provide specialised expertise unavailable internally, as well as a network of key contacts that can open doors in the areas of new business or capital. They may also bring industry-wide connections and links to the public sector. A non-executive director can act as a sounding board on issues and changes facing the business, and can provide objective guidance. A non-executive director can assist the family in resolving disagreements and in facing difficult issues such as succession planning. Some family business run meetings can be too informal, with indistinct lines drawn between the different roles of director/shareholders, and between family meetings and board meetings. A non-executive director can introduce appropriate standards of corporate governance. The Higgs Review, commissioned by the UK government in 2003, undertook a detailed review of the role and effectiveness of non–executive directors in the UK. While companies are not required to adopt the report, it can assist boards of directors in implementing the relevant provisions of the UK Corporate Governance Code. The Higgs Review suggests four key areas in which non-executive directors can be particularly valuable:

—   *Strategy:* Non-executive directors can contribute to and challenge the development of strategy.

—   *Performance:* Non-executive directors can scrutinise the performance of management in meeting agreed goals, and monitor the reporting of performance.

—   *Risk:* Non-executive directors must satisfy themselves that financial information is accurate and that financial controls and risk management systems are robust and defensible

—   *People:* Non-executive directors are responsible for determining appropriate levels of remuneration for executive directors in larger corporates. They have a prime role in appointing senior management and in developing succession plans.

Selecting a non-executive director

When selecting a non-executive director, you are looking for someone able to get on with the existing board of directors/management. They should be well respected on the strength of their prior business experience, and they must be prepared to offer constructive advice. Their experience, skill sets and overall attitude must complement those of the other directors in the company. You must strike a balance that introduces new perspectives and new skills to the business. You must consider where the non-executive director is at in their own career. Retirees can bring a wealth of experience to a family business. Be careful about employing professional advisors, such as solicitors or accountants. This could result in conflicts of interest where they formerly advised or continue to advise the firm. If you have enjoyed a long-standing relationship with them, questions will be asked about how objective they can be. The company should prepare a profile of an ideal candidate. Existing advisors may be able to assist you in the recruitment process, offering their opinion on potential candidates or individuals they are aware of in the marketplace. It is worth checking with the Boardroom Centre of the Institute of Directors, which has a database of potential candidates.

There is no legal distinction between executive and non-executive directors. Both own the same duty of care to the company. The primary difference is that executive directors owe additional duties under their employment agreements, whereas non-executive directors do not usually have such an agreement. Even though non-executive directors may not be directly employed by the company, it is good practice to have a statement of the terms under which they are retained, outlining the company's expectations and the level of remuneration for attending meetings during the year. The statement should also indicate their responsibilities, such as chairing meetings, commenting on succession plans or fixing directors' remuneration. To avoid ambiguity, the statement should outline what information they are entitled to receive and the lines of reporting and communication. The contribution of non-executive directors should of course be reviewed regularly. It is useful to establish guidelines for how the board of directors should function. This will clarify expectations, and send a message that the roles of directors are taken seriously. It will also outline the criteria for recruiting candidates to the board of directors. Non-executive directors are usually remunerated based on how much time they devote to their activities, such as the number of days a year they need to attend board meetings and perform other activities. There may also be a performance related element to the remuneration, depending on their overall level of contribution. The initial term of the directorship should be limited to 2-3 years. This gives the company space to monitor the director's performance, with the opportunity to renew the arrangement.

OUTSIDE BOARD OF DIRECTORS OR BOARD OF ADVISORS

The dynamics in family businesses need to be properly managed. If these dynamics are ignored, there is potential for unravelling the business. When the dynamics are acknowledged, it is easier to achieve common purpose. Communication with key stakeholders, particularly in second, third or fourth generation businesses and beyond, should be addressed through formalised governance structures that separate the business of the family from the business of the business. Establishing a board of directors that includes independent outsiders is often crucial for a large number of family businesses if they are to achieve long term success. They can help optimise company profits while maintaining family harmony. Such a board of directors can bring experience to operational and strategic decisions, be objective in decision making, provide board diversity, and send a positive message to customers, shareholders and employees. Boards structured on this basis make recommendations on what they believe represents the best interests of the shareholders and the company.

Outside directors and advisors can also play an important role in implementing management succession plans. They can serve as mentors for succession candidates, assist potential successors with their concerns and assist the existing generation with their concerns over successors. They can also make valuable suggestions for the development of successor candidates.

Many owners of privately-held businesses do not take full advantage of the benefits provided by such formal governance structures. Some treat the board of directors as a mere rubber stamp for management. Founders often attribute their success to the fact that they pursued their own objectives and did not pay heed to others' opinions. The introduction of outside directors, and the move towards a more accountable system of governance, may not always be viewed in a favourable light. Some founders see this as nothing more than an administrative nuisance. In many family businesses, the board's function is to fulfil the minimum statutory requirements and to rubber stamp all decisions of the owner/manager. The board exercises few of the management functions or authority that could potentially be vested in it and availed of. There is often a misconception among family businesses that only larger publicly listed companies should have broadly-based boards with independent outsiders involved. In reality, businesses that do not have a functioning board of directors or outside board of directors may be missing an opportunity to improve the management and profitability of their company, especially during a period of succession transition.

WHEN IS IT TIME TO CONSIDER TRANSITIONING TO A MORE FORMAL BOARD OF DIRECTORS?

Although a functioning board of directors should have real powers, first-generation entrepreneurial owners of smaller businesses may not need an outside board, because at this stage, the business structure and management hierarchy are relatively simple. As the business develops, the picture can become much more complex, particularly where the business reaches a certain scale or when it transitions to the second generation and beyond. As the company increases in size, the owner's role changes. More of their time is devoted to performing high-level managerial tasks and less time is spent on day-to-day issues. The success and growth of the company may make it necessary to consider outside board members. Owners of family managed businesses are often guilty of resisting, at least initially, the appointment of outsiders, fearing interference and having strangers becoming involved in their business.

The first essential question to be asked is whether existing key stakeholders are committed to making the idea work. It becomes a futile exercise if the board of directors is not allowed function in a meaningful way. It is time to consider appointing outside directors if the business has sufficient resources to benefit from the decision and recommendations of a well-constituted board, and if the size and growth of the company merits greater and more diverse constructive involvement at management level. You need to think of the composition of the board, and the number of outside or non-family members to have on the board. When a board consists mostly of family members, meetings can resemble family meetings rather than board meetings. Family members should, like non-family directors, be appointed on the basis of their experience, judgement and wisdom. It is not advisable to have spouses or relatives with little to contribute to professionally orientated business meetings on the board. The main duties of the board are to oversee management performance; to consider the major decisions facing the company in the area of strategic planning, investments and financial management, and changes to organisational structure; to protect the interests of shareholders; and to interact with family about the family's involvement in the business.

It is worth examining publicly available guidance regarding the make-up of boards of directors:

1. The UK Corporate governance Code (formerly the Combined Code) available on the FRC (Financial Reporting Council) website. This also has links to both the Walker Review and the Higgs Review.

2. The National Standards Authority of Ireland and the Institute of Directors have jointly published a code of practice for corporate governance assessment in Ireland.

3. The OECD principles of corporate governance, available on the OECD website.

THE ROLE OF THE BOARD IN SUCCESSION PLANNING

Outside directors and advisors can assist the owners in selecting successors from the pool of candidates, in implementing and monitoring management talent assessment, and in a management grooming plan. The board can help ensure that a management development plan is not tainted by family issues or family bias. Non-executive family directors can serve as mentors for succession candidates. An independent board lends credibility to the management succession process.

Your existing advisors may be able to help you organise a board of directors that will formalise corporate governance arrangements and provide a greater degree of continuity at a sensitive and potentially disastrous time for the business where succession is not managed appropriately.

CHAPTER 5 – ACTION PLAN

– Assess the stage the business is at and whether it will benefit from outside experience.

– Consider whether full-time assistance is needed by employing outside talent.

– If yes, proceed to assess candidates and recruit management for certain roles.

– If part-time high-level input is required, take on a suitable non-executive.

– Consider how external involvement can support the succession process.

CHAPTER 6

CORPORATE GOVERNANCE – FAMILY AND SHAREHOLDER ISSUES

OUTLINE:

By the end of this chapter you will have understanding of:

Why to hold family meetings.

– The concept and role of a family council.

– How to set up a family council.

– The family charter or constitution.

– Shareholders agreements.

Family issues and business issues are different. The requirements of the family and the business do not always coincide. The complicated dynamics in family businesses need to be properly managed to avoid the unravelling of a once-thriving business. Communication among key stakeholders who are often family members can be improved by implementing formalised governance structures that play a critical role in separating the business of the family and the business of the business.

A family's governance structure is the family's rules and systems governing the holding and preservation of the family's business and wealth. This structure allows the family and its professional advisors to work together, to create a family vision and a road map to guide the family as it grapples with family business decisions. The ownership structure within the business affects the overall governance requirements. In the first generation, ownership may be held by two shareholders. By the third generation, ownership may be held by twenty or more individuals. The greater number of individual shareholdings always brings the potential for conflict among shareholders and among family members. Different criteria apply from a governance perspective, depending on whether the business still remains an owner-managed business, or is being run by siblings in partnership, or where the business has moved to the third or fourth generation, involving cousins or more distant relatives. A good governance structure must achieve organised accountability and a balance of power amongst various interests in the family, including family members, shareholders, directors, trustees of family trusts, family advisors, and others.

It is useful to contrast this with the conventional corporate governance requirements of a listed company or a large-scale private non-family company. Assumptions on which traditional corporate governance guidelines are based do not always apply to family businesses. These assumptions include:

Conventional corporate governance	Family business
Listed public companies	Mainly private companies
Disbursed ownership	Concentrated family shareholders
Predominant role of the financial institutions	Predominant role of the owning family
Shareholder value is paramount	Family value returns on investment that are not entirely economic. Preserving and extending a legacy, control over one's own life and the availability of careers for family members, might be acceptable.
Short-term investor commitment	Long-term family commitment
Short-term performance measurement	Long-term investment horizon
High financial leverage	Low financial leverage

Conventional corporate governance is based on shareholder protection, and usually leads to greater regulatory costs. This is why conventional corporate governance does not always suit even large-scale family businesses. Most family businesses prefer structures and practices that reflect trusting relationships and which encourage teamwork. When a family business is established, the founder constitutes the governance structure, since he/she controls most aspects of management and governance. Formal structures are often absent. When the business passes to subsequent generations, a more formal governance structure is required to facilitate management of relationships between personalities involved. Formal frameworks may include:

- Family meetings

- A family council

- A family constitution or charter

- Shareholders agreements (since family constitutions are not usually legally binding documents)

There are no hard and fast rules about the detailed roles of governance in family businesses. Families must find what structure and governance processes suit their needs and provide enough flexibility to adapt and change as the circumstances require.

This chapter explores family governance issues and their role in a succession context. The diagram below shows different governance structures.

	Governance Structure
Family Council ▼	– Interface between owners (family members) and business – Represents interest of the family in the business
Group Board ▼	– Consolidated ownership of all family businesses
Corporate Centre ▼	– Decision supports and coordination between company board and operating management
Business Units	– Entity responsible for operations' execution

FAMILY MEETINGS

Communication is the essence of good corporate governance. The starting point for working and planning together as a family is to hold appropriate meetings that discuss the aspects of the business that impact on the family and its relationship with the family. Family meetings should be a mechanism to encourage family participation in producing a shared family vision. Family meetings are a decision-making forum for providing a cohesive family position in connection with decisions relating to the business, and a forum for resolving potential family conflicts. If a family does not meet, there will be inadequate communication on business issues, particularly to family members not involved in the business. There will also be no forum where family members involved in the business can focus on how family issues could impact on the business. When families are unable to meet together, they clearly will have difficulties working together within the business. If families cannot arrange or agree to hold regular meetings, there will be doubts regarding the family's ability to work together if a conflict arises. When families cannot organise constructive and effective meetings, it may be best to bring in a family business consultant to assist the family in establishing an appropriate structure for holding and running meetings.

There are several advantages of family meetings:

1. Disputes can be raised. All family businesses face the challenge of resolving the different needs and expectations of family members.

2. Family meetings can encourage family participation in planning, problem solving and decision making. Family meetings can provide a framework for supporting family members whose grievances or issues may otherwise not reach the awareness of other family members, and for taking appropriate action.

3. Family meetings can bring new ideas to the surface, and provide a framework for monitoring the younger generation and examining a framework for discovering and nurturing talent.

4. Family meetings serve to educate the family.

5. Family meetings can provide a support framework for a family, and can become a cohesive decision-making unit that balances the tasks

and demands made on the family with personal and social interactions among family members.

Family meetings are a precursor to a family council, which is usually a more formal structure. The participation in family meetings or the family council meetings is a question of balance between the age and maturity of the participants, and of confidentiality. Should all family members be invited to attend, regardless of age? Should the audience be limited in terms of the issues being discussed? Is it more appropriate to have a two-tier structure, with family meetings involving the wider family, and the more select family council involving individual members from different families who represent their families to provide an overall cohesive family view? This is particularly relevant in family companies that have progressed to the third or fourth generation, where a large number of different families constitute the overall family unit.

There are several reasons why all family members should attend family meetings:

–   In-laws, spouses and partners can learn about family business plans and issues first hand, and gain a more realistic picture of where the family business is at.

–   The younger generation and in-laws may bring different perspectives.

–   Having as wide a group as possible exposes attendees to family traditions, the overall family vision and an indication of the family commitment to the business.

It makes sense to hold an initial meeting to plan how family meetings should be run, rather than expose the wider family to an unstructured format that could end up discussing difficult issues that discourage long-term participation. Family meetings should be held relatively regularly. A formal agenda supports communication, encourages participation, and allows sensitive issues to be raised. Family meetings need a chair. This role should be rotated in order to encourage participation, nurture talent in the next generation and broaden the family leadership base. An external consultant could perhaps assist with the initial meetings, until a formal process has been established that the family is comfortable with.

A family council could be composed of a smaller number of family members, possibly drawn from different branches of the family and from different generations. The family council provides executive leadership to the family, formulating issues for discussion at the family meetings and ensuring a communication and information flow between the family and the family's business. A family council can be the driving force behind calling and running family meetings, and can also liaise on behalf of the family with the business.

FAMILY COUNCIL

A traditional board of directors governance structure is generally less suitable when managing family dynamics. By holding family meetings and creating a family council, families can improve communication, accountability and harmony. In some situations, a family council can encompass a wide number of family members. Sometimes, informal family meetings may be held, with the family council becoming a smaller representative group appointed to represent the family in its dealings with the business. The co-ordination and organisation of such structures needs to be appropriate for the family.

Participation in a family council or family meetings could lead all stakeholders to consider themselves part of the family business system. Family issues may be addressed separately from business issues, rather than being inappropriately exposed in front of non-family board members. The key is communication and management of familial interpersonal relationships. As the diagram below illustrates, the family is run by the family council, the board of directors is selected by the business owners, and the day-to-day operation of the business is handled by the management team.

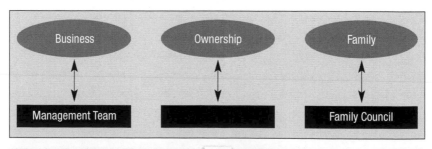

What is a family council?

Just as the board of directors addresses issues concerning the company and protects the financial interest of the shareholders, so a family council protects the interests of all the members of the family. It is the main forum through which the distinctive interests and concerns of all family members and shareholders may be addressed. It enables family members to participate in the development of the family's strategic plan and in future policy making. Just as procedures and protocol at a directors meeting may be established by the company's articles of association and shareholder agreements, so procedurally the framework within which a family council will operate is usually determined by the family constitution (or charter) which will establish ground rules for meetings and a vision or mission statement.

The family council provides its members with a structured forum within which the various families holding shares in the business may agree on courses of action for the business, communicate with each other and decide on roles for family members in dealing with the family business. The family council deals exclusively with family issues facing the business, rather than with business issues per se. The family council should elect or appoint certain members of the council to act as a liaison with the board of directors, and to co-ordinate, manage, articulate and align family goals and expectations with the company's strategic plan. The family council will assist in clarifying and establishing the family's values and vision, and will help the family unite behind common goals. Clear communication with the board of directors should provide a clear signal regarding long-term strategic issues, business risks, the return on investment sought by the family, and the family's attitude to ethical issues.

The function of the family council is to keep family issues out of the boardroom, and to keep certain corporate operational issues out of the realm of family debate. Overlapping issues are managed and communicated by the liaison between the family council and the board of directors. A structure of this nature gives the family a clear communication channel to the board, without the board having to be composed solely of family members. This way, experienced outsiders who can bring different skill sets and new perspectives to the business can be part of the board.

The council should operate on a consensus basis, not by majority vote or by shareholding percentages. The council's role is to create a family bond and to encourage a cohesive family approach that allows issues to be presented, information shared among family members, and misunderstandings cleared up. This provides a framework for resolving issues before they get out of hand and threaten the overall business.

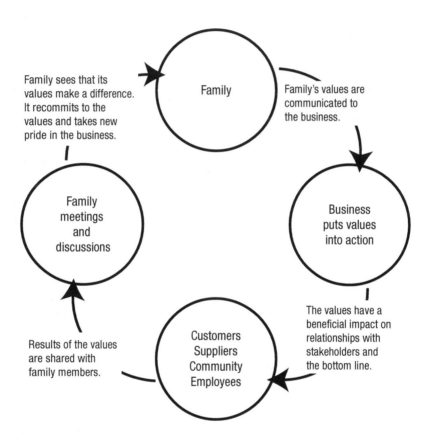

Reinforcing values between family and business
Source: Ward John L., *Perpetuating the Family business the Family Business* (Palgrave Macmillan, 2004)

Benefits of family council

Many of the benefits of a family council are similar to the benefits of family meetings. Principally, the family council ensures cordial family relations and mends relationships that may have been fractured when family members work together. The family council provides a support structure for its constituent members or family units during difficult times.

Family council meetings serve to maintain family participation and interest in issues concerning the business, to foster family involvement in philanthropy or giving back to the community, to educate family members on financial or other issues, and to teach the wider family on business issues, on the family's history or involvement in the business, and on appropriate family business values. The family council and family meetings provide an opportunity for family to get together and bond outside of the business.

Setting up a family council

A trusted advisor such as your succession planning specialist can help organise the establishment of a family council. It is usual practice to establish a family council in conjunction with a formal family charter or constitution. Sometimes, the council is established as part of a wider governance process, with outside directors invited to participate on the board. The process is obviously one which most business owners are not familiar with. That is why seeking outside help in its establishment and to ensure it operates smoothly is initially a good idea until it is up and running.

The advisor will usually attend the first few family council meetings to observe and make recommendations. Once the family governance structures are in place and operating, the advisor's involvement will diminish over time.

The critical steps in setting up a family council:

1. **Call a family meeting to explain the concept and outline the requirement for a family council.** It is important that all key relevant stakeholders are invited to the meeting. You may choose to conduct this initial meeting in an offsite setting so that family members feel more at ease, and understand from the outset that a family council is separate from the business. It is advisable for an advisor to be present to help facilitate the meeting, to educate the wider family as to the aims and purposes of having a family council, and to assist in gaining family buy-in.

2. **Develop the family mission and vision statements.** The first order of business is to compose a mission and vision statements that spell out the objectives for the family. Under the guidance of more senior

family members, the entire group should participate in composing and ultimately ratifying the statements. The aim of such statements is to develop a cohesive family message that sets out the overall family influence or culture that they wish to portray towards the business. These statements help family members develop a common sense of purpose. The statements should define who the family are, their most important values, and how these values should be reflected in their dealings with the business.

3. **Develop the family constitution.** The family council needs to develop the structures for conducting family business. A family charter or constitution outlines the rules and formalities governing family meetings and the operation of the family council. The family charter can be amended where requirements change over time. It usually takes a number of family meetings to establish such a charter, and requires assistance from outside advisors to facilitate a final working document.

4. **Set a schedule for family council meetings.** Family council meetings should be co-ordinated like board meetings. Dates should be booked for twelve months ahead.

5. **Elect family officers.** Various family members may be entrusted with roles within the family council. Family officers are entrusted with conducting the business of the council. The roles are similar to the roles on a board of directors: a chairperson, a vice-chairperson who chairs the meeting when the chair is absent, and a secretary to record the minutes, note the matters discussed and decisions made, ensure that the minutes are circulated, and circulate the agenda prepared by the chair in advance of meetings.

6. **Establishing council sub-committees.** Specific issues may require a sub-committee that addresses a particular topic of interest to the family. Sub-committees could cover charitable/philanthropic issues, family health and welfare issues, issues related to providing adequate information to family about the business, a community relations, and a corporate liaison committee that acts as the conduit between the family council and the board of directors. Other issues that could be examined by sub-groups of the family council include employment policy for family members and/or dividend policy.

7. **Start the meetings.** Family council meetings should be conducted with all the formalities and respect of formal business meetings. Circulate the agendas in advance, and establish quorums for attendance at meetings. Meeting ground rules should be established and posted, and minutes should be kept recorded and re-read. Introduce, follow up and revisit issues where required. Reports from sub-committees should be prepared and recommendations approved or rejected by the main council. Meetings should have a defined purpose and should monitor the family's progress and objectives.

Decisions should be made on the basis of a consensus. If unanimous consent is not obtained, the matters should be discussed again, and if necessary referred to a sub-committee for further examination. Sub-committees may then establish a formal policy for presentation at a general council meeting. The overall requirement is to reach a family consensus. Policies should match the family vision and mission statements and family charter. If matters cannot be agreed, they may be abandoned or reconsidered later. Once matters have been agreed, they become a part of family policy in dealing with the business.

FAMILY COUNCIL: SUGGESTED ROLES
Family Issues
– Draft and amend family constitution based on inputs from family members
– Facilitate selection of family council
– Manage sale of shares of the owners
– Train and develop next generation
– Plan family gatherings and help to create healthy family relationships
Business Issues
– Elect family members for the Group board
– Deal with macro business issues, ownership, return on equity, dividends, etc
– Understand the rationale of family executives
– Debate issues
– Express agreed views through appointed chairman

Family constitution

A family constitution is a written statement of a family's shared values and policies in relation to ownership and operation of the business. The relationship the family wants to have with the business should be formally written into a constitution. This is the single most important building block for any system of family governance. This formal document clearly sets out the guiding principles and defines the rules of the family business. The central aim of the document is to set out guidelines that will help the family work together. This is a consensus-based system that enables all relevant issues to be aired, and ensures that the system of governance developed by the family is appropriate for the family and is not imposed on the family. The family constitution usually covers the following issues:

–   Sets out the core family values that all the members should strive to follow.

–   Outlines the process for decision making and holding of meetings.

–   Clearly sets out what financial benefits each family member can expect to receive from the business both in terms of salary, share ownership, etc.

–   Establishes long-term goals for the family including commitment to the family business, whether it is intended to continue to pass the business from generation to generation, or whether it is intended to ultimately sell the business.

–   Provides a mechanism for introducing younger family members to the business and its governance structures.

–   Establishes mechanisms for dealing with family members who are involved in the business, including how their performance should be evaluated, how their roles will be determined and what criteria should govern their being allowed to enter the business.

–   Provides a dispute resolution procedure.

–   Establishes criteria for selecting leaders and leadership transition.

–   Establishes whether the business should have independent directors.

–   Outlines how the business should operate within the wider community and articulates any philanthropic ambitions of the family.

In the early 17th century, the Mitsui brothers began business in Tokyo. In order to ensure that succession issues were successfully handled, the Mitsui family developed a family constitution which included details about the amount of property due to each branch as well as the duties of the family council, a periodical assembly that controlled business and other personal matters. Each male Mitsui, on coming of age, swore sacred Shinto oaths to uphold the Mitsui constitution and further the family interest. Today, the Mitsui family, owns nearly one-fifth of Japan's car market and nearly one-sixth of its textile production.

Formulating the family constitution is a time-consuming process, and may reveal issues not previously considered in the family context. There might be a question about the legally binding status of the family constitution. Family members expect the family constitution to be a confidential family statement of intent, rather than an enforceable legal agreement. The constitution has moral rather than legal force. A family constitution is usually considered in conjunction with a shareholders agreement covering issues requiring legal enforceability. The more modern view is that, where possible, all aspects of governance should be condensed into a single legally enforceable document. This has the advantage of ensuring that all issues are taken into account in relation to the formal aspects of governance of the business. If two or more governance documents are involved, there may be gaps in the structure that cause confusion or misunderstanding.

The legal issues that may merit inclusion are addressed in the section below on shareholders agreements. The prime requirement for the family constitution is that it is flexible and regularly updated to meet changing circumstances. Avoid an overly rigid constitution, since it could prove unworkable or obsolete due to changing circumstances.

The roots of Japan'sthe Kikkoman Corporation stretch back to the 17th century. Best known for its soy sauces, the company originated when eight families joined together to form a trading consortium. The company was incorporated in 1917 and went public in 1949. The company has a tradition of allowing only one member per generation from each of the founding families to work at Kikkoman, thus preventing any one branch of the family from gaining dominance. One of the principal challenges for the business was balancing the competing needs of its several branches. To this end, they produced a simple statement of twelve philosophical principles. The statement was adopted to facilitate the integration of the varied family interests, and has served them well for over a century. Among the ideals articulated in the statement are peaceful behaviour, faith, mutual respect and discipline.

Shareholder agreements

A well-thought-out governance system operates at a number of different layers at both the family level and the ownership level, whereby the interaction of owners is covered under a shareholder agreement, and the articles of association are drafted or amended to reflect the agreement among shareholders. The shareholders agreement directs how shareholders in a family business act in relation to the business. Shareholder agreements serve a number of important purposes, including a framework for defining ownership relations, creating a framework for resolving disputes and conflicts over ownership issues. These agreements influence the ownership structure and transmission of shares to support the family's intentions regarding future devolution of ownership.

The primary issues of concern in drafting any shareholders agreement include:

– Voting rights – how they will be exercised and how voting control devolves.

– Ownership of shares and how shares can be transferred.

– Liquidity – in private companies, serious family conflicts can erupt when shareholders who want to sell are locked into an ownership position.

– The transferability of shares.

– A policy covering dividends or value being paid to shareholders.

Shareholder agreements – voting rights
Voting entitlements are usually enshrined in the company's articles of association, detailing the specific rights relating to the class of shares held. Under basic company law or as provided for under the articles of association, certain decisions will only require a majority vote among the shareholders to decide in favour of it. Other decisions require a special resolution passed by a 75% majority. A clause in a shareholders agreement governing voting issues on various decisions may override

these provisions, and require higher effective percentages for decisions to be carried. The clause may also have specific voting requirements for certain decisions such as the election of directors or strategic acquisitions.

Shareholder agreements – issues relating to transfer of shares
Shareholders agreements will usually include restrictions on the transfer of shares by gift, sale or will, and pre-emption rights that ensure that the shareholding in the business remains within the family. Families will need to consider who can hold the shares, particularly once the ownership devolves past the second generation. For example, can shareholdings transfer within individual branches of the family, as opposed to the wider family or to third parties? Where individual shareholders wish to exit the business, the valuation placed on their shares can give rise to different scenarios based on the size of shareholding and the basis of valuation utilised. Ideally, a shareholders agreement should include a valuation formula to represent the calculated value of the stock for any shareholder who may wish to exit the business. The shareholders agreement may provide for exit mechanisms for shareholders under a buy/sell arrangement, or could provide for the company to buy back or redeem shares in certain situations. A pre-determined valuation mechanism reduces the potential for dispute if an individual wishes to exit the business at shareholder level, and if other family members or the company itself are prepared to finance such exit.

Shareholder agreements – setting a distribution/dividend policy
Liquidity, or the ability to derive value in cash terms from one's shares, can be an overriding concern for shareholders, especially in a family business where some family shareholders are employed in the business and others are not. Family shareholders not employed in the business may perceive those employed in the business as deriving value from it, yet in the absence of any distribution policy, they see no economic benefit to them.

Liquidity can be provided by dividends or by share buybacks/redemptions that are usually covered as an exit mechanism for family members who wish to sell their shares and have no future part in the business. These issues are identical to the issues discussed earlier with the transfer of shares. For those family members who wish to retain their shareholding or to prevent having it diluted, as against other family shareholders by way of partial share redemptions, in the absence of a dividend policy, they may receive no immediate or annual cash benefit from their shares. While their shareholding may appreciate in value, if they can't sell it, it is an asset with a paper value only. It has no material financial impact on their daily lives, particularly if the family attitude is to preserve and hold the business for future generations.

Creating dividend policies can be challenging and complex, particularly in a family business. Once a business reaches a certain size and shareholder ownership becomes more diverse, dividend policies can be essential in maintaining family unity and harmony, and in ensuring the future of the family business.

Clearly, the first consideration should be the burden any dividend policy places on the business, and the degree of flexibility that can be incorporated to provide for times when the company needs to retain cash for reinvestment. Ideally, some mechanism should exist for identifying surplus cash resources that can occasionally be distributed to shareholders. Dividend policies vary significantly between family businesses, and often reflect what has worked well in the past, and what the overall family values are.

If a dividend policy is put in place, shareholders employed in the business can become concerned about the difficulty of changing it in the future should the need arise. This only happens when the dividend policy needs to be reduced at some future stage, in which case a low annual dividend may provide the necessary flexibility. It may not be too onerous a burden, and can be topped up with an additional discretionary payment should the business be able to finance the additional amount on an annual basis. This gives some certainty to shareholders about the minimum annual amount, while also having potential for a larger payout in good years on an ad hoc basis. Any element of discretion, however, contains the potential for dispute.

A dividend policy is usually based on any of the following:

–   A fixed amount. This could be a relatively low figure, but has the advantage of being a commitment the company can easily keep each year. It may therefore provide some degree of certainty to shareholders.

–   A percentage of net annual profits. The amount will vary depending on company performance.

–   An amount based on company cash flow.

–   A rate based on return on share value or capital employed in the business. This can be a hybrid using percentages of net earnings, or part of a formula where a minimum floor and maximum ceiling is set for the range of dividend payments made in any one year.

–   A residual dividend policy. Where a company relies on internally generated equity to finance new projects, it may wish to balance its debt/equity ratios before making any dividend payout. In this situation, dividends can only come out of the residual or leftover funds after project funding/capital requirements are met. This entails paying out an amount that cannot be reinvested in the business at a pre-stipulated rate of return.

A critical consideration in establishing a dividend policy is sustainability in managing shareholder expectations. It is important to strike the right balance between the needs of the business and the needs of the owners.

Evolution of corporate governance through generations

A carefully managed business will transition from its initial inception as an entrepreneurial owner managed enterprise through the generations to a structure with many different stakeholders, especially at shareholder level. The transition phases of the business are illustrated below:

Refer to next page

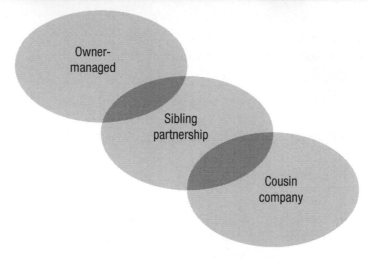

Source: Gersick, Kelin, John David, Marion McCollom Hampton, Ivan Lansberg, *Generation to Generation: Life cycles of the family business* (Harvard Business School Press, 1997)

By the time a business reaches the third generation and beyond, decision-making will become unwieldy without appropriate structures in place. There is potential for conflict. The more complex a family business becomes, either through a diverse number of family shareholders or through the complexity of the business enterprise itself, the greater the need for efficient systems. These systems will ensure appropriate and timely communication and appropriate strategies and governance structures that ensure transparency and clarity surrounding all issues impacting on key stakeholders. This will reduce the potential for ambiguity and friction.

At owner/manager level, there is usually no need for family meetings, a family council, a family charter or a shareholders agreement. Once the business has transitioned to the second generation, on the assumption that more than one child is involved in the business, there may be a requirement for at least some family meetings and possibly a shareholders agreement. Once the business has devolved to a much wider range of family members in the third generation or beyond, it may be time to consider a family charter and a family council. There should also be a detailed shareholders agreement, governing issues that impact on all key stakeholders, and covering issues that may arise from the different interests and priorities of ownership, the family and the business. There is no one-size-fits-all solution. Each individual family-run business must implement the appropriate family governance structure for its requirements. A governance structure is what it says on the tin: a "structure." The main requirement is the commitment and enthusiasm of family members for making the governance system work. The most important aspect of the system is continuous and effective communication.

While a business remains in the first and second generation, most families will have individuals working in management. In later generations, as the family gets bigger or becomes more removed from the business, most of the owners will become less involved in the day-to-day running of the company. The German company Haniel is a good example. Since it was founded in 1756, Haniel has developed from a commodities trading company based in Duisburg into an international group. It remains a family-owned business to this day. The 600-strong Haniel family undertakes social responsibility projects primarily via the Haniel Foundation. Family policy dictates that none of the family shareholders are allowed to become part of the management of the business. The family has effectively created a clear delineation between management and ownership, with family involvement restricted to the Foundation's charitable activities. This separation remains a core principle of Haniel's corporate governance. The exchanges that take place between family and management take many forms. The family can influence major strategies through the supervisory board and advisory board. The family has a ceiling of 25% of profits, the rest being reinvested in the company. The common goal is to increase the value of the company as a going concern. Sustainability remains Haniel's most important guiding principle. The traditional values created by the family complement the entrepreneurial spirit of management. Haniel is an excellent example of how a business has diversified and embraced new markets, industries and products over the course of its development.

CHAPTER 6 – ACTIONS

– Start some form of forum for communication amongst the family.

– With an owner managed or first/second stage generation business, hold family meetings.

– With a second generation business, consider a shareholders agreement.

– With a business in its third/fourth generation and beyond, consider setting up a family council, drafting a family constitution and shareholders agreement.

WEALTH MANAGEMENT

Although business succession focuses on transitioning the business from one generation to the next, it encompasses many other issues. The business is often the primary source of a family's wealth or the main contributing factor to generating value at a family investment level. If the business is not the main source of family wealth, it is a contributing factor to wealth creation via dividends or salary invested outside the business, via pension arrangements, or via the sale of the business and subsequent reinvestment of the proceeds. At a basic level, the business is the family's "livelihood." Apart from basic annual income generation, it can represent and facilitate a myriad of other planning alternatives that assist in enhancing, developing, protecting and retaining the wealth represented or derived from it, for both the current shareholders, who are often the founders of the business, and future generations. Individuals can become too focused on the business. They immerse themselves in the commercial and managerial issues that confront them, even though they went into the business in the first place to provide for the daily needs of themselves and their families, and if the business prospered, it would provide for their future needs and potentially the needs of future generations.

People often claim that they started business in this area because they enjoyed it, or because it intrigued them, or because they found it challenging. Yet these reasons would have been swiftly abandoned and an alternative activity pursued if the business had failed to put bread on the table. As businesses develop into successful and more complex larger operations, these basic needs are easily met. It is assumed that the business will continue to meet all the lifestyle requirements of the family. At a micro level, the focus is on the "business." It is assumed that the business will provide for all. At a macro level, it is prudent to consider what would happen if the business was not there. In such a scenario, where would the family or shareholder needs be met? When wealth management is part of an overall succession planning process, the individual welfare and personal financial security of the business owners and their families are looked after. In this context, many non-business issues will influence decisions, including the date on which individuals involved in the business wish to retire, and the financial resources they wish to have at their disposal in retirement. This means determining their retirement goals, the pension provision and life cover they have, their cash flow requirements, their attitude to risk when investing, and tax efficiencies to be made when structuring alternatives. Ultimately, most families want to protect their wealth. They want to enhance each individual's pursuit of happiness in the overall pursuit of long term preservation of the family.

THE REINVESTMENT DILEMMA

During its foundation and initial growth phase under first generation ownership, it is usual to reinvest business profits in upgrading systems, acquiring new plant or business premises, and expanding into new markets. The founders often make personal sacrifices in forgoing immediate personal return, in return for ensuring the business's viability and in anticipation of future returns. These sacrifices comprise part of the founder's effort to establish the business. They foster the founder's pride in achieving success. The founders' endeavours and sacrifices have made the business what it is today. At a generational level, this can contribute to different attitudes when deciding salaries, dividends and other forms of extracting value from the business. Different individuals have different wealth requirements and varying degrees of involvement in the business.

A critical decision for all businesses is determining the rate of reinvestment in the business, rather than the shareholders extracting wealth. Where there is a wish to preserve ownership of the business within the family, the family's shareholding in the business is an illiquid asset. Recourse must be made to the business if the family wishes to access value from it. An alternative is to sell the business in order to realize the family investment. However, even when the long-term family goal is to sell the business, in the short to medium term, the family's shareholding is essentially an illiquid asset which may limit overall opportunity for diversification of family wealth.

Cash or value that can be released from the business must serve both the businesses requirements and the requirements of the family. Getting this balance wrong can be potentially disastrous. For example, extracting too much value to satisfy demands of family members may result in the business suffering. Extracting too little value may leave certain family members disgruntled. This results in potential for personal conflicts that could impact negatively on the business. There has to be a balance between the business's requirement for capital and the family's demands for payouts. The future strength of the family business depends on continued financial reinvestment. The decision to extract minimal value may however result in the family placing all their eggs in the one basket. Wealth needs to be examined through the perspective of wealth held "inside" the business and wealth held "outside" the business. The more wealth held outside the business, the less the family has to rely on it, and the greater protection afforded to any deterioration in its performance or value.

Having a liquidity strategy in place removes uncertainty for shareholders around how capital or income will be distributed to them, while also providing for an alignment of the needs of the business and its requirements. The key components are:

–   Ensuring harmony among stakeholders in the business, and managing expectations by having clear and unambiguous guidelines on how and when wealth can be extracted, who can extract it, and at what level it can be extracted.

–   A proactive approach that ensures that family investment decisions are made in a professional and objective manner, and take into account future needs and strategies, as opposed to individual decisions based on personal investment criteria.

–   Assessing the market value of the business. This will focus on an examination of the level of family wealth represented by the business, and potentially the need to diversify either at a business level or at an individual level by individual family members.

–   Balancing the requirements of those family members involved in the business and those shareholders not directly involved in the business.

–   Examining the financial requirements of the business and communicating these requirements to all stakeholders.

Any examination of the financial requirements of the business should be in the context of a business or strategic plan that will drive the financial requirements of the business. This plan should include the current status of the business, financial figures, annual sales turnover, product lines, competitive environment, number of employees, location of facilities, marketing and distribution structure. The plan will include a financial plan that examines current liabilities, debts, long term obligations, funding needs, financial forecasts and a valuation of the business. The financial forecasts are based primarily on the balance sheet, profit and loss account, cash-flow and future financial projections over a number of years. The business plan should also incorporate a strategic assessment of the prospects for the business, the risks in its market, its key strengths, how well it is represented in its market, growth opportunities, and how all this impacts on operating costs and capital expenditure.

In contrast, the family usually extracts value from the business by one of the following means:

– Salary and bonuses, which would both be liable to income tax.

– Pension provision, which may be tax relieved.

– Dividends, which would be liable to income tax.

– Capital repayments/share buybacks.

Existing profits may be extracted by the owners or reinvested in the business. In meeting financing requirements of the business, other sources of finance (which may facilitate greater profit extraction) would primarily consist of:

– Improving working capital cycle of the business. This is a one-off form of finance that generates cash savings by shortening debtor periods and potentially lengthening creditor periods. In the short term, this will provide a one-off cash-flow benefit for the company.

– The company may raise debt against some of the existing assets of the business.

– Existing assets may be disposed of either by outright sale or by a sale and lease back transaction. Deferring asset acquisitions over a period of time, or using hire purchase or leasing arrangements, may result in a deferral of long-term capital investment which could release funds in the short term for alternate use.

– New business opportunities may be proceeded with on a joint venture basis in order to limit the capital investment of the business.

This involves securing a partner for certain activities, and is either a simple financial arrangement or a strategic arrangement.

–   Finance could be raised by equity release, whereby a private equity investor or venture capitalists subscribe for shares in the business. In a family business context, this is not a common way of realising finance, because the family always prefers outright control over the business.

Examining the various options for raising finance gives the family an indication of the level of value available for reinvestment in the business or for potential extraction and use outside of the business. If the family goal is the long-term future prosperity of the business, their rate of reinvestment must be higher. Conversely, the longer the business owners live, the lower the reinvestment rate is likely to be, as over time they will take out money to satisfy their own needs as well as their families. Founders often regard the family business as a long-term payback for the overall family investment in the business. This can have the unfortunate effect of making their family comfortable at the expense of the business. Early warning signs include declining turnover, declining profitability, cash-flow problems, inefficient use of cash, declining value of the company, decline in business capabilities, increased weaknesses in its market, declining reinvestment in plant and machinery, research, marketing and people. When this happens, the family needs to consider the strategic direction of the business and the level of reinvestment required, or whether it is time to dispose of the business. The decision about the business's finances regarding the family can be broken down into three distinct alternatives:

–   Reinvest heavily in the business for long term gain.

–   Dispose of the business.

–   Maximise value extraction from the business pending its future discontinuance.

The key issue in the overall assessment is the risks to the family in managing its wealth. Can these risks be managed through diversification of interests outside of the business, without jeopardising the wealth accumulated to date within the business?

ASSET AND WEALTH PROTECTION

Protecting wealth is about recognising risks and taking appropriate action. Risk can be examined either in respect of one particular asset in isolation, or on a cumulative basis relative to the entire family's asset holdings. Risk can usually be categorised as follows:

—   *Business risks:* Risks arising from trading exposures and creditors.

—   *Financial risks/debt management:* This usually depends on the underlying nature of the investment, the level of gearing, or debt arrangements with financial institutions.

—   *Tax risk:* Concern that inefficient planning will allow the tax authorities to claim a disproportionate share of an individual's wealth, see Chapter 10 for some planning alternatives.

—   *Marital risk:* This involves protecting assets from non-family members or estranged spouses.

Business Risk

Operating more than one business through one company increases the risk that one profitable and well-functioning business could be jeopardised due to the performance of an unprofitable debt-ridden business. The basic rationale for incorporation is limited liability, so that different operations conducted by different companies provide a degree of protection. In a group situation involving a number of companies, the financial performance of one entity may be directly or indirectly linked to the performance of the other entities through provision of assistance or finance across the group. In such situations, the performance of one company may still jeopardise the wider group operations. Alternative ways of keeping businesses separate include:

1.   Hiving off businesses to separate entities.

2.   Parallel trading structures.

Chapter 10 provides an overview of tax issues in succession planning, and outlines the tax implications of hiving off one business from a group of businesses. This can easily be done as part of a risk minimisation strategy or a diversification strategy that separates two or more businesses so that they are not directly interlinked.

Another alternative is parallel trading structures. This involves the establishment of new companies separate from existing companies/groups of companies, that carry out certain activities. From a succession planning perspective, the benefit is that it enables new business or asset acquisitions to be acquired through a new company with potential financial assistance from the existing group. At the same time, this provides a shareholding structure that allows value to accrue in the hands of the next generation. From a risk perspective, the most important issue is the separation of the new company from any existing business, so that financially it has no obligations to them.

Since most parallel trading structures are established by leveraging value in the existing businesses, the latter are normally exposed to potential underperformance of the new business. Ideally, once the new business/company starts to perform well, the financial assistance offered by the existing group is removed and the links between the two companies severed. Financially, future performance is not interlinked or intertwined with the existing group structure. There are two financially separate operations. The wealth represented in each is immune to any risks associated with the other. It is strongly advisable to obtain professional advice on the tax and company law implications of such structuring.

Mayer Amschel Rothschild founded the Rothschild banking dynasty. Each of his five sons set up a banking business in one of the five principal European financial capitals of the 18th century – Frankfurt, Vienna, London, Paris and Naples. The father in effect established a family banking system whereby he lent money to each son to start their banking business in their own specific geographic location, on the understanding that they would repay him so that his "family bank" could make further loans to family members. Once the original loan was repaid, each son retained the profits of his own particular banking division. Interest was charged on the loans. The father's main demand was that each son relate to him all the financial information they obtained in their own geographic location. This information was then shared amongst the wider family, in effect creating an international information sharing network. By sending his sons to different countries, he diversified his family's human resources geographically both politically and in terms of economic risk. Had he failed to diversify, and kept all his sons in Frankfurt where he first started his business, it is unlikely that any part of the business would have survived the Holocaust. So while the branches of the family business in Frankfurt, Vienna and Naples were wiped out by the ravages of history, the London and Paris branches survived. This clearly demonstrates that a family's wealth is both its human capital and its intellectual capital. Furthermore, the way the Rothschilds used financial capital and long-term wealth preservation was better served by lending rather than giving money to the next generation. By lending money and having it repaid, Rothschild senior could re-circulate the money to advance other business opportunities. By lending money rather than giving it to his sons, the father also showed them what business was like for people who do not have the facility of obtaining family finance. Most importantly, from a risk perspective, the overall structuring delivered diversification without which the family business would not have survived.

Debt/banking risk

The global financial crisis that began in 2008 has delivered a number of significant challenges for individuals/companies who have existing debt or who are looking to borrow new funds. A critical issue facing individuals/companies today is developing a financial strategy with an appropriate level of debt leverage. In the past, debt was frequently seen as simply a cheaper form of finance than equity/cash resources. The volume of debt in corporate structures was maximised to whatever the bank would lend. This created two key issues for individuals/ companies with existing debt in the current recessionary climate:

1. Their financial model was sized and structured to accommodate the maximum amount of cheap debt finance, as in Euribor rates at a low point in the cycle and low interest margins. This inherited structure brings significant risks in today's environment.

2. When such highly leveraged structures default, shareholders run the risk of losing all their equity in a debt restructuring. This is crit-

ical, since in many cases when debt was cheap, shareholders were prepared to use high leverage to avoid diluting their ownership. The corollary of this approach is that inappropriate levels of debt today could result in full loss of equity in a restructuring.

There are also several challenges for individuals/businesses who are looking to raise new debt in today's environment:

1. The impact of the financial crisis on the banking system has left many banks with weak balance sheets and a requirement to shore up their existing capital. This has resulted in a lower volume of credit being made available. The second quarterly business trend survey in summer 2010 published by ISME (Irish Small and Medium Enterprises Association) showed that 13% of respondents indicated that "lack of access to credit" was their main concern.

2. Lack of competition in the banking sector, higher funding costs and internal competition for capital within the individual banks, has also led to higher borrowing costs for individuals/companies.

3. Several banks in Ireland are overweight in certain sectors, such as property, so that new lending in these sectors has been constrained. This has significantly impacted the way in which individuals/companies can operate in these markets.

These issues highlight the importance of a model that can be used to design appropriate debt strategies in the future, and to reflect the changing environment for raising debt in Ireland today. The model described below can be used to help companies identify, analyse and resolve the key issues in developing a company's debt strategy. The model examines a number of key considerations which should drive the formulation of any company's debt strategy. The model comprises four interlinking cornerstones which must be viewed simultaneously when assessing debt requirements:

1. The financing requirements of the business.

2. The level of appropriate security offered.

3. The stability of the debt structure.

4. The required level of financial flexibility of a company's cash flows.

1. *Business objectives:* An effective debt strategy should be aligned to the short – and long-term objectives of your business and to your future financing requirements, in order to support business growth through, for example, mergers or acquisitions.

2. *Properly structured security:* Any charges over assets, parent company or personal guarantees provided to financial institutions should be considered in light of any future plans for these assets. The risks of security being exercised following a potential default should be fully evaluated. Personal guarantees can prove lethal from a wealth protection perspective, since they defeat the limited liability a corporate structure would otherwise offer.

3. *Stability of Debt:* The stability of a company's financing arrangements is vital, including the term of the loans and the reasonableness of the covenants applied. In general, you should apply the principle of matching your debt tenor to the life of the asset. A key consideration in today's environment is the requirement for stable, medium-to long-term financing arrangements which reduce or eliminate refinancing risk and the risk of a covenant breach in the business. However, such medium – to long-term arrangements typically have a cost implication. The appetite of the business, and the ability of its projected cash flows to support any such cost increases, must be examined in detail.

4. *Financial Flexibility:* The cost of the debt package in place is a key consideration for any business that wants to evaluate its debt strategy. There is a trade-off between increased stability, including longer term loans; and sustainable covenants, the level of security given, and the margin cost of the loan. Debt margins reached historic lows during 2007 before increasing dramatically in the four years since. These margins are expected to remain high.

Current debt market conditions have created a complex and difficult environment for borrowers. Organisations are currently facing challenges both with raising new debt and refinancing and repaying existing debt obligations. The level of debt in your capital structure must be sufficiently balanced to support your business model, and to meet the risk appetite of the equity providers. The steps outlined above can serve as a guide to help individuals and organisations consider the range of interactive issues upon which to base any debt strategy.

Asset transfers to reduce risk

With a number of the other risks, whether business or debt related/financial, transferring assets to stand-alone holding structures may help reduce particular exposures, usually in the form of creditors having access to assets. As part of any asset protection strategy, two main issues arise when deciding to transfer assets to a holding structure:

1. The tax issues in respect of the proposed asset transfer.

2. A legal impediment that might impugn the transfer and subsequently render it void.

Other personal and commercial requirements can also arise in respect of a specific transfer:

–   Any arrangements relating to the asset being transferred involving third parties, such as tenants or parties (e.g. banks) that may have a charge over assets.

–   The proposed structure to which the asset may be transferred.

–   If transferred to an individual directly, their capacity/ability to deal with the asset prudently, and any other issues that might arise in connection with holding the asset in a personal capacity.

Quite apart from the legal implications of any vehicle to which the asset may be transferred, when you examine the specific capacity to transfer an asset, assuming no other issues such as undue influence and duress, your main focus is whether a creditor could in future seek to have a transaction set aside under bankruptcy law Section 59 of the Bankruptcy Act 1988 provides as follows:

a) That any transfer at undervalue/gift of property shall be void as against an Official Assignee in bankruptcy where the individual making the transfer is adjudged bankrupt within two years after the date of the transfer, and

b) if the transferor is adjudged bankrupt at any subsequent time within five years after the date of the transfer, it shall be void as against the Official Assignee, unless the parties claiming under the gift / settlement prove that the transferor was, at the time of making the transfer, able to pay all his/her debt without the aid of the property comprised in the gift / settlement.

In effect, a transfer can be set aside absolutely within a two-year period of being made. For the three years thereafter, it can potentially be challenged. There is little to no risk for that three-year period if there is certainty around the solvency position of the transferor at the time of the transfer. In addition, Section 74 of the Land and Conveyancing Law Reform Act 2009 provides that "any conveyance of property made with the intention of defrauding a creditor or other person is voidable by any person thereby prejudiced." This applies not only to land but also to personal property such as shares.

At the time of writing, this is an issue of concern for individuals due to deteriorating financial circumstances. In particular, where individuals have given personal guarantees for corporate debt, individual asset transfers to family members do, from an asset protection perspective, merit examination in light of overall requirements under bankruptcy law. The prudent course when effecting any asset transfer at undervalue, or when making any gift, is to prepare a statement of net worth with up to date valuations. The statement, which would include all assets and liabilities, should be attached to a declaration of solvency signed in the presence of a solicitor at the time of the making of the transfer. This verifies your solvency position and substantiates that you can at that point in time meet all your debts without recourse to the assets you propose to transfer.

This should all be effected well in advance of any deterioration in one's position. It is advisable that you effect such transfers while you are in a financially strong position, or where you have given personal guarantees for corporate debt while your businesses are financially healthy. Planning of this nature is designed for a "rainy day," and is best facilitated by having assets held in different unconnected structures, or held by different family members.

Holding assets separately on an unconnected basis should be a consideration where all new asset acquisitions are being made, unless you are just looking at possible transfers of existing assets. There is little point closing the door after the horse has bolted. This is all too apparent in respect of some of the attempted restructuring implemented in the recent past. This is likely to be subject to creditor scrutiny and creditor challenge over the validity of the transfers effected.

Creditor and marital risk

The other risks mentioned, such as financial risk, tax risk and marital risk, are usually protected by ring fencing and protecting assets through a combination of steps which may offer some protection. While there is no single solution, there are several options:

—   *Use of trusts:* Trusts are an extremely effective means of creditor protection, provided the asset transfer is made while you are solvent. In respect of the wider use of a trust to protect against claims in a marital breakdown situation, the situation is much less clear, since the courts have power under both divorce legislation and judicial separation legislation to vary the terms of any trust when imposing a financial settlement between two parties to a marriage. Obviously, if the trust was settled by either of the parties to the relationship, the situation is much more clear-cut for the courts if they decide to vary its terms as part of any financial settlement. When a trust has been settled by the parents of one of the parties, the courts are less inclined to interfere, particularly where it relates to family business assets. There is a lack of certainty here. The best advice is to be proactive, in the hope that the court might be more inclined to leave the trust assets alone and make provision for a spouse out of non-trust assets.

– *Letters of wishes:* Letters of wishes for a trust could be specifically worded so that the trustees would only consider children and grand-children (and not non-family members) as beneficiaries of the structures.

– *Beneficiaries under trusts:* Similarly, the classes of beneficiaries under a trust could be designed so as not to include the spouses of family members. They could be specifically excluded as beneficiaries.

– *Shareholders agreement:* These can be drafted in such a way that it becomes very difficult for individuals (particularly non-family) to deal in shares that they have either inherited or acquired in some other way. These restrictions could also apply to creditors who have taken a charge against shares that at the time of charge are subject to a shareholders' agreement. It is advisable, despite the tax cost, to hold a certain level of shareholding in trust so that surviving family members' shareholdings, together with the trust shareholding, give de facto control against any shareholding held by a creditor or non-family member. Certain provisions of the Companies Acts, such as protection of minority shareholders from oppression, limit the absolute control a family may have. However, it does still ensure a far preferable position, compared to a situation where a creditor/non-family member could end up with a 50% shareholding. Some shareholders agreements provide that if a shareholder becomes bankrupt, there is a forced sale of their shares to the company or to the other shareholders. This serves to protect the remaining share-holders, so that they no longer face a situation where a third party creditor succeeds to the shares.

– *Pre-nuptial agreements:* Traditionally, the courts in both Ireland and the UK have refused to enforce pre-nuptial agreements on the grounds that they are contrary to public policy. Other common law systems (such as the US, Australia) have historically adopted a similar approach, but things are changing, either through judicial intervention or legislative change. The Irish government recently appointed a study group on pre-nuptial agreements. In its report,[i] the group expressed the view that pre-nuptial agreements are enforceable under Irish law, although subject to variation if matrimonial proceedings reach the courts. The extent to which a pre-nuptial is recognised and the significance attached to it, would be determined by the courts on a case-by-case basis, in order to meet the constitutional requirement for a proper provision for the respective spouses and children of any marriage in a divorce situation. Interestingly, the report called for a change in existing law to provide specifically that pre-nuptial agreements be taken into account in the event of a separation or a divorce. The report also recommended certain procedural safeguards, including that a pre-nuptial agreement be in writing, signed and witnessed, that each party obtains separate independent legal advice, that both parties make full disclosure of their financial information, and that the agreement is made at least 28 days before the parties' marriage. It therefore appears that pre-nuptial agreements may be enforceable in Ireland, subject to the rights of the courts under existing separation and divorce legislation to vary any agreement where warranted. It would appear to be only a matter of time before the issue comes before the courts for consideration, or is subjected to specific legislative reform. A more modern progressive approach will emerge once pre-nuptial agreements are recognised.

> In the age of multiple marriages, it is inevitable that step-families will disagree more frequently. The children of one of the Johnson & Johnson shareholders took a much publicised and costly lawsuit against their stepmother. Seward Johnson was one of the sons who inherited a majority ownership in Johnson & Johnson. He had children with his first wife, and his last spouse had been his companion for more than a decade before he died. When he died, his children went to court against their stepmother. Ostensibly, the fight was over finances, but in fact it was over the feeling of the children that were denied recognition and respect by their father. Like most family feuds, the only result was that no one was victorious, both sides paid huge legal fees, and both sides attracted unwarranted publicity.

RECENT IRISH EXPERIENCES

Wealth creation, protection and transition to the next generation have occurred very haphazardly in Ireland in recent years.

Partnerships

Large numbers of highly leveraged family partnerships were put in place from a wealth transition perspective, with a view to facilitating future value accruing in the hands of the next generation. Now that so many children are overly burdened with debt, they are arguing before the courts that they knew nothing about the structure, did not receive independent legal advice, and that they should not be tied into the obligations created as a result of the arrangement.

Many individuals also structured their affairs through partnership arrangements with third parties, often in respect of illiquid assets, with lack of clarity around exit. Many of the partners in such arrangements are now left in a difficult situation where business dealings of another partner also impact on them. One example is a prominent property developer who had more than 200 partnerships/co-ownership ventures. Following his insolvency, other individuals will now potentially share a greater than pro rata part of any loss. Clearly, the individuals who entered into arrangements with this developer should have ring-fenced their exposures by ensuring that the pertinent banking arrangements could only impact or have recourse to them on a pro rata basis.

Debt

Where possible, debt should be structured as non-recourse. Mistakes have emerged recently on this, not only as regards capital but also as regards interest being recourse only to particular assets, thus ring-fencing exposures.

From a family governance perspective, consideration should be given to the level of debt that any family member can undertake. In particular, how they may apply family assets as security for such debt. In one case, a member of a high-profile business family pledged their shares to a domestic banking institution. When the person subsequently defaulted, the bank enforced the security by taking the shares as a bank asset. The other family members had no choice but to purchase the bank's shareholding. In other situations, individuals who passed away with substantial debts have now left their family facing the burden of their financial arrangements. It is critical to remember that if a highly leveraged individual dies, the debt in their estate passes to the beneficiaries of the estate along with the various assets. In a number of estates, beneficiaries are contesting the level of such debt.

Marriage breakdown

In a marriage breakdown, one result of the dispute between the parties is that the business assumes the burden, or part of the burden, arising from the financial deterioration in the party's circumstances. The business can thus become collateral damage of the marital breakdown and debt situation.

There have been several media reports of estates being contested after a marital breakdown, where the deceased is in a second relationship and their estate is contested between their first partner or children and their second partner and/or children. In some marital breakdowns, it is only assets held in family trusts (which are often not burdened by debt) that are available for the claimant's spouse. All other assets held by the other spouse may carry a significant debt burden. The courts are generally reluctant to prejudice creditors by giving assets to the dependent spouse, where such assets might otherwise be utilised to meet creditor obligations.

Trusts

In some instances where clients have been advised to settle funds in trust, those funds have not been appointed to any beneficiaries. This money is often the sole unencumbered and protected family asset, a true "rainy day" fund. When all other assets are in negative equity, the family value is effectively wiped out because of debt obligations.

General

The arrangements entered into by many Irish individuals in the recent past lack diversification in investments and business interests. They carry far too high levels of debt, and the debt arrangements are not structured appropriately. The interlinking of debt obligations compounds the difficulties. A problem in one area can bring all their assets into play. Like a house of cards, when one obligation is called in, everything can be lost. That is why the past two years have witnessed a change in the way individuals are structuring their affairs. Many are now taking appropriate advice in this area. For many others, it may be too late, but those with a viable business have learned a valuable if expensive lesson.

Privacy and Confidentiality

Certain trust and company structures will help prevent your level of wealth or asset holdings entering the public domain. This was covered in Chapter 3.

Retirement considerations

Business owners can place too much reliance on cash-flow from their businesses to fund retirement related living expenses. If the senior generation within a business has not made adequate financial provision for retirement, it can be prompted by a desire to maintain control of the business so as to protect their overall financial position. This is clearly inconsistent with a strategy for passing the business to the next generation, and can lead to situations of conflict as retention of control and the imposition of financial constraints on the business may impact on the next generation. If the retiring founder has an inadequately funded retirement plan, or little to no investments outside of the business, he or she will typically continue to draw a salary or arrange to receive a consulting fee from the business. In may sometimes be possible for lump sum payments to be made to the retiring person's pension plan. The primary issue here is that no coherent plan for retirement was established at an early stage, to ensure adequate financial provision for the retiring family member outside of the business.

Retirement goal setting

Given the high cost of funding retirement, individuals should plan for their future financial provision at a relatively early stage. It is advisable to ask the following questions:

–   Do I want to reduce the amount of time spent at work or would I prefer to remain active in the management of the business or participate in a new role within the business?

–   What sort of retirement lifestyle do I and my partner/spouse envisage?

–   What are my goals and the timeframe within which to realise or accumulate the amount of value required to satisfy such a lifestyle?

–   How much income and capital can the business provide to fund my lifestyle?

–   Do I have sufficient wealth within the business or external to the business to fund my proposed lifestyle? If not, what options do I have?

–   Does my wealth need to be restructured in order to provide for my retirement? Does it depend on a sale of the business?

–   What effect will asset performance, inflation and the risk weighting of my investments have on my overall retirement plan? Do I have a well thought out investment strategy to achieve this?

–   What are the other issues likely to impact on my situation, including family obligations, provision for family members outside the business, my health and life expectancy and funding tax liabilities in passing assets to family members as part of any estate plan?

Once you have established your goals, contact an appropriate professional advisor, who will examine your financial position relative to what you wish to achieve during your retirement. Establishing a plan and liaising with an appropriate professional advisor will assist in determining the level of capital required to fund your retirement. It will also assist in recognising other needs, such as lifestyle choices including a holiday home or boat, or philanthropic activities you plan to become involved in post retirement. Financial planning usually involves securing the financial position of your spouse and dependent family members, including provision of care for a disabled relative. This can all be incorporated into an overall retirement plan. Having a formal plan and a timetable for implementing the plan is an important exercise. It provides a benchmark against which you can determine or evaluate the performance of your investments, the level of capital to be extracted from the business and how that impacts on any liquidity plan for the business. The absence of a plan increases the likelihood of having insufficient assets to meet your requirements in retirement.

With your goals established and your financial information collated, you are now able to make a detailed assessment of how realistic and achievable your goals are. This will help manage both your expectations in retirement and your existing expectations as to how you apply available resources, both within and outside the business. Any retirement plan should be consistent and coordinated with all the other elements of your overall succession plan. To achieve tax efficiency, make sure that pension provision is part of any overall investment plan. Review your retirement plan regularly to ensure that you are meeting milestones. This review also gives you an opportunity to address changes in personal and financial circumstances and to revise the plan as required.

Pension provision

For the self-employed, pension provision is an important part of any overall wealth management strategy, allowing you to diversify wealth away from the business while simultaneously providing for retirement. This book offers only a brief overview of pension alternatives as they impact on the self-employed or on people who are substantial shareholders in their company through which their business operates. The alternate arrangements in providing for your pension are:

1. Retirement annuity contracts (RACs).

2. Personal retirement savings accounts (PRSAs).

    An executive pension plan (EPP), an individual pension scheme set up by your employer company with you as the key or executive individual. The EPP is subject to the rules governing occupational pension schemes. For private companies, there are three types of EPP:

    i) A scheme administered by an insurance company and investing solely in traditional 'off the shelf' unit linked managed funds and unitised with profit funds.

    ii) A scheme administered by an insurance company in association with a stockbroker, with the power to invest in a much broader range of equities. This is known as a self directed equity pension scheme.

    iii) A small self-administered pension scheme with its own trust deed and rules and investment mandate. This encompasses a broad range of asset classes agreed between the member and the scheme trustee within the parameters permitted by Revenue. The rules that apply to schemes of this nature are different from those applying to larger occupational pension schemes.

Costs of running each of these scheme types differ. Seek professional advice on which scheme is most suitable to you.

RACs

An RAC is a contract between an individual and a Revenue-approved service provider, structured either by life assurance contract or provided under a trust arrangement. RACs have been the traditional form of personal pension. The contract provides retirement benefits through an annuity and lump sum which can be taken from age 60 onwards. There is no obligation to purchase an annuity after drawing down a lump sum. You can invest in an approved retirement fund (ARF), a post retirement fund discussed below. Usually the annual sum contributed does not exceed the available level of tax relief.

PRSAs

A Personal Retirement Savings Account is a contract between an individual and an authorised PRSA provider in the form of an investment account. PRSA benefits are determined by the contributions paid by and on behalf of the contributor and the investment return on those contributions. The annual sum contributed is usually equal to or less than the available level of tax relief.

Executive Pension Plans (EPPs)

An executive pension plan is a form of occupational pension plan that en employer sets up for an employee who is usually an executive or director of the company. Executive pension plans operate in much the same manner as a regular defined contribution occupational scheme.

The maximum ordinary annual contribution including administration costs to be paid on or on behalf of an individual employee (combined employer and employee), is significantly higher than that possible under RAC or PRSA regulation. This maximum is defined by the **greater** of:

$$\text{Contribution} = \frac{\text{B x CF} - (\text{value of assets plus retained benefits})}{\text{Term in years to normal retirement (Min 1 Year)}}$$

$$\text{Or} = \frac{\text{N/60ths pension x CF} - \text{value of assets}}{\text{Term in years to normal retirement (Min 1 Year)}}$$

B   =   Revenue maximum pension based on current remuner-
             ation but service to normal retirement date

CF   =   Maximum benefit capitalisation factor (an actuarial fac-
             tor based on age)

N/60ths =   The pension that can always be provided from a scheme
             regardless of retained benefits

Note: Any new pension funding proposal must take account
             of existing pension assets in aggregate.

Unlike employee contributions which are liable to PRSI and universal
social charge, employer contributions are fully tax deductible, and can
be increased or decreased at any time subject to the maximum limits
based on the cap on personal contributions, and the overall restriction
on the level of funding permitted within the pension fund. This makes
EPPs very flexible, and they can be very efficient in funding for maximum benefits over a short time period. EPPs also offer flexibility in retirement age. Normal retirement age is between 60 and 70, but with
EPPs, the member can opt to take early retirement from age 50 with
the employer's consent.

Certain rules apply to pensions schemes classed as "small self-administered pension schemes." An occupational pension scheme is classed by
Revenue as a small self administered pension scheme in the following
circumstances:

–   The scheme has less than 12 members.

–   65% or more of the scheme's assets relate to the provision of benefits
    of directors with a 20% shareholding or more, their spouses and
    dependents.

To obtain Revenue approval, a small self-administered pension scheme
must have a "pensioneer trustee" who is approved by Revenue. This pensioneer trustee is an outside, independent professional trustee with a
duty to ensure that the scheme operates in accordance with Revenue

guidelines, and that pension assets are not misused for tax avoidance purposes.

One of the main attractions of self-directed and small self-administered pension schemes is the control that small companies and their 20% directors have over investment of scheme assets. The trustees may invest directly in the stock market, deposits, property or hire external investment managers. To prevent abuses, clear restrictions on investments apply:

–   Loans to scheme members or their families are prohibited.

–   Restrictions are placed on certain property investments.

–   Self-investment is not allowed, e.g. the acquisition of company assets such as property, shares or debentures.

–   Schemes may not invest in what are known as "chattels" or "pride of possession" articles including works of art, jewellery, yachts, etc.

–   Investments in private companies must be limited to 5% of scheme assets and 10% of the private company's share capital.

Full details of restrictions can be found in the Revenue Pensions Manual. In order to ensure approval, Revenue requires regular submissions of information about the scheme. Actuarial reports must be submitted at least every three years, detailing the assumptions on which the funding of the scheme is based. Revenue also requires audited accounts for each scheme year no later than nine months after year end. Information on how the funds have been or will be invested must also be given to Revenue.

Tax relief on contributions

The self-employed can claim tax relief on personal pension contributions to an RAC or PRSA. Members of an occupational pension scheme can also claim tax relief on their own contributions, as distinct from contributions made by the employer.

Age	Tax Relief Limit (% of Remuneration*)
Under 30	15%
30 to 39	20%
40 to 49	25%
50 to 54	30%
55 to 59	35%
60 and over	40%

From 2011, the maximum remuneration figure used to calculate relief is €115,000.

A single earnings cap of €115,000 applies for all types of pension contributions made by individuals. There is no cap for employers contributions to an occupational pension scheme. Personal contributions are
not tax relieved from PRSI or the universal social charge.

The recent National Framework Document on pensions recommends
changing the tax relief infrastructure so that all scheme members enjoy
a flat rate of relief on pension contributions (possibly 30%). There is
no definite timescale for this, but 2014 has been mooted as a possible
target date. Following the 2011 election of a new government, the basis
under which any tax relief is afforded may change and the recent jobs
initiative confirmed a new levy of 0.6% on private pension scheme assets
that will apply in each of the next four years 2011 to 2014. The levy
will result in a direct reduction in the pension fund of those individuals
saving for retirement.

Options on retirement

A self-employed individual or proprietary director (a director with more
than a 5% shareholding) may avail of the following options on retirement:

A. Tax-free lump sum.

B.   Pension/retirement annuity.

C.   Transfer their pension to an approved retirement fund (ARF).

A.   Tax-Free Lump Sum

A tax-free lump sum may be taken up to €200,000. An additional amount of 25% of the value of the fund, less €200,000, up to an overall limit of €375,000, can be taken subject to the standard 20% rate of income tax. Maximum limits apply to the overall amount which may be taken as a lump sum, tax-free or taxable: 25% of €2,3000,000 which is currently not subject to indexation (referred to as the Standard Fund Threshold). In December 2010, this stood at €5,400,000.

B.   Pension/Retirement Annuity

The remainder of the fund can be used to purchase a retirement annuity (annual income) from a life assurance company. This is the traditional alternative. The retirement annuity is guaranteed for life, while the capital is lost to the individual. Annuity purchasers should therefore choose an annuity which has a guaranteed option of at least five years to protect some of the capital used to purchase the annuity. The annuity is liable to income tax, which is collected by the insurance company operating PAYE in paying the annuity to you.

Most life assurance companies do not limit the purchase to the life assurance company in which the monies were originally invested. This is usually referred to as an "open market option." The level of the annuity payable will depend on the type of annuity purchased. There are a number of options here:

1. A level (or non-indexing) pension will remain constant for the life of the policyholder. This may commence at a satisfactory level but will reduce in real terms over time due to inflation effects.

2. An escalating (or indexing) pension may be purchased with increases at a set percentage every year. For example, the consumer price index amount or 5% p.a. The obvious advantage with this is that the pension payment increases in line with or above inflation.

3. A married retiree may wish to provide a retirement income for his/her partner. A spouse's pension will ensure that the pension will continue to be paid to a spouse in the event of death in retirement.

4 There is also an option of providing escalation on the spouse's pension.

Notes:

(1): The more benefits added to the annuity, for example, escalation, the more expensive it becomes. It has the effect of reducing the pension amount to the policyholder.

(2): The 'Annuity Rate' is the rate at which the pension is purchased. For example, it will typically cost €100 for every €5 pension (increasing) payable. A level annuity may provide an income at 6.5% of the fund.

(3): A policyholder may build in one final option which ensures the full pension amount is paid to the next of kin on death for a limited period typically 5 or 10 years.

C. Approved Retirement Fund ("ARF")

An Approved Retirement Fund (ARF) is an investment account into which part of an individual's retirement fund can be transferred upon reaching retirement age. ARFs are an alternative to the more traditional route of purchasing an annuity or pension on retirement. The benefit of an ARF is that the individual retains control of the investment, can take any annual income or gains from the fund and then leave the investment to the next of kin on their death. For example, an ARF could be a deposit account, a portfolio of equities, a property or a life assurance company's managed fund. The individual is the beneficial owner of the assets.

An individual can withdraw funds from an ARF at any time. There is no maximum withdrawal. Income tax and the universal social charge are payable on any amounts drawn down from the ARF. There is an imputed distribution on all ARFs every February. Currently, this is 5% of the value of the ARF. ARF holders are required to pay income tax and levies as if they had withdrawn 5% of the fund, whether or not they actually did.

Tax is calculated by reference to the ARF value on 31 December, and is regarded as a distribution made no later than February of the following year. No imputed distribution will be made from an ARF in February, if in the previous year the ARF holder took total withdrawals from the ARF equivalent to the rate of imputed distribution for that year. It is therefore more tax-efficient to take sufficient actual withdrawals in any year to avoid double taxation.

Before being allowed to invest in an ARF, you must first meet one of the following requirements:

–   Be in receipt of a guaranteed pension/annuity for life of at least €18,000 p.a. which can include the state pension if it is being received at the time.

–   Invest at least €120,000 in an Approved Minimum Retirement Fund (AMRF). An AMRF is the same as an ARF but cannot be drawn until age 75.

TAXATION OF ARF ON DEATH

Unlike the annuity option, the ARF remains your property and can be passed on to family just like any other asset. The tax implications of ARFs are outlined below:

A.   *Passes to spouse*
     A surviving spouse will not suffer any liability to income tax or capital acquisitions tax ("CAT"), on the basis that the assets then pass to an ARF in the name of the surviving spouse.

B.   *Passes to a child*
     If the spouse subsequently dies and leaves the ARF asset to a child, or if the assets are left directly to a child (rather than passing first to the surviving spouse), any tax liability depends on the child's age:

     If a child is under 21 years of age, the receipt is regarded as a benefit for CAT purposes and may result in a liability to this tax. The current CAT threshold is €332,084 per child. Any amount in excess of the threshold will be taxable. There is no income tax liability in this situation.

For any child over the age of 21 years, there is no liability to CAT. However, income tax is charged at the standard rate on receipt of assets.

C.   *Other individuals*

Where an ARF is passed directly to an individual (who is not a spouse/child), income tax is charged at the marginal (top) rate. There may also be a CAT liability with appropriate CAT thresholds applying. If, however, it passes to a spouse first and then on to an individual (other than a child), income tax will apply at the standard rate. There may also be a CAT liability with appropriate CAT thresholds applying.

Summary of retirement options

The options available to self-employed individuals are:

–   Use all of the retirement fund/pension to purchase a retirement annuity.

–   Withdrawal of up to €200,000 of the total retirement fund as a tax free lump sum, and a further amount subject to an overall cap with a 20% tax rate. The balance of the fund can be used for the following options:

–   Purchase a retirement annuity.

–   Draw down the balance subject to their top rate of income tax.

–   Invest in an ARF.

When deciding whether to purchase an annuity or avail of the ARF, you may wish to consider some of the relative advantages/disadvantages of both alternatives:

ARFs compared to Annuities

Guaranteed Annuity

Advantages	Disadvantages
Provides a guaranteed level of income for life. There is no chance of it running out.	The cost of purchasing an annuity has continuously increased over the last ten years. Once a sum is invested in an annuity, the capital is lost.
Funds are not exposed to the market so there is no investment risk.	Annuities cannot be passed on death except where a spouse's pension is built in or there is a guaranteed period.
Range of options such as guaranteed periods, spouses benefit etc.	Annuity rates are linked to interest rates and the rate you receive will ultimately depend on interest rates prevailing on the day.
No ongoing advice is necessary as they are simple and easy to operate.	There is a risk of inflation, unless an escalating pension is chosen.

ARF

Advantages	Disadvantages
Capital is preserved for dependents. On death the ARF will pass to the spouse or estate.	There is a risk that the fund could be fully drawn down or "bomb out" while the individual is still alive, not least because of the imputed distribution of 5% per annum.
Income flexibility. ARF holders can take income at any time and there is no limit to the amount of the drawdown.	Investment risk due to market exposure.
Gives the opportunity to defer the purchase of an annuity. An individual could set up an ARF in the hope that annuity rates will improve.	If the ARF is used to defer annuity purchase there is a risk that rates could fall further.
Capital and income are rolled up free of tax until a withdrawal is made, subject to a deemed annual drawdown.	Ongoing advice may be necessary if the individual does not have sufficient investment knowledge.
Exposure to the investment markets with potential for capital gains.	The annual imputed distribution reduces the benefit of gross roll up and estate planning opportunities.
Control over investment policy. ARFs can be set up with a wide variety of fund managers with a wide range of investment products.	

General investment planning

Given the time commitment involved in a family business, many business owners have neither the time nor the energy for personal investment management. It can be challenging to establish an investment strategy, and to find the time to focus on investment possibilities outside of the business. As a result, even where investments are made, too little time is spent reviewing and monitoring investment performance. Where a liquidity strategy has not been established to accumulate assets outside of the business, many business owners establishing a succession plan discover that after concentrating solely on the business, they must now suddenly change focus and consider managing a certain amount of liquid wealth. This is often outside their comfort zone.

Some individuals approach this as a retirement project. They analyse and research various investments, they collate advice from service providers, they decide on asset allocation, they review performance and they manage their investments themselves. Most individuals would be better served by obtaining professional investment advice from an appropriate advisor.

In establishing an investment strategy, there is no optimum investment strategy that you can adopt in advance. By definition, no one can predict the future. Your investment strategy should therefore cater for your personal situation and your attitude to risk. If you want to remain risk free, you can achieve this at the expense of growth in your capital. A spread of investments is generally advisable, giving some security but with a potential upside if investments do well. In deciding on an investment, it is important to decide on how long you want to tie up your funds. For example, cashing an investment before its term is up can result in early encashment penalties. In general terms, you should consider:

–   **The size of the investment:** The size of funds you have to invest can limit the type of investment you can make. For example, some investments have a minimum entry level. The more funds you have to invest, the more you can spread your risk.

–   **Risk vs. reward:** Usually, the higher the risk, the higher the potential for gain. Adopting a higher risk strategy could result in a loss of some or all of your investment. Your investment strategy should also take account of the overall purpose of the investment and the age of the investor. Generating a reasonable return on your investment requires a balance between risk and reward. This means spreading your investments, giving you potential for gain while not over-exposing you to undue risk.

– **Time frame:** You need to take into account when you will need access to your funds. If the time frame is relatively short, you should invest in a product specifically designed with this in mind. Some investments tie up your funds for a number of years. Early encashment can result in very severe financial penalties.

– **Requirement for income:** If you need to take income on a regular basis from the investment, the investment or product should have this facility. Remember that some investments do not have a facility to take income.

– **Tax efficiency:** The tax treatment of investment products can vary. Since tax will reduce the gain on your investment, it becomes an important, but not the sole, element in investment decisions.

Investment planning using an advisor

It is essential that your investment advisor understands your requirements in order to enable them to anticipate and plan for your future needs. Your investment advisor should be aware of the following:

– Your level of knowledge in relation to investing.

– Your current investment strategy.

– Your current investment portfolio.

– Your personal risk level.

– Your overall life goals and objectives and how your non-financial objectives interact with the financial provision required.

In order to establish an appropriate investment strategy, an investment advisor should also be familiar with wider business and financial issues:

- Your overall succession plan.

- Your short term and long-term individual liquidity needs.

- Your will.

- Your insurance requirements.

- Your overall retirement plan.

- Future financial provision for family members.

- Level of capital or income required from the business to support an investment strategy.

4-Stage Investment Planning

Your investment process can be easily broken down into four simple stages:

1. *Assessment:* Your existing investments, strategy and risk tolerance will be assessed. Your investment advisor will educate you on various alternatives, on investment principles, and on how your investment plan should coincide with your retirement plan and specific financial goals.

2. *Analysis and recommendations:* Your advisor will develop asset allocation models and help you determine an investment policy.

3. *Implementation:* Your advisor will provide information on investment manager and stock selection, manager monitoring, and details of all dealings and trade settlements.

4. *Reporting:* Your advisor will provide, usually on a quarterly basis, an investment report, including details on investment portfolios, valuations and performance data, special investments, values of

properties, details of expenditure and costs in placing or disposing of the investments, together with ongoing supervision of investment policy.

Philanthropy

Philanthropy comes from the Greek, "philos anthropos", meaning love of my fellow man. A family business' social and philanthropic activities are often based on family business values. Family members seek to have their values and vision reflected in their behaviour and in the policies of their family trusts or their business.

Philanthropy in the industrial world reflects trends in wealth, family make up and demographics. Greater wealth is concentrated in fewer hands. In many countries, there are tax incentives or tax deductions available for charitable giving. Philanthropy is a socially responsible path and a way for many people to express their values, using their wealth to create a lasting positive influence. It has become a powerful ideal. In our age, Bill Gates and Warren Buffett are leading the way. In past eras, it was the Rockefellers, the Carnegies, the Mellons and the Fords. Andrew Carnegie said: "It is more difficult to give away money intelligently than it is to earn it in the first place".

> Sir Tom Hunter is a Scottish billionaire who has decided to give his fortune away during his lifetime. «My wife Marion and myself are going to leave this world as we came into it – pretty much with nothing. I don't want to take £1 billion to my grave with me.» Hunter has stated that while he will not leave his three teenage children destitute. «They will be taken care of. I don't want to burden my kids with great wealth. Warren Buffett said that he would leave his kids enough that they can do something but not too much that they will do nothing.»

In assessing charitable donations, the first question you must ask is whether that contribution should be from individual family wealth or family wealth located outside of the family business. Maybe it should be by corporate donations from the family enterprise. Donations can also be funded from income or from capital. Donations are often funded from income from a cash-flow perspective, unlike donations of capital which can sometimes represent a significant impact on net worth.

There are a number of philanthropic options:

–   Direct gifts or bequests by way of a will.

–   Donations to donor advised funds.

–   Establishment of a private foundation.

Most donations are direct gifts to existing operating charities. Usually such charities are well established, or the donor may be personally acquainted with individuals involved in the charity.

If you wish to benefit a number of charities, or if at first you are uncertain as to the charities, you can choose the preferable option of donor advised funds, intermediary entities which enjoy charitable status. They exist to receive and manage donations, and they use the donations to fund a number of other charities. This intermediary funding vehicle allocates funds to charities which use them for charitable purposes. Donor advised funds usually allow the donor and their family to continue their involvement in charitable decisions after the donation has been made. Sometimes, the donor family provides the funding, without specifying which charitable cause will benefit. This is left up to the intermediary, which provides certainty and assists the donor family in developing a long-term strategy for application of the funds.

Another alternative is a private foundation which an individual or family sets up and is involved in the operation of. A charitable foundation is usually formed under a trust instrument or is a company limited by guarantee. The directors or trustees are usually related to the donor through business or family relationships. This option is only recommended if you wish to operate your own charity. Many of the characteristics required in running a successful business translate to the operation of a private foundation. Charitable foundations provide a structure for transferring and segregating wealth within the family, and provides an opportunity for family members to become involved and to make a an active and meaningful contribution to the work of the foundation. It is only worth establishing a private foundation if a sizeable donation is involved, if the family wish to be directly involved, if the family has the requisite skills and talent, and a long-term commitment to the charitable entity.

In Ireland there are a number of tax reliefs for charitable giving, including relief from capital acquisitions tax and capital gains tax and income tax in certain circumstances. There is also a stamp duty relief on transfer of certain assets to registered charities. This tax relief applies for a direct gift, a gift to a donor advised fund, or gifts to a private charitable foundation where the relevant charities enjoy charitable status with the Revenue. If you are setting up a private foundation, you can register it with the Revenue so that it ultimately achieves charitable status for the purposes of donations to it.

In all situations, before you make your donation, clarify that the relevant charity is registered with the Revenue. You may also consider donating funds to a donor advised fund. Several such funds exist in Ireland. Details are obtainable from the website www.philanthropy.ie.

Family office

Once a business has successfully matured or transitioned through a number of generations, wealth management becomes more of an issue for stakeholders than it was during the initial start up entrepreneurial phase. Over time it can be possible for the level of wealth outside of the business, or the level of liquid as against the illiquid wealth represented by the business held by the family, to be quite substantial. How the family deals with this wealth has implications for the devolution of business versus non-business assets among family members. There are also implications for overall family harmony regarding those family members involved in, and possibly inheriting, the business, as against those who are not. When a business has been sold, the family wealth can sometimes be preserved in a corporate or trust structure. The family remains connected to the business through the coordinated management of their wealth. Decisions faced by families who continue to own and operate a business can be very different from decisions faced by families who have sold their business. For those continuing to operate a business, it might be convenient for others to manage their wealth. Once the value of the business has been realised, however, the primary question is whether the family should remain together from an investment perspective, or whether they should each pursue their separate destinies. If they do remain together, what is the appropriate basis for managing that wealth into the future?

John Davidson Rockefeller Sr had one son, John D Rockefeller Jr, who decided at an early age that he had no interest in a business career. With his father's agreement, he devoted the rest of his life to family governance and philanthropy. John Sr's wisdom in not forcing his son to remain in the family business, and his willingness to allow him to follow his own path, was one of the best wealth preservation decisions ever made. John Jr set up the family office that serves to manage the wealth management needs of each family member. He thus made a significant contribution to the overall wealth preservation of the family. It also encouraged members of the family to contribute to philanthropy, to go into politics, and to enter various industries, all with the backing of the family office.

The purpose of the family office is to protect the family wealth and to promote harmony. It does so by applying business structures and theory to managing the family's personal wealth. A family office can form part of the family governance structure, as outlined in Chapter 6. When properly organised and staffed, a family office replaces emotional, subjective and historical processes with rational, objective and forward-looking plans. It is an advantage to hire skilled professionals who will devote their full attention to the protection and growth of family wealth and are accountable to family members This frees up family members to focus on other activities. There are various approaches to planning management of wealth:

– A do-it-yourself approach, with a family member taking on the role of investment manager. This family member liaises with external consultants in managing the family's overall wealth.

– Utilising a number of different service providers. This means that the investment management is handled by a number of different firms, each managing separate investment portfolios. The family has a degree of involvement, but someone will have to co-ordinate, report and oversee the activities being carried out by the service providers. In this situation, it is unlikely that any one service provider will provide a consolidated reporting or oversight of the whole. Reporting services would have to be developed or else sourced elsewhere. An existing advisor, such as your accountant, may be able to fulfil this role.

– Utilising the services of an independent multi-family office. This usually serves a number of clients, and is developed on the principle of diversifying investment management across a number of service providers, each offering customised services for each family across the area of reporting, administration and investment.

– Establishing your own family office. This necessitates investment of significant wealth, given the costs of directly employing all the appropriate individuals who provide administrative and reporting services for the family.

The appropriate structure depends on what you perceive as right for you. Bear in mind that a family office has to centralise and manage often tedious and overwhelming administrative functions: reconciliation of bank/investment statements, payment of bills and taxes, preparation of financial statements, assessing investment reports and family expenses, dealing with tax and trust coordination, charitable trust administration, cash management, executing investment strategies, dealing with insurance needs, managing tax compliance for all family members, and maintaining confidential records in a central location.

Owners of closely held businesses who anticipate involvement of family in either the business or in investment of the wider wealth, should consider the role of a family office in their overall succession plan, and consider how it could assist in laying the foundation for an affluent and harmonious lifestyle and family legacy for future generations. The expertise of the family office can help educate the next generation from an early stage about the challenges and responsibilities of managing the family wealth, its investment, philanthropic and other activities, offering the opportunity of hands-on experience.

Wealth preservation across generations

The broader picture

Many family businesses do not survive beyond three generations. The same can be said for the wealth generated by a family, either through its business, or its disposal, or subsequent reinvestment of the proceeds. Family wealth is not self-perpetuating. Without careful planning and stewardship, a hard-earned fortune amassed throughout a lifetime can easily disappear within a generation or two. The real question is: Can a family successfully preserve its wealth over a number of generations, or even for longer periods like 100 years? The failure to preserve wealth has given rise to the proverb, *"Shirt sleeves to shirt sleeves in three generations"*. The principles that apply to succession in a business context also apply to long-term wealth preservation. A family's ability to remain in business for a long time is due to excellent long term succession planning, regardless of how successful the family is financially. Families do not always realise that their approach to long-term wealth preservation should be similar to their approach to a business. The shirt sleeves quotation describes a three-stage process: the creation of wealth, stasis, and dissipation. The real issue for families is whether they can extend the period of creativity through several generations, thereby postponing for as long as possible the period of stasis and ultimate dissipation of the wealth. Some of the issues facing families include:

— In most cultures, wealth preservation has always meant the accumulation of wealth measured as financial wealth. Few families understand that their wealth consists of human capital, intellectual capital and financial capital. Few families understand that without active stewardship of their human and intellectual capital, they cannot preserve their financial capital.

— Families often fail to apply appropriate timeframes for successful wealth preservation. Planning for use of the family's resources, including its human and intellectual as well as its financial capital, is often far too short term. It is specific to individuals, rather than measured on a generation by generation basis when viewing the collective wealth of the family. Short-term for a family is 20 years. Intermediate term is 50 years and long-term investment is 80-100 years. When this type of measurement is applied to a family's investment strategy, the discipline of patience which highlights the success of investors such as Warren Buffett or the Rothschilds shines forth. Patience is a virtue in everything that a family does. For families setting their long term strategies for preserving financial wealth, time is a better friend than to most other investors.

— Families often fail to understand that the preservation of family wealth over a long period of time involves hard work.

If families wish to invest together and preserve their wealth for future generations, a number of principles emerge:

–   Human behaviour determines whether a family preserves its wealth. The actions of family members are more critical than what they own.

–   Wealth preservation should be a dynamic process of group activity/governance. If the family recognises that its decision-making process is a form of governance, it will understand that by organising itself to make joint decisions instead of individual and ad hoc decisions, it has a better chance of averaging more good decisions than bad decisions.

–   The assets of a family are its individual members. A family might know as part of its overall planning that no matter how much they save in taxes (which may be the cost of an investment or doing business), such savings pale in comparison to the revenues lost through poorly educated family members.

–   The wealth of a family consists of the human and intellectual capital of family members. The family's financial capital is a tool for supporting the growth of the family's human and intellectual capital. With the growth of human and intellectual capital comes a high probability of growth of financial capital, just by making each family member the best family shareholder, beneficiary or family representative they can be. The family's financial capital is a powerful tool for promoting the growth of its human and intellectual capital. Without human capital, the family has no assets. Without intellectual capital, under-educated family members will make poor business decisions, resulting in the dissipation of the family's wealth. Growth of a family's financial capital relies hugely on the investments in its human and intellectual capital.

When the next generation displays entrepreneurial flair, it may be best to invest in this flair, rather than involving them in the family business. This is what Stelios Haji-Ioannou's father did. When Stelios was in his 20s, he became bored in running a division of his parent's shipping empire in Athens. His father gave him working capital of €5 million, and told him to run his own business. Stelios travelled, examined various businesses, and chose a business that was not too far removed from his father's. He had seen budget airlines operating in the United States, and as a fan of Richard Branson and his Virgin operation, he decided to create a low-cost airline called Easyjet. Within four years, the airline had 20 routes, over 100 flights a day, a staff of 1,000, and an estimated market value of €120 million. Worthy of note is that Stelios achieved all this in an environment that was very different from the comforts to which he would be accustomed if he had continued to work in the family business. The father recognised his son's entrepreneurial talents, and had the foresight to fund him in establishing his own business, rather than force him to remain in a large family business. The father facilitated an outlet for his son's natural talents.

Family Balance Sheet

A traditional balance sheet or financial statement measures the financial state of a business at a certain point in time. With a family's financial balance sheet, this includes a statement of assets, liabilities and overall family equity in light of the family's overall financial holdings. A family balance sheet, however, expands on the human and intellectual capital issues as they relate to the family and the family's overall wealth holdings. The chart below presents a brief overview of how a family balance sheet might look:

Refer to table next page

The Family Balance Sheet

ASSETS ➡ MINUS	LIABILITIES
The family's total human capital, including: – Each family member's intellectual capital – Each family member's financial capital – Each family member's social capital	Long-term family risks – Failure to understand that success requires a one-hundred-year plan – Failure of family governance – Failure to comprehend and manage all forms of family, human, intellectual and financial capital Intermediate family risks (internal) – Death – Divorce – Addiction and other "secrets" – Creditors – Poor health – Poor beneficiary/trustee relationships – A geometric increase of family members in each generation – Investment programs of less than fifty years Intermediate family risks (external) – Inflation – Inadequate trustee management – Estate and others forms of transfer and wealth taxes – Changes of political system – Lack of personal security Short-term family risks – Income taxes – Market fluctuation – No mission statement – Lack of financial education
EQUALS	SHAREHOLDER EQUITY
➡	– Are the family's human capital and intellectual capital increasing when measured against the family's liabilities? – Is the family as a whole dynamically preserving itself? – Are individual family members successfully pursuing happiness? – Is the family's governance system producing more good decisions than bad by taking a seventh-generational view?

Source: Hughes, James E. Jr, *Family Wealth, Keeping it in the Family* (Bloomberg, 2004)

These criteria should be taken into account in the overall context of managing and preserving the family's wealth across generations.

> The Pitcairn family sold its interest in Pittsburgh Plate Glass in 1923, and invested the entire proceeds into a trust company named The Pitcairn Trust Company. Today, over 100 family members hold a beneficial interest in the trust, which has assets in excess of $1bn. A professional elected board of management manages the company, according to the directives of a written mission statement. The Pitcairns hold annual family meetings, and communicate constantly with one another. All family members have signed a stock purchase agreement. Any family member who wishes to end their participation can cash-out their shares on redemption. Although the values held by the trust are significant in today's terms, it began modestly after the sale of the business. The growth came from the family staying together and investing together, obtaining appropriate advice to maximise the value of the original business sale.

Managing financial wealth for the long term

The preservation of wealth for significantly wealthy individuals usually entails:

–   Wider diversification at the expense of higher returns.

–   Reducing volatility.

–   Focus on real assets such as property and gold which are expected to maintain an intrinsic value.

–   Investment in illiquid and unlisted securities and companies.

–   Management of tax liabilities.

However, not all wealthy individuals practice the preservation of wealth through diversification. Many self-made entrepreneurs retain a huge portion of the businesses they founded. This makes their net worth very dependent on the day-to-day value of their business. While in percentage terms the wealth tied up in their businesses may be substantial, the lesser share of money held outside the business may still be enough to ensure a very prosperous lifestyle, whatever happens to their core company.

Entrepreneurs generate wealth by being risk-takers. Unsurprisingly, they are often comfortable taking the risk of not diversifying, even though as individuals age, they tend to become more risk adverse. Many wealthy people are simply badly advised. Those with recently acquired wealth may simply be ignorant of how to professionally manage their money. One example is famous sports professionals who go from millionaire status to bankruptcy in just a few years. They typically manage this by putting their cash into do-or-die business ventures that they have no ability to evaluate, as well as leaking money to friends, family and advisors as quickly in retirement as when they still were earning millions.

Of particular interest in this context are the investment policies of Warren Buffett or the Rothschilds. Look at the annual reports of their investment vehicles. Look at the investment habits of those who have held wealth across generations, such as the reports of RIT Capital Partners, the Rothschild family's investment trust. Listed on the stock market, its reports indicate the level of diversification in their asset allocation. Here is how RIT Capital Partners' assets were allocated as of March 2010.

Quoted equities	39.2%
Long equity funds	18.6%
Hedge Funds	7.8%
Unquoted direct investments	10.2%
Unquoted fund investments	10.5%
Real assets	9.6%
Absolute return fixed income and currency	2.4%
Liquidity	19.4%
Borrowings	(16.8%)
Other assets/liabilities	(0.9%)
Total net assets	**100%**

Another notable aspect of Rothschild's strategy is currency diversification. They do not do this to generate exchange gains, but to diversify from a risk perspective. The key to wealth preservation is massive diversification that guards against all conceivable forms of investment failure:

–   Massive vertical diversification means choosing investments across the whole spectrum of asset classes, from property bonds, private equity and stocks to more exotic investments, like unlisted businesses, land, art and teak furniture and intellectual property such as publishing rights.

–   Horizontal diversification means that holdings in the different asset classes are spread widely among baskets of stocks, different fund managers, various sovereign bonds and into different currencies.

–   Political and legal diversification means considering management of taxes, the legal structure of asset holdings, political risk, some of which can be managed through holding assets offshore or holding of real assets like property or gold.

Investor allocation

There is an assumption in most families that the older generation wishes to increase the financial wealth of the younger generation. However, it is often the case that the way in which various types of assets are allocated across individual family members or via their holding vehicles, is not necessarily chosen on the basis of who is most appropriate to hold particular types of investments, but rather by who had the cash when the investment opportunity arose. In terms of long term tax planning, it is often the oldest family member who is the wealthiest. They have the available cash when the investment opportunity arises, so they buy it. As a result, the oldest family members often hold many of the fastest growing assets on the family financial balance sheet. Older family members are often encouraged by their investment advisors to structure their portfolios to ensure more funds for later generations. Yet these same older members of the family are often more risk adverse and wish to hold assets producing more income. When assets with the greatest likelihood of appreciating in value are held by the oldest family members, there is greater potential that the family will pay more inheritance tax in the future.

Investment allocation must take inheritance tax implications into account when deciding which family members should hold the investments being made. The oldest family member would then buy the investments offering the lowest growth, and the youngest family member would buy the investments offering the highest growth.

The younger generation often lacks the capital to make such investments. Appropriate structuring can leverage the value in the hands of the existing generation, or receive loans from them. This facilitates faster growing assets being held in the younger generations' investment vehicles or trusts. The more stable income-producing assets, such as bonds and deposit accounts, are held by the elder generation.

There is no one definitive approach to protecting family wealth, just as there is no one definitive way of solving technical problems in a family business. It is critical that the challenges that are unique to families in business are understood and addressed. These challenges will also apply in connection with the preservation of wealth across generations.

CHAPTER 7 – ACTIONS

- Analyse your wealth both inside and outside your business and future demands on your capital.

- Assess the various risk to your wealth and take steps to minimise these risks.

- Develop a plan for retirement and consider your financial needs in retirement.

- Put a pension plan in place or look to enhance an existing pension arrangement.

- Consider your investments and any charitable donations you may wish to make.

- If you have significant wealth, consider using a family office. Consider how well prepared the next generation are to manage that wealth.

CHAPTER 8

CONTINGENCY PLANNING

OUTLINE:

By the end of this chapter you will have understanding of:

– The various types of life policy.

– Provision for loss of income.

– Provision for critical illness or disability.

– Life insurance considerations for loss of key staff.

– Life cover arrangements between owners of a business.

– Why you should implement an enduring power of attorney.

Owners and management are very good at protecting businesses. Most businesses have some forms of insurance, including employers liability insurance, public liability insurance, insurance for loss of profits and insurance for other potential risks to their business. Key management, however, is by far the most important asset of most businesses. Owners seldom make appropriate arrangements to cover the loss caused by an unforeseen event to a key person, and seldom make appropriate provision for their family. It is not possible to plan for every possible scenario and outcome, but it is worth considering measures to help prepare for the unexpected.

LIFE INSURANCE

Life insurance provides liquidity that would not otherwise arise on an event that may have a catastrophic impact on the business, and which may also significantly impact the financial position of the deceased's family. Life insurance is a basic tool to manage the risk of loss, and can provide income replacement for a family or business on the death of a key employee or earner. In addition, proceeds from life insurance policies may be used to purchase the shares of deceased shareholders in the company. This facilitates the transfer of the business from one generation to the next or between the families of siblings. Life insurance may be used to pay gift or inheritance taxes. There are certain tax efficiencies in respect of policies to fund those tax liabilities. Life insurance should be examined as part of any overall financial plan and as part of any retirement and succession strategy. Old insurance needs may have become obsolete, while new insurance needs may not yet have been catered for. Life insurance can take many forms, and is usually categorised as follows:

Type of Policy	Product Features
Term assurance	Level term assurance Decreasing term assurance Convertible term assurance Increasing term assurance
Whole of life	Non profit policies With profit policies Low cost profit policies Unit linked policies

Term assurance policies are the oldest form of life cover. The term or number of years for which the policy will provide protection is chosen by the customer/policy holder. On the death of a named individual, the amount of the life cover is paid to the policy holder. Term policies can be set up so that monies will be paid on the life of one person or on the lives of two or more persons. Typically, a husband and wife can be insured on the same policy, with the intention of providing a lump sum for the survivor, money to cover education, or money to clear financial liabilities. Term policies can also provide monies if both parents die prematurely. Term assurance is usually recommended when an individual's need is linked to a finite term. There are several types of term assurance:

- *Level term assurance:* The amount payable on death remains unchanged for the term of the policy. If there is no claim paid under the policy, the policy expires without value.

- *Decreasing term assurance:* As the life assured gets older, the initial sum assured payable decreases, usually on a fixed scale. This is used in connection with mortgage protection.

- *Convertible term assurance:* Similar to level term, but provides an option to convert the policy into a new policy. The policy is effected for a certain period, say 10 years. At its expiry, the policy can be renewed for say another 10 years.

- *Increasing term assurance:* The sum assured increases as the policy holder gets older. Most policies increase by a fixed amount each year, or by a rate linked to inflation, or as otherwise agreed under the terms of the policy. This policy costs more than a level or convertible term assurance policy, but ensures that the policy holder has a level of protection which is relatively inflation protected. When the increase in policy cover arises, so does the premium. This may be the case when the cover increases, or when the rate of premiums may have been guaranteed from the inception of the policy for a predetermined period, and set to increase only after the expiry of that initial period.

The other general category of assurance is whole of life policies, which provide life cover plus the facility to pay additional contributions which will be returned to the policy holder in the event that there is no claim under the policy. Policies can be effected on a single, joint or dual life basis. The policies can usually be categorised as:

- *Non-profit policies:* The traditional design of such policies provides a guaranteed sum assured at death in return for a guaranteed premium. The amount of life cover chosen at the outset remains unchanged throughout the life of the policy. There is usually a small encashment value if the policy is surrendered. These non-profit whole of life policies are quite similar to term assurance for life. Provision can be made for indexation or an increasing level of cover, with the premiums increasing in line with such increases.

– *With profit policies:* Under these policies, policy holders pay a higher premium in return for a guaranteed sum assured, along with a share of the investment profits of the with profit fund maintained by the life assurance company to which the policy is linked.

– *Lost cost with profit policies:* This is a with profit policy with decreasing term assurance. Only part of the sum assured is in the earlier years, provided out of the with profits element. However, as the with profit element increases and the level of term assurance decreases, the life cover element decreases and can usually be met or is exceeded by the with profits sum payable. The reduction in the life cover element reduces the overall cost.

– *Unit linked policies:* These policies do not provide guaranteed returns. The returns are linked to the performance of the life insurance company's investment managed fund. The contributions made to the policy are allocated to purchase units in the underlying investment fund. The return on the policy is linked to the performance of the underlying fund, and to the value of the units when the policy either matures or is encashed.

PERMANENT HEALTH INSURANCE (PHI)

These policies provide protection against long term disability, and are designed to replace lost income in the event of disability. They are payable after a deferred period of 13, 26 or 52 weeks. The payments continue until the policy holder recovers, reaches the usual rate of retirement or dies, whichever occurs first. All life companies have predetermined limits of the level of permanent health insurance an individual can insure themselves for. The maximum is generally 75% of earnings / salaries, less any State disability benefit to which they are entitled. Premiums for permanent health insurance are tax relieved at the top rate of income tax for that individual, but there is no tax relief for PRSI or the universal social charge in respect of the payment. The benefit in payment will be taxed at the relevant rate of income tax.

SERIOUS ILLNESS COVER

Serious illness cover provides a once-off lump-sum payment after a specified period, following diagnosis of a life-threatening illness (e.g. heart attack, stroke, cancer) covered by the policy. Premiums for this cover do not qualify for tax relief, but the benefit is tax free.

DISABILITY AND CONTINGENCY PLANNING

Business owners have more responsibility regarding disability and contingency planning than regular employees. If a regular employee with disability cover is injured or becomes ill and is unable to work, the employee will receive payments from the insurance company to replace their income until they can eventually return to work. It is less straightforward with business owners. Although cover may provide an income replacement for their families in the event of an illness or disability, there is an added problem. That is, planning for the survival of the business if the business owner has diminished capacity and cannot play a management role or be involved at a competent level in directing the business.

DISABILITY BUY OUT INSURANCE AND THE SHAREHOLDERS AGREEMENT

In Chapter 6, we saw that shareholder agreements govern the transfer of shares in closely-held companies to ensure protection for all shareholders. The disposal of shares under such agreements usually covers death of a shareholder, or where a shareholder may wish to exit the business. Under the agreement, provision is made for their shares to be purchased by the other shareholders or by the company. However, the disability of a shareholder, particularly a shareholder who plays a key role in the business, is often overlooked in many shareholder agreements. This can result in a loss of leadership at board level and at management level, an inability to take critical decisions in the best interests of the business, a lack of vision, and diminished input into strategic decisions. The responsibilities and voting power of the disabled shareholder may devolve to family or relatives who lack the abilities, appropriate experience or willingness to make informed and appropriate business decisions. Ultimately, this must be to the detriment of the business.

It therefore makes sense to ensure that as part of an overall business protection and shareholder protection mechanism, a shareholder agreement must define long-term disability or incapacity as an event that generates redemption or cross-purchase of the individual's shareholders shares. The company, or other shareholders, would make appropriate financial provision to fund any buyout in such a situation. This is usually arranged through an appropriate assurance arrangement, whereby the purchase provision under the shareholders agreement defines the nature of the disabilities covered, which is identical to the appropriate insurance policy. These circumstances are covered in more detail in the Business Protection section below.

DISABILITY ACTION PLAN

Apart from any arrangements made at shareholder level, the disability of a key stakeholder may leave a detrimental void in the business, resulting in a loss of key customers, reduced profits, poor management decisions, higher employee turnover, and the potential for disputes among shareholders. Any plan for long-term development of successors may become derailed if the incapacitated individual may have acted as mentor and educator to the next generation. Customers that sense that the business is experiencing difficulties will walk, and key employees may be similarly inclined. A contingency business plan must be developed to cover such an eventuality. Appropriate individuals should be identified to step into the shoes of key persons if they become ill. These individuals should be made aware of the plans and what is expected of them in such an eventuality. These contingency plans should be reviewed periodically and updated as appropriate, outlining who exercises which responsibilities. Plans should be formalised and put in writing to answer the following questions:

–   Who would fill various roles if a key individual became ill?

- What procedures would be followed if the business was interrupted through a natural disaster?

- What procedures would be followed if the business was interrupted by a terror attack?

- What procedures would be followed if the business was interrupted through a serious disease outbreak, such as swine flu?

BUSINESS PROTECTION

Every business has a key person or persons. The success of the business depends greatly on their knowledge and expertise. In an owner/managed business, this is usually the owner of the business, but there might be other key individuals such as the chief financial officer, an ace salesperson, or an engineer or scientist responsible for developing the company's proprietary IP. If a key person dies, the business may find it impossible to readily find a replacement. This could lead to the closure of the business, severe financial difficulties, and a much-diminished ability to continue to operate. The death of a key employee or director may cause financial loss for a business in a number of ways:

- The business loses the individual's management expertise

- The business loses the individual's contacts.

- The business loses goodwill.

- A reduction or withdrawal of credit facilities by banks or suppliers worried about the future profitability of the business.

- The repayment to the deceased's estate of any loans made by the deceased to the company.

Key person insurance provides a closely-held business with protection if a key employee dies. This is life assurance effected by the company on the life of one of its employees or directors, with a view to compensating the company for an anticipated financial loss in the event of that individual's death. This insurance is not designed to improve the company's financial position, but exclusively to compensate it for loss. When drawing up business protection insurance, you will need to complete a detailed financial questionnaire that calculates the exact level of financial loss that may arise in certain circumstances on the death of the employee covered. The usual procedure to be followed is as follows:

1. The management of the company, usually at a meeting of the board of directors, decides to establish cover for key individuals.

2. An application form is completed, showing the company as the proposer for the policy and listing the key individuals to be covered. A company director who is not a key person signs on behalf of the company.

3. A detailed financial questionnaire is completed, showing the insurable interest and ascertaining the potential loss to the business as a result of the death of the key person.

4. Once the life company accepts the proposal, the business or company starts paying the premiums. At this point, a binding contract arises and the policy is in force.

In some cases, the premiums can qualify as a business expense for tax purposes. Revenue regards the premiums as tax deductible when the following conditions are met:

–   The individual insured does not have a substantial proprietary interest in the business.

–   The policy has no encashment value.

–   The policy is intended to cover loss of profits in the event of death or serious illness of the key employee.

When these conditions are met, the premiums will be allowable deductions for corporation tax purposes. The proceeds of any payout on the policy are classified as a trading receipt and liable to corporation tax. If the conditions are not met, no tax relief is available, but even if premiums do not qualify for tax relief, the proceeds can still be taxed if the policy is intended to cover loss of profits.

PROPRIETOR INSURANCE

This insurance is primarily designed to provide surviving business partners or directors of a business/shareholders with a lump sum that enables them to buy out the dependents of deceased shareholders or partners, or to pay a lump sum to these dependents in order to provide them with some degree of financial security on the death of their family member. Provision can also be made for the serious illness or disability of a director/shareholder, allowing the remaining individuals to buy out their interest.

BUSINESS PROTECTION FOR SHAREHOLDERS

If a director in a private company dies, the director's dependants who are not involved in the business may wish to dispose of their shares immediately, possibly in order to pay inheritance tax where no provision has been made for same. The Memorandum and Articles of Association of private companies and any associated shareholders agreements will contain provisions whereby shareholders must first offer their shares for sale to existing shareholders. Failing this, the shares can be sold to outside interests. If surviving shareholders cannot afford to purchase the shares, they may have no alternative but to offer them to outside interests. Most third parties would not consider commercially purchasing a minority stake in a private company. So unless the shareholding of the deceased constituted a majority interest, there may be little or no opportunity for the deceased shareholder's family to realise value in respect of their shareholding. Even if the shareholding constitutes a majority interest, the surviving shareholders may see the majority shareholding disposed of to an outsider with whom they may not be comfortable operating the business.

In these situations, it is advisable to provide for a lump sum to provide the surviving shareholders with the necessary funds to effect a purchase of the deceased shareholder's shares. There are two methods for providing for these situations:

— *Co-directors Insurance*

All the shareholders enter into a purchase agreement usually referred to as a buy/sell agreement, a put/call option agreement, or a contingent purchase contract, whereby on the death of an individual, their shares are purchased by the other shareholders. This agreement provides for a basis of valuation for the shares and any other conditions deemed appropriate. There may not always be an automatic obligation on the deceased family to sell their shares. There may be an option of participating in the business, in which instance the proceeds of the policy are retained by the other shareholders.

One way of providing life cover is by a life of another policy, where each director/shareholder effects a policy on the life of each of his or her fellow directors/shareholders. This policy is simple to put in place. There is an equitable distribution of costs, with each director paying for a policy on behalf of their fellow directors. This may not be appropriate where there are a large number of shareholders/directors, because if each director has to effect a policy on the life of every other director, there will be a significant number of policies in place.

An alternative form of life cover is when each shareholder takes out a life insurance policy on their own life in trust for the benefit of the other shareholders/directors. The advantages are flexibility, and the fact that the funds are in the right hands at death. This option is most suitable where there are a large number of directors/shareholders. The primary disadvantage is that there is an incorrect distribution of costs, with a younger director paying a much lower premium than an older director.

The position of Revenue on this is that where the proceeds of a trust arrangement are payable to the other directors on the death of a director, the proceeds will be exempt from inheritance tax if they are used to purchase that director's shares. Any excess amount is liable to inheritance tax. In respect of payment of the policies, it is a personal arrangement. If the company pays for the policies, the money paid is treated as a benefit in kind in the hands of the directors, and is liable to income tax. There is no tax relief either for the company or for the director/shareholder on payment of premiums to effect the policy.

— *Company share buyback insurance*
Another way of achieving the same result is for the company to take out cover on the lives of the director shareholders. This resembles a Keyman policy, except that the proceeds are intended to enable the company to buy back the shares from the director/shareholder in the case of serious illness or death.

The company enters into a share buyback agreement with the directors which is similar to a buy/sell agreement and sets out the terms under which the shares are to be bought back. The requirements for a company to buy back its own shares under the Companies Acts are outlined in Chapter 10. From a taxation perspective, as the objective of the policy is clearly of a capital nature, the premium is not tax deductible for corporation tax purposes. However, the proceeds are also not taxed as trading receipts.

PARTNERSHIPS

As with companies, surviving partners in the partnership may be under an obligation to buy out the family of a deceased partner. The general framework is similar to that for co-directors insurance. The partnership discharges the cost of the premiums which are treated as partners' drawings. The premiums are not allowable for deductions for tax purposes. The receipt by the surviving partners of the proceeds of a policy on the death or disability of a partner are not liable to capital acquisitions tax, as the arrangement is made on an arm's length commercial basis, and there is cross-consideration among all of the partners. The proceeds realised are paid to the deceased partner's family in return for the transfer of his/her interest in the business to the remaining partners.

Enduring power of attorney

Another consideration concerns what happens to an individual's wealth if they become mentally incapacitated prior to effecting any gift of assets to the next generation. This can often be a matter of concern both in terms of ensuring that one's wealth (and the business) is passed on in the manner intended, and also in terms of ensuring that one's own needs are looked after such an event. This situation may require an enduring power of attorney, which only comes into effect when a person becomes mentally incapable of managing their own affairs. It has no power or effect prior to that date. If the individual dies without suffering any prolonged period of mental impairment, the enduring power of attorney may never take effect.

If someone becomes mentally incapable of taking care of their own affairs, that person's attorney will take responsibility for dealing with all financial affairs, and may be authorised to take personal care decisions on his/her behalf. If someone becomes mentally incompetent without having executed an enduring power of attorney, the family cannot deal with that person's assets without applying to the High Court for the person to be made a ward of court. Administratively, this is a much more difficult procedure than an enduring power of attorney. The family will also have less control over the application of assets under a ward of court arrangement than they would if an enduring power of attorney had been executed.

Under an enduring power of attorney, you can direct what is to happen if you become incapacitated, and you can make sure that the individuals exercising control over your affairs are the people you want rather than a court-appointed individual. If at a future stage, the attorney forms the view that you have become mentally incapable of managing your affairs, their power of attorney only takes effect after they apply to register the power of attorney with the High Court. As part of the application process, they would produce a medical certificate evidencing incapacity. Once the attorney has applied for registration, they are permitted to take certain essential actions regarding maintenance, the maintenance of dependents and the protection of the estate pending finalisation of the registration. Once the enduring power of attorney has been registered, the attorney can act in accordance with whatever powers have been granted under the document. This is something that anyone concerned with the potential application of their assets should consider, especially if there is concern about how the business affairs would be handled in the event of incapacitation.

CHAPTER 8 – ACTIONS

– Consider purchasing:

  – Permanent health insurance as income cover.

  – Keyman insurance to protect your business.

  – Disability and death provision/cover as part of any share-holder arrangement.

– Put an emergency plan in place to cover situations where there is a sudden leadership void.

– Consider making an enduring power of attorney in case you become incapacitated.

CHAPTER 9

EXIT OPTIONS: TRANSFER OF OWNERSHIP OR SALE?

For most families, the decision whether to transfer ownership of the business to the next generation or to sell is shaped by the following factors:

- Does the founder wish the business to transition to next generation of the family? Since family members are typically already involved in executive management prior to the founder's exit, the transition will be planned and effected in an orderly manner.

- If there are no suitable family members to run the business, but professional management has been employed, ownership may transition to the next generation, who will typically be involved through board participation;

– If there are no suitable family members to take over from the current generation, or if none of the next generation have an interest in the business, and the existing ownership does not wish to bring in professional management, the business may well be sold.

– If the owner dies unexpectedly, ownership will transfer under their will or on intestacy. In such a situation, the family may unexpectedly be required to run the business;

– The family may obtain a once-in-a-lifetime offer, as a result of which they sell the business.

The transfer of ownership is one of the most significant events in the life of a family business. In the past, the first a family might become aware of the terms of the business transition is when a shareholders' will is read at their solicitor's office. Today, greater emphasis is given at an early stage to planning the organisational forms through which shareholdings are held (such as trusts, holding companies, shareholder agreements, etc.) and the creation of structures to preserve family harmony in the future and, where possible, minimise inheritance taxes.

There are two main approaches to transitioning a business from the current owners: where the existing owner's shares are transitioned to the next generation, and where the owners decide to sell the family business rather than to transition it to the next generation.

TRANSITIONING OWNERSHIP THROUGH GENERATIONS

Family businesses can have a range of ownership configurations, including an owner managed business, a partnership involving parents and children, a sibling partnership, a cousin collaboration, or once it goes past four generations, a more diverse loose collection of relatives. Life cycle events, such as marriage, retirement, death and birth create the potential for changes in the ownership group. The family should anticipate and plan for individual and family life cycle transitions, since they change the goals of stakeholders, change investment objectives, and could impact on the overall financial situation. Life cycle transitions are often trigger events for changes in ownership.

Family decisions around ownership have significant implications for the future of the family business. The ownership scenarios below show how ownership decisions made by the previous generations can impact on ownership configurations that evolve by the time a business passes to the fourth generation:

– Equal distribution to all family members.

– Distribution to male family members only.

– Distribution only to family members employed by the family business.

Scenario one: ownership based on distribution to all family members of each generation

Note 1: Ownership percentages are rounded so they do not total 100%
Note 2: Shading = ownership

In the above example, equity in the family business has been distributed equally at each generational level. By the fourth generation, one member in branch B holds one third of the shares, with the remaining shares split across 13 individuals, the next largest shareholdings being 8%.

Scenario two: ownership based on family tradition limiting ownership to male heirs

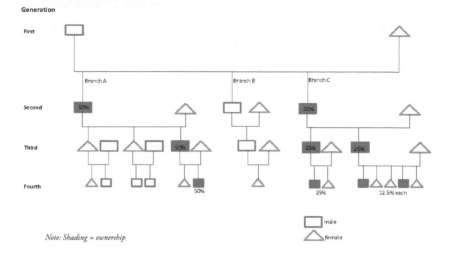

Note: Shading = ownership

In this scenario, none of the members of branch B of the family hold any stock, while one family member in branch A controls 50% of the stock after four generations.

Scenario three: ownership based on employment

Generation

First

Branch A   Branch B   Branch C

Second

Third

Fourth

Note 1: Ownership percentages are rounded so they do not total 100%
Note 2: Shaded symbols are family employees and owners. Some younger family members have not yet been allocated shares

male
female

In this scenario, only employee members are ever allocated stock. When they cease employment, their stock is repurchased by the company. The company awards stock as compensation to family members. More senior and more long-term family employees end up holding a greater portion of the stock. This allows family members to join the business and obtain ownership, even if no one else in their immediate family was ever involved in the business. The shares are effectively redistributed at each generation based on those employed in the business.

As these three scenarios show, ownership configurations can vary significantly, depending on the ownership decisions taken by the family. The extent to which ownership can fragment as shares pass down generations is clear.

UNDERSTANDING THE RESPONSIBILITIES OF OWNERSHIP

It is important that, when considering transfers of interests in a family business to the next generation, that they display a level of maturity and an understanding of the responsibilities of ownership. One task of the existing generation in anticipation of the ownership transfer process, is to outline or consider the boundaries of the family as they pertain to the inheritance of risk, burdens, opportunities and assets and access to financial information. Will all future shareholders be willing and able to honour access to financial information in a responsible and confidential manner? Who will be entitled to what share of the wealth, and why? Are all children to be shareholders in companies owned by the family? If so, what portion of shares and voting rights will be allocated to whom? How are in-laws that have married into the family treated? What about adopted children and stepchildren?

Once the existing generation considers these issues, a decision has to be made about whether intended transferees are capable shareholders:

— Will they have the business information, knowledge and acumen to participate meaningfully at shareholder meetings and contribute to shareholder decision making?

— Are they aware of the long term consequences of any decisions or actions they may take at shareholder level?

— Are they willing to share their thinking and decisions openly with other stakeholders in the business?

–   Do they understand the family's business culture, the family's commitment to the business, and ways in which they might contribute to it?

CHOICE OF METHOD OF TRANSITIONING OWNERSHIP TO NEXT GENERATION

There are many different structures under which ownership transitions from one generation to the next:

–   Distribution of shares to all family members.

–   Distribution of shares to all family members employed by the business.

–   Distribution of shares to all family members employed in senior executive positions.

–   Distribution of shares to a select group of heirs, usually male.

–   Distribution of shares to the oldest child in each family.

–   Distribution of more than one class of share, e.g. voting shares, to family members employed in the business, and non-voting shares to other family members.

–   A family agreement that redistributes stock at each generational level to balance ownership across different branches of the family.

–   Splitting ownership of various family enterprises, so that different enterprises are owned outright by separate family units post transfer. This can be achieved by hiving off or reconstructing the family businesses, see Chapter 10.

Parents usually strive to achieve a degree of equality among their children, and try to display fairness in the distribution of their estate. However, applying equality of treatment to a family business may be destructive and dangerous. A reluctance to choose one child over the others can result in the next generation all having equal shareholdings in a business in which they have very different roles and relationships, with some employed in the business and some not. Some family members are clearly better suited to manage the business than others. This can be to the detriment of the business, as well as providing the basis for future family disputes among the children. Equal shareholdings can cause deadlock in decision making. The current generation can minimise the scope for potential future conflict by considering potential problems in advance, and by holding an open discussion with family who will be better disposed to accept an arrangement if they understand the overall objective of ensuring continuity of the family enterprise.

DECISIONS ON OWNERSHIP

There are four basic ways in which decisions on future ownership can be made:

–   The existing generation retains all the authority and makes the decisions on their own.

–   The existing generation, while retaining all decision-making authority, consults with their children, gives them access to relevant information, seeks their opinions and preferences, and takes all this into account when reaching an overall decision.

–   The existing generation chooses to share their authority with their children, and invites them into a joint decision-making process.

–   The existing generation allocates all of their authority to the next generation, and has them make the ownership decisions.

Long experience suggests that the second or third methods of arriving at a decision are the most effective way of ensuring successful ownership transfer, for the following reasons:

1.   The successful implementation of ownership decisions often requires the involvement of those whose lives will be affected by them.

If all stakeholders participate in the decision-making process, they are more likely to accept and commit to decisions made.

2.   Existing senior generation often make incorrect assumptions about what the next generation wants for their future. Engaging with the next generation and involving them in the decision process can lead to better informed choices.

Any discussions around ownership transfers should start by outlining the family's common objectives and shared identity, before engaging in discussions around more difficult issues, where individual family members' needs or aspirations are not necessarily aligned with what is best for the family. Before discussing the allocation of equity in the business between those employed and those not employed in it, or the level of wealth to be passed to each family member, it makes sense to start by discussing the family's history in an ownership context. Talk about what has and what has not worked in the past in respect of ownership transfers, and discuss the lessons that the family has learned from past experience, and how these lessons might shape expectations.

EFFECTING THE OWNERSHIP TRANSFER

Considerations when transferring ownership to family members:

–   Should I make a gift of some of my interests in the business to family members?

–   Should I sell the business to family members in return for partial or equal value of the business?

–   If I sell the business, how will my exit be funded?

–   Should I leave my interest in the business in my will?

–   Should I have an enduring power of attorney to deal with a situation where I become incapacitated before I can gift the business to family members?

–   Should I consider transferring some of my interest in the business to a family trust?

– How will I fund associated costs and taxes?

Where owners of family businesses wish to pass ownership of a business to their chosen successors, this will usually happen as a gift, partial sale or bequest in a will. The owners must co-ordinate the specific mechanics of the share transfer arrangement with their individual retirement plans and their overall estate plan. They must take account of any shareholder agreement, of how the share transfer coincides with any management grooming programme and the overall corporate structure of the business, and how the company is valued at that point in time. All of these issues directly affect the method selected to transfer ownership to the next generation of owners. Different considerations apply to each option.

GIFT OF SHARES

The main question when gifting shares for nil consideration is whether the owner of the business has extracted enough value from the business for the purposes of facilitating their retirement. A gift of shares may not be possible if the founder relies on the proceeds of sale of the shares to fund their retirement. The other main consideration is the tax issues, discussed below in Chapter 10. All options naturally assume that appropriate governance structures, a management grooming plan, and all other aspects have been addressed. Another issue worth considering is the area of protecting the family member from a spouse or potential spouse, where shares in the family business are being gifted. This was partially addressed in Chapter 7.

The mechanics of share transfer in a family situation is usually relatively straightforward. There is little requirement for the level of detail or complexity that can arise in share purchase agreements where businesses are being sold to third parties.

SALE OF A BUSINESS TO SUCCESSORS

The primary issue here is that often the younger generation does not have the financial resources or access to enough capital to buy the business for a cash sum. Depending on the financial strength of the business, the younger generation may be able to raise some debt to finance the acquisition of shares from the current owners. In today's more constrained debt markets, the ability to leverage significant levels of debt may be limited. This may not be a bad thing, as there are many examples of families over leveraging to buy out the older generation, and where the very continuation of the business was put at risk in a subsequent downturn in trade. The pricing of any debt will depend on the duration and security of the finance available, as well as on the broader economic environment. Most banks will require secured loans and may demand personal guarantees. There will usually be fixed capital and interest re-payment periods, as well as operational and financial covenants. Financial penalties will be applied to breach of covenant.

In the absence of adequate initial debt raising, the younger generation may seek to find an equity partner to finance the buyout. This leads to a dilution of ownership that the wider family may not find acceptable. Equity finance carries a higher cost of capital as it is unsecured. Raising private equity results in third-party involvement in the ongoing strategy and governance of the business. In return for their investment, the private equity investor can bring strategic thinking, and can demand that specific targets are achieved for the business over an agreed time frame. Private equity partners often allow the family remain in control of the business, but will require representation on the board of directors. They may also require a separate class of share to prevent them from being diluted on any further equity raising.

Private equity investors may assist in raising additional finance. They may require that the corporate governance structure of the company be updated, and they may encourage clear management practices and appropriate succession planning. Private equity can also assist with the following:

– Providing an exit mechanism for shares awarded to executives.

– Providing an exit mechanism for family members who wish to realise their shareholding, where the family ownership base has become fragmented.

– Allowing the existing owner to realise part of their equity.

- Providing increased professionalism in the management of the business.

- Facilitating new investment in order to illustrate to management and staff the owner's commitment to the company's future growth.

To bridge the financing gap on a transfer from one generation to another, the current owner may agree some element of deferred consideration, to be paid over a number of years out of the future profits of the business. The obvious difficulty for the retiring generation is that they no longer control the business, yet they still have a considerable financial stake in the continued future success of its operations through deferred consideration. If the successors fail to manage the business profitably, the existing generation's deferred consideration may ultimately not be discharged or only partially discharged.

ISSUES IN PASSING SHARES ON DEATH

When passing family wealth or shares in a business on death, you must be aware of entitlements that individuals may have under the Succession Act. The entitlements for individuals vary depending on whether you die leaving a will ("testate") or without leaving a will ("intestate").

Intestacy

Where a person dies intestate, the following entitlements may arise:

- If they leave a spouse but no children, the spouse is entitled to the entire estate.

- If they die leaving a spouse and children, the spouse is entitled to two thirds of the estate and the remaining one third is divided equally among children.

- If the spouse has pre-deceased them and they are survived by their children, the children share the estate equally.

Since the passing of the Status of Children Act 1987, non-marital children have the same rights and entitlements as marital children. If you die without any spouse or children, the Succession Act provides for other orders of entitlement. Your assets usually pass to parents and/or siblings, or to more distant relatives if you have no surviving parents or siblings.

Testate succession – legal entitlements under a will

It is not possible under the Succession Act to disinherit a spouse. Legally, they have a minimum entitlement to your estate, despite the provisions of your will. A surviving spouse's share is commonly referred to as a 'legal right share,' which can be either:

– If the deceased leaves a spouse and no children, the surviving spouse has legal right share to one half of the estate.

– If the deceased leaves children, the surviving spouse has a legal right share to one third of the estate.

Where the deceased makes no provision for their spouse under their will, the spouse has an automatic entitlement as a result of their legal right share. If the provision under a will for a surviving spouse is less than the value of the legal right share, the surviving spouse can choose between their entitlement under the will or their legal right share. The value of the legal right share is separate from any assets held jointly between the deceased and their spouse. These automatically pass to the surviving spouse by survivorship.

The succession rights of a spouse can be effected or extinguished in the following circumstances:

– Under a deed of separation, the parties may renounce their succession rights to each other's estates.

– Under a judicial order of separation, succession rights may be extinguished.

–   A spouse can renounce their legal right share before a marriage under a pre-nuptial agreement, or separately during the marriage, subject to obtaining independent legal advice.

–   In a divorce, the court can also make an order extinguishing succession rights of the spouses.

The Succession Act also provides that any transfers made three years prior to an individual's date of death, where such transfers were made to defeat or reduce the share of a spouse, on application to the court such transfer may be treated as a bequest under the deceased's will, thus forming part of their estate and part of the overall assets divisible to the spouse in lieu of their legal right share. This prevents attempts to disinherit a spouse or children from taking effect within a certain timeframe prior to an individual's death.

CIVIL PARTNERSHIPS

The Civil Partnership and Certain Rights and Obligations of Cohabitants Act 2010 extends marriage-like benefits to same sex couples in the areas of property, social welfare, succession, maintenance, pensions and tax. While the Act concentrates mainly on same sex couples, there are provisions for cohabiting couples, offering them additional rights and protections. Cohabitants are two adults living together as a couple in an intimate and committed relationship, and who are not related. There is no automatic redress for cohabitants. They must apply to court for a variety of property orders to be made if the court believes that this is just and equitable. To qualify for redress, the couple must have been living together for five years, or two years where there is a child of the relationship. In respect of succession rights:

–   Under the legislation, a civil partner has the same succession rights as a spouse in either a testacy or intestacy situation.

–   A qualified cohabitant may, after the death of the other cohabitant, but not more than 6 months after representation is granted to the deceased's estate, apply to court for an order for provision out of the net estate. If the cohabitant fails to notify the personal representative of the deceased, the latter can distribute the estate without taking account of any potential claim the cohabitant may have. The total value of any court order will not exceed what the applicant is entitled to if they were a spouse or civil partner of the deceased.

CHILDREN

Children of a deceased have no specific right to any specific part of the deceased's estate, but they do have a right under the Succession Act to apply to the High Court. If the High Court decides that the deceased failed in their moral duty to make proper provision for the child, it can order that such provision be made out of the deceased's estate, taking account of the overall circumstances including the level of wealth of the deceased, the position of the child and what provision had been made by the deceased for the child during their lifetime.

Effect of Succession Act provisions

You do not have full testamentary freedom in determining where your assets pass when you have a spouse or children. If the family business is only to pass to certain family members, you must make provision for your spouse and/or other children who will not be inheriting the business. This ensures that the transfer of the family business is in accordance with your wishes.

CONSIDERATIONS IN MAKING YOUR WILL

Other issues to take into account when making a will include:

– Who will you appoint as your executors to administer your affairs? Apart from choosing someone you feel will competently deal with your estate, you must avoid the potential for conflict, particularly if the executor is also a beneficiary under your estate.

– Who will you appoint as guardians to any minor children you might have?

– Arrange a trust clause to administer assets on behalf of minor children or incapacitated or improvident beneficiaries. Your trustees will usually also be your executors, but they do not need to be. The power given to trustees to deal with assets can vary significantly. Care should be taken when considering this.

– The division of your estate, particularly how business assets are to devolve.

– Obtaining appropriate tax advice on the provisions of your will and any structuring alternatives possible.

– Will previous gifts or advances made to beneficiaries during your lifetime be taken into account or ignored for the purposes of your will.

– Should you and your spouse make "mirror wills", where you both broadly agree between you whom your combined assets are ultimately to pass to. Usually, all assets pass to the surviving spouse, and then pass to the pre-determined beneficiaries.

– Address any issues relating to foreign assets and the interaction of any foreign will with your Irish will.

– Consider an enduring power of attorney (see Chapter 8) in the context of any will being prepared.

Always let the executors know that you have made a will. Let them know where it is located for safekeeping. So many legal complexities can arise in making a validly constituted and executed will that it well worth seeking appropriate legal advice. Do not attempt to draft your own will.

SELLING THE FAMILY BUSINESS

Where the decision is taken that transition of the business to the next generation is not an option, the current owners will have to consider selling the business in order to realise value from the business. Since selling the family business is likely to be the biggest business decision you will make in your entire business career, this needs to be carefully planned and properly executed.

There are various reasons why an owner of a family business may wish to exit the business through a sale. Financial security is usually the foremost concern, as continued operation of the business by the family may not generate a high enough return or generate a comparable amount of liquidity. The decision to sell can be an emotional one, and is usually based on a combination of factors:

–   A once-in-a-lifetime, too-good-to-be-true offer for purchase.

–   Reaching a decision that the business has reached a premium value.

–   A realisation that next generation of family lacks the requisite ability to run the business.

–   The next generation of family has no interest in running the business.

–   There is likely to be sharp disagreement in the next generation of family over running the business. The ensuing conflict may be to the detriment of the business.

–   The requirement for capital injection demands new ownership.

–   Opportunities that new ownership bring for expansion of the business into new markets or overseas.

–   The retirement plan of main shareholders envisages a sale of the business.

–   External factors in the wider economy: legislation, regulation, technological developments, M&A activity in the sector.

Family businesses can also be sold in response to an opportunistic approach from an acquirer. Since there is no certainty that an exit can be achieved on this basis, the owners must take control of the disposal process. Planning the exit may take a number of years, and will require careful consideration of the following factors:

1. What is the business worth?

   Sellers should seek an independent opinion on the worth of the business. A good advisor will also consider the factors that influence value on a sale. Is the earnings trend likely to result in value increasing over time? Might the business be sold in parts to optimise value? Are there surplus assets in the business that can be separately sold or distributed to shareholders on a sale? Do the reported earnings need to be adjusted for non recurring items, in order to more fairly present maintainable earnings to a buyer? Knowing the likely range of value and whether it can be enhanced prior to sale, is a key consideration in planning an exit.

   It is critical to identify whether the vendor's price expectations are reasonable and attainable. Owner managers can be too closely attached to their business to value it as an acquirer would. An independent professional view is always useful in planning a disposal. The valuation process will be informed by a valuation exercise using valuation parameters including recent disposal transactions in the sector, and the proper identification of key differentiators within the business: cutting edge technology, niche customers, growth prospects and future plans of the business.

2. Who might buy the business?

   Finding the right buyer is not only important to optimising value. In a family-owned business, the current owner must be satisfied that the buyer is right for the business, its customers and employees. Management of the business might offer an exit option to the current owner. The biggest challenge to this form of exit is likely to be raising the finance to execute the management buyout (MBO). In current market conditions, the ability to significantly leverage transactions is likely to be difficult. This may put pressure on the vendor to accept deferred consideration or a loan note as part payment of the sale price. This may render this option less attractive than alternatives. An MBO team backed by private equity may enable the transaction to be structured without the need for any form of deferred consideration. If management are a realistic and likely buyer of the business, a period of prior discussion and planning is required to enable an MBO to be put in place.

Another alternative is a sale to a trade player. This can be the best exit option, particularly if the acquirer has a strong balance sheet, which eliminates the financing risk on a transaction. A trade player can often generate synergies from the integration of a business in the same sector: distribution savings to shared customers, economies in administration overhead, consolidation of warehousing and logistics operations, improved purchasing power, joint marketing and other factors. In theory, a buyer should not pay for any synergies it creates on an acquisition. In reality, a competitive bidding process means that synergies do come into play when trying to justify a higher price. Early consideration of the identity of potential trade buyers is worthwhile, particularly as in the years prior to sale, forging a business relationship with these entities gives insight into their strategies and confirms whether they are a likely acquirer.

Finding the right buyer for the business is important financially and commercially. Detailed acquirer research is carried out, with A and B lists based on strategic fit and the ability to do a deal of the scale in question. The greater the strategic fit, the higher the value in your business. You must also examine how acquisitive the company has been historically, and the financial track record of the potential acquirer.

Larger private family-owned companies should also consider a public flotation. This option is only viable for a small proportion of family entities, and may not fully realise the family shareholding on flotation. Since flotation is a costly process, and because many family companies shy away from the public scrutiny and regulatory compliance that accompanies a listing, flotation is not usually an option.

3. Timing
    The timing of commencing the formal sale process is critical, and is determined by proper planning. For example, a founding shareholder who also acts as Chief Executive might consider becoming chairman for a few years prior to a sale, putting in place professional management to run the business, while keeping close scrutiny over

operations and performance in the lead up to sale. This will convince an acquirer that the owner is not key to the business, and that his departure at the time of sale will not leave a gap in the management structure. Following an acquisition or the sale of a business division, it is helpful to wait for a while before establishing a normalised trading track record. Tax considerations such as the availability of retirement relief to the vendor may also affect timing.

In addition to value, buyer profile and timing, the successful execution of a sale can benefit significantly from a thorough planning process, enabling a buyer to optimise the timing and the value on a sale. Owner managers have become more sophisticated, and are primarily concerned with personal wealth maximisation. The decision to sell your business should be accompanied by a big "Health Warning." It is a complex and challenging process which you must get right first time around. You are unlikely to get a second chance.

The following is a useful checklist of the questions a vendor might address in the disposal planning process:

Pre-planning for a sale

Key questions to be addressed prior to considering a sale:

- Where do I see myself five years from now?
- Will my services be required post disposal and can the business function without me?
- What will make my business more attractive to prospective buyers?
- Does the business need to change in preparation for sale?
- How can I maximise profitability in the coming years?
- What are the profit patterns of the business, such as trends in turnover, gross profit and pre tax profit?
- Do I have sufficient human and financial resources to grow the business?
- How can I retain and secure key employees?
- Are there gaps in the senior management team?
- Are key supplier and customer relationships critical to the future success of the business?
- Are the current business systems and controls appropriate to the size and complexity of the business?
- Are there key problem areas or issues that need to be addressed e.g. share ownership issues, legal cases, employee matters, tax issues?
- Are there tax considerations that need to be addressed?
- What is a realistic price assessment of a likely sale?
- Does this price meet my objectives?

EXECUTING THE SALE

When the timing for a sale is right, the vendor should engage professional advisors to help execute the disposal. This process involves the following stages:

1. *Review of Planning assumptions*
    Immediately prior to sale, review the key planning assumptions regarding valuation, timing, and likely buyers, in order to confirm the validity of executing a sale process at the current time.

2. *Market Testing*
    Produce a short anonymous teaser document to test buyer appetite for the opportunity. The teaser will not contain confidential or commercially sensitive information, but would give sufficient information to prospective buyers to enable them form a view on the attractiveness of the opportunity and likely scale of acquisition.

3. *Information Memorandum*
    Qualified buyers who have signed up to a confidentiality agreement will be given an information memorandum on the company. This sets out detailed information on the business, its markets, competitive position, management team and financial position. The memorandum enables bidders to make informed indicative bids for the company.

4. *Bid evaluation*
    Bids are evaluated to assess comparative values and conditionality. A key element is the confirmation that the bidder has the financial capability to complete the transaction. At this stage, the number of bidders will be reduced to a smaller number of candidates likely to pay the price sought and possessing the more general capability to execute.

5. *Data Room*
    Qualified bidders are given access to a confidential data room to enable them to conduct due diligence to a standard that enables them make final offers.

6. *Negotiation and choice of preferred bidder*

Negotiations take place with bidders, ultimately a preferred bidder is chosen, and non-binding heads of agreement are entered into, setting out the terms of the deal. The heads of agreement should be relatively detailed, in order to avoid undue further negotiation during the concluding stages of the process.

The ability to negotiate a transaction on terms attractive to the owner manager is critical, and is based on a combination of human skill and understanding of the prospective acquirer's motives. This stage is based on proactive engagement with interested parties. Bid management is key to the process until a preferred purchaser is selected. Advice on price, terms, negotiation tactics and structuring the deal are important parts of the sales process, and will be influenced by tax planning considerations and the purchaser's integration plans.

Tax is always an important element in structuring a sale. Details of the main tax considerations are outlined below:

Tax considerations

- The different tax implications on an asset sale as opposed to a share sale. The quantum of tax liabilities may vary significantly.
- The purchaser may wish to obtain part of your business. If you have a number of businesses, the purchaser may want just one of them. The purchaser may wish to acquire the business without obtaining non-essential trade assets such as the premises where you currently operate. A pre-sale reconstruction may be required to package the business for sale separately. This can be implemented on a tax effective basis, if it carried out early enough.
- Depending on how the transaction is structured, the timing of the payment of tax liabilities and cash-flow could be critical. Deferred consideration and/or earn-outs linked to future performance of the business are taxable immediately, although it may be some time before the purchaser is obliged to discharge these sums in your favour.
- If you receive stock in the purchaser company as some or all of the consideration, it may assist in deferring part of your capital gains tax liability. Market factors need to be accounted for if payment is wholly in stock. Another option is consideration of equity collars/hedging arrangements that minimise exposure to market fluctuations.
- Examining your position in advance of the sale also provides ample opportunity to review your post retirement income position, as well as pension provision or increased benefits under an existing pension arrangement.
- Your residency position for the year of sale will impact your position. If you reside overseas, it may provide opportunities or disadvantages.
- Disposing of your business may provide an opportunity to share the benefits of sale amongst family members on a tax effective basis. Making gifts from the net proceeds of sale is tax ineffective. Advance structuring can maximise the overall benefit to your family.

7. Completion

The completion process involves the interaction and provision of services to both parties from advisors to both parties, including auditors, taxation specialists, pension consultants, legal advisors, wealth management consultants and corporate bankers.

The corporate finance advisor plays a critical role in project managing all parties to the transaction. This will dictate the overall effectiveness and efficiency of the sales process. The sale documentation must reflect your expectations of your responsibility for any past tax liabilities of the company.

9 Top Tips

While each business sale transaction is separate, here are nine top tips – lessons learned by colleagues from their experience in corporate finance:

1. Ensure sufficient advanced planning prior to sale. Two to three years in advance is not unreasonable. Flexibility is required, because a lot of unpredictable things can happen in this time period.

2. Understand the motives of the ideal acquirer for the business, and prepare the business for the most advantageous sale. The creation of a competitive bidding environment will maximise value for the shareholders, so pre-qualify potential acquirers.

3. Know the value of your enterprise. You may need to separate specific assets (e.g. properties) from the business being sold.

4. Beware of deferred consideration/earn outs. If there is a deferred consideration/earn out element to the sales price, find a formula that provides the shareholders with sufficient control over the business to maximise same.

5. Commit fully to the sales process. If you withdraw at any stage, it can be difficult to reinvigorate the sales process.

6. Agree detailed heads of agreement. This reduces the scope for misunderstanding during the sales process. Try to get difficult negotiation issues out of the way pre due diligence. This will ensure that due diligence is confirmatory only, and could result in other benefits like maximising benefits from the completion accounts process.

7. Maintain focus on the business throughout the sales process. Do not lose sight of the financial performance of the business through this period. Your credibility is at stake.

8. Be prepared to haggle and to burn the midnight oil. The sales contract marks the culmination of the sales process. This involves lengthy and detailed documents, protracted and complex negotiations involving both you and your professional advisors.

9. Make sure you are aware of the tax position and alternatives at an early stage. This will impact on negotiations and on the structuring of the transaction. It will also provide an indication of a purchaser's attitude in facilitating your tax planning.

More and more owner managers are seeking to release shareholder value by disposing of their business. Whether you are selling to a trade buyer, the internal management team, private equity investors or to an external management team backed by high net worth individuals, the sales process can be difficult and challenging. As selling your business will tend to happen only once in your lifetime, it is vital that you maximise your return and get it right first time around. With the right relationships and the right team of financial, tax and legal advisors, the transaction can run smoothly, and you will continue to reap personal and commercial benefits post sale.

CHAPTER 9 – ACTIONS

–   Determine the future ownership configuration you wish for the business.

–   Consider whether you will sell the business or pass it to family members.

–   Make a gift or partial sale of the business to family, or obtain advice on your will if the business were to pass under it.

–   If you need recourse to value build up in the business to fund your retirement or exit, examine whether it would be more appropriate to raise finance via debt or equity alternatives. This is also an issue for any purchaser or family member looking to fund a buyout of your ownership stake.

–   If you are selling the business, plan in advance. Have a pre-determined sales process to guide you through the sale.

CHAPTER 10

TAX ISSUES
IN SUCCESSION PLANNING

OUTLINE:

By the end of Chapter 10 you will have an understanding of:

- The various taxes involved.

- The different tax reliefs applicable in passing business assets to family.

- Some of the tax-based structuring alternatives.

- Providing equity incentives for management.

Any business succession or estate planning process involves the application of various taxes. The cornerstone of any successful estate plan from a tax planning perspective is flexibility. Regularly review both your estate plan and your will to take account of changes in the business, changes in the regulatory and tax environment and, most importantly, changes in family circumstances. Similar to changes in the wider commercial environment, the basis under which charges to tax operate and the various tax reliefs available may change annually. When viewed over a ten-year period, tax changes may have a significant impact on overall wealth preservation.

Tax issues are usually examined in the specific context of distribution of assets to family members, and in a business context, the succession

of some or all of the family to the business. Tax issues must also be examined as part of the overall estate plan, with particular reference to:

– The balance between the financial security of the senior generation,
  and the ability of the business to remain financially viable and competitive.

– The anticipated future ownership structure of the business, and
  whether business interests pass to all or only some of the family mem-
  bers/children.

– Retirement funding for the generation that may be exiting the business

This chapter focuses primarily on the succession issues, on the transfer
of assets to family members, and on the division or sub-division of business interests to facilitate distribution amongst the family.

Businesses run by private groups can be complex, and this chapter cannot cover every conceivable structure and potential outcome. It is highly
advisable to talk to specialists about your business. This chapter relates
to:

– Business relief for gift and inheritance tax purposes.

– Retirement relief for capital gains tax purposes.

– Reconfiguring share rights.

– Demerging family businesses.

VARIOUS TAXES INVOLVED

Three primary taxes must be considered when transferring the business
to family members:

– Capital Acquisitions Tax (CAT) which comprises both gift and inheritance taxes.

- Capital Gains Tax (CGT).

- Stamp Duty.

In addition, in the context of trusts, a tax charge under the CAT code known as discretionary trust tax may also arise, and shall be addressed later in the chapter in the specific section addressing trust taxation.

The application of these taxes vary, depending on whether the current owners of the business gift their interest in the business to family members during their lifetime, sell the business, or allow the business to pass on death in their will. The taxes arising are:

- *Sale:* In the event of a sale to a third party, the business owner will be concerned primarily with capital gains tax.

- *Lifetime transfers:* As part of a transfer to family members during their lifetime, the following tax issues will materialise:

    - Just like a sale, it is considered a disposal of the business for capital gains tax purposes. There is a need to consider whether a CGT liability arises or not.

    - The element of undervalue or gift on the transfer may give rise to CAT.

    - Where documents are required to effect the transfer, stamp duty may be imposed.

- *Death:* Where assets pass under a will or on intestacy, the tax position is:

    - No CGT or stamp duty.

    - CAT applies to the inheritance. This is the only tax for consideration.

Leaving assets to pass under a will does not encourage timely participation of the next generation in the business. Gifting assets early at a lower value may be much more tax effective than allowing them pass under a will in the future when the market value of the business could be much higher, with potential for higher tax liabilities.

OPERATION OF TAXES INVOLVED

Capital Acquisitions Tax (CAT)

CAT comprises both gift and inheritance tax. The tax applies on receipt of a 'benefit' – any situation where you receive an asset at undervalue by way of gift or inheritance. The computational rules are identical for both gift and inheritance taxes. In each case, the tax is payable by the recipient of the gift or inheritance.

The tax applies in any of the following situations:

– On a gift or inheritance of any Irish property, including shares or interest in an Irish business.

– Where either the person providing the gift (the 'donor') or the recipient of the gift are Irish tax resident. This primarily applies to a gift or inheritance of a foreign business, with CAT applying by virtue of the residency status of the person providing the gift or the beneficiary.

Charge to Tax

CAT is charged on the value of the gift or inheritance in excess of an exempt limit or threshold that is determined by the relationship between the parties. Only amounts in excess of the threshold are chargeable to tax. There are three exempt class thresholds (which are index linked), depending on the relationship of the recipient to the person providing the gift or inheritance. The following are the basic thresholds for 2011:

Refer to table next page

Category	Relationship	Amount
Class A	Child or minor grandchild of the person providing the benefit where the parent is dead. Parents also fall within this threshold in certain circumstances, as do nieces and nephews who have worked in a family business for a period of time.	€332,084
Class B	Brother, sister, niece, nephew or lineal ancestor/descendent of the person providing the benefit.	€33,208
Class C	All other cases.	€16,604

All gifts and inheritances received since 5 December 1991 are aggregated, within their individual category. The tax free amount in each category is the cumulative amount that can be received before paying tax, where benefits are received from a number of individuals within the same classification. Gift and inheritance tax applies at a rate of 25% on the value of any gift or inheritance in excess of the exempt threshold amounts. Where a tax liability arises, the tax return outlining the details of the gift/inheritance and a cheque for the tax payable must be sent to Revenue, based on the date the gift/inheritance is received.

Gifts/inheritances received between 1 January and 31 August	Return and payment due by 30 September*
Gifts/inheritances received between 1 September and 31 December	Return and payment due by following 30 September*

* It is anticipated that the return filing date and payment date of 30 September will be changed, in line with the income tax filing date of 31 October.

Where the tax is paid later than the due date, penalty interest will apply to the outstanding tax from the date of the benefit, i.e. the penalty interest will also apply for the period leading up to 30 September when the tax is due.

There are a number of exemptions and reliefs for CAT. But in the context of succession to business assets, business relief and/or agricultural relief is the main consideration and is addressed below.

Capital Gains Tax (CGT)

CGT is payable on chargeable gains arising on the disposal of assets. The tax is applied for disposal of assets since 5 April 1974. A disposal of assets usually takes place where the ownership of an asset changes, and includes a situation where you dispose of part of an asset. For example, if you wish to transfer only part of your business to the next generation, it is not necessary that you receive a cash sum or capital amount on the disposal. A disposal is treated as arising on a simple transfer of ownership, regardless of whether you receive anything for it. A gift is accordingly a disposal for CGT purposes. When assets pass on a death, they are not treated as a disposal for CGT.

The tax currently applies at a rate of 25% against the 'gain' arising on the disposal of the asset. This is simply calculated by deducting the original cost of the asset, the costs of acquisition and the costs of disposal from the price received/market value of the asset, to arrive at the taxable gain. Payment of the tax is based on when the disposal is made:

| Disposals between 1 January and 30 November | Payment due on 15 December |
| Disposals between 1 December and 31 December | Payment due on 31 January |

On receipt of a gift or inheritance, the beneficiary is regarded as having acquired the asset at its market value should they dispose of the asset at some future stage. In business succession terms, there are two primary reliefs from CGT:

– A retirement relief exists in certain circumstances when an individual is over 55 years of age and is disposing of their interest in a business, see below.

– In certain circumstances where both a CGT and a CAT liability arise, the CGT liability may be offset as a credit against the CAT liability.

Stamp Duty

Stamp duty is a tax on documents. Where the transfer of an asset necessitates a document (e.g. a stock transfer form for transferring shares) or a conveyance or a lease (when transferring a property), a stamp duty charge will arise. Where assets pass under a will, no stamp duty applies. Stamp duty only applies in the context of lifetime transfers of assets. Stamp duty rates are as follows:

Stamp duty on shares	1%
Stamp duty on non-residential property	6%*
*Varying rates apply for non-residential property, but the 6% rate is reached once the market value exceeds €80,000.	

Transfer of most business interests will either attract stamp duty at the rate of 1% for a share transfer or up to 6% for all other asset transfers. There is relief for transfers between blood relations which serves to reduce the stamp duty by 50%. This does not apply in the case of the transfer of shares. A transfer of shares between family members is liable to stamp duty of 1%, yet a transfer of other business assets is liable to stamp duty at 3%.

Once a document transferring an asset is signed and dated, stamp duty must be paid within 30 days of when the document was completed.

MARITAL POSITION

Marital status impacts on transfers as follows:

— *Married and together:* Transfers of assets between husband and wife are totally exempt from CAT, CGT and stamp duty.

— *Separated:* If the parties are separated, exemption from stamp duty and CAT still applies. The exemption from CGT only applies where the parties are living together. However, a transfer of assets under a deed of separation or under a court order for a separation will not give rise to CGT.

— *Divorce:* Where assets are transferred voluntarily between former parties to a marriage following their divorce, CAT, CGT and stamp duty would arise. Where parties are divorced, provided that a transfer of assets occurs on foot of a court order made under the Family

Law Divorce Act 1996, there is an exemption for CAT, CGT and stamp duty purposes. This is another reason why any asset transfers in such situations should be made on foot of a court sanctioned order.

The Civil Partnership and Certain Rights and Obligations of Cohabitants Act 2010 extends similar property rights to same sex couples and provides certain rights for cohabiting couples. No changes have as yet been made to the tax system to reflect this position, but changes are expected during 2011. It is expected that similar tax treatment as that afforded to married couples will apply to same sex couples who register as a civil partnership. The three categories of tax treatment are broadly similar for a same sex couple, depending on their relationship status.

Co-habiting couples are not married for tax purposes. Property transfers between them would give rise to CAT, CGT and stamp duty. However, just like court orders can be made in a divorce or separation situation, assets can be transferred (between cohabitants) when one cohabitant applies to court for redress. It is anticipated that the tax legislation will change, and reliefs from the various taxes will apply.

Some individuals have more than one partner (or a spouse and another partner). In addition to the legal complexities that will arise, there will be different tax treatment afforded the different 'partners' by virtue of their relationship status, i.e. a spouse, civil partner or partner not covered by the other two categories. Seek specific advice on both the tax and legal issues in such situations.

DIFFERENT TAX 'RELIEFS' APPLICABLE

Business Relief for CAT

The ability to avail of business relief on a gift or inheritance of business property significantly reduces the tax liability on receipt of those assets. The effect of the relief is to reduce the market value of the property by 90% in determining tax liability on the gift or inheritance. Tax is thus only payable on 10% of the value of the assets received. With the current CAT rate of 25%, the net effect of being in a position to avail of business relief results in an effective tax rate of 2.5% on a gift/inheritance of business assets.

The relief was introduced in April 1994, and was applied at various levels until the current level of relief at 90% was introduced on 23 January 1997. There must be some concern as to whether the relief will continue to apply at its current advantageous level. In other countries, the relief can reach 100%.

Property qualifying for relief

The relief applies to business property as follows:

- Property consisting of a business or interest in a business.

- Shares in a company (subject to certain conditions).

- Land, buildings, machinery or equipment owned by the person providing the benefit but used by a company controlled by that person or by a partnership in which they are a partner. The property interest must pass at the same time as the shares in the qualifying company or interest in the partnership.

Conditions relating to shares

In the context of a gift/inheritance of shares in a company, the beneficiary must fall within one of the following three situations for the relief to apply:

1. The beneficiary and various family members must together have control of the company. The relief applies regardless of the size of the shareholding inherited by the beneficiary.

2. The beneficiary receives a shareholding entitling them to 25% of the voting control of the company.

3. The beneficiary receives a 10% shareholding in the company and has been a full-time employee of the company in excess of five years.

When the beneficiary and family members do not together control the business, the relief will only apply in situations 2 or 3. This can cause problems where two unrelated individuals own a business equally. If one of them wishes to pass their 50% to their family and they have more than two children who they wish to pass it to, problems may arise if some of their children do not work in the business. Since they do not fall under 1 above and may have difficulty with qualifying for situation 2 or 3, a restructuring of shareholdings may assist in resolving this issue.

Where assets used by the company operating the family business are held personally outside of the corporate structure, those assets may also qualify for business relief, provided they pass with a controlling shareholding in the company. The controlling shareholding requirement must be considered, as the shareholder who owns the property assets outside of the company must clearly have more than 50% control of the business. This would not be the case where a business is held 50:50 by husband and wife. In such a situation, the individual who holds the assets outside of the company is given 51% of the shares, to ensure the assets held outside the company also qualify for the relief.

Non-qualifying activities

Remember that the relief only applies to business interests. Value in the business derived from investment activities from dealing in land, shares, securities or currencies or holding of any other investments, will not benefit from the relief. Where over 50% of the activities of a corporate group relate to the making of investments, the relief is totally denied. However, where the activities of a company consist of wholly or mainly the carrying on of a business, relief will apply to that part of the value of the company relating to its business activities and business assets, but will be denied to the portion of the value of the company/business relating to its investment activities.

For example, if a company worth €20m derives 75% of its value from business activities and the other 25% from investment activities, a gift or inheritance of shares in that company business will carry relief on €15m. In effect, €15m of the business is treated as having a value of €1.5m for tax purposes, and the other €5m is not subject to relief. Accordingly, €6.5m out of the overall €20m value of the business will be the taxable value for CAT calculations.

Conditions relating to ownership

The business property must have been owned by the person providing the benefit and/or their spouse for at least five years prior to the transfer on a lifetime gift or for at least two years prior to the transfer on an inheritance.

Where a beneficiary receives a gift/inheritance of business property, the property must be retained in order to preserve the relief. The relief is clawed back if they dispose of their interest in the business within six years of receiving it. Where any part of the value of the business or assets on which business relief is claimed relates to land with development value, the claw-back period is extended from six to ten years in respect of the portion of the value of the gift/inheritance that relates to that land.

A similar relief with differing conditions applies for agricultural property, reducing the value of that property by 90%. This is known as agricultural relief. But if an individual does not qualify for agricultural relief, they can still claim business relief, if the agricultural property is being used in a business (including farming).

STRUCTURING YOUR AFFAIRS TO AVAIL OF BUSINESS RELIEF

Without proper structuring or appropriate advice, business relief will often not be maximised, or not be available at all. Outlined below are some considerations and alternatives in availing of business relief:

—   *Shareholdings* – Where an individual's shareholding is 50% or less, they do not have control of the business, in which case only a certain level of shareholding may be passed to family members to qualify for relief. A 10% shareholding for a family member who has been employed in the business, or a 25% shareholding, qualifies for the relief. However, where an individual has a 50% or less shareholding and wishes to give shares to two or more children, then relief may not be available. It is worth passing the shares only to those family members involved in the business, and providing for the others with non business assets.

- *Shareholdings* – Where two non-related families operate a business and have a particular shareholding split, such as 60/40, 50/50, 70/30, it may be possible to reconfigure the rights for both classes of shares so that when the number of shares in issue is also taken into account, both shareholdings have control as defined under the Companies Acts. This reconfiguration of the shareholdings enables both families to qualify for business relief, even though one family will have less than a 50% shareholding. This ensures that family can leave its shares to a wider number of family members, as opposed to leaving only a 25% or greater shareholding to one individual or a 10% shareholding or more to a family member who worked in the business. It should be possible to reconfigure the shareholding without jeopardising the de facto status quo as regards the relative control they both actually have.

- *Holding Company* – If an individual does not have a controlling shareholding in a company, and wishes to leave their shares to a number of family members, it may be advantageous to transfer those shares to a separate family holding company. For example, if someone has a 40% shareholding in a company, and it would not qualify for business relief if left to two or more children, it may be possible to transfer it to a holding company, and then for the shares in the holding company to qualify for the relief. There will be capital gains tax and stamp duty implications on the transfer of the shares to the holding company. If structured appropriately, the transaction may be treated as a neutral event for capital gains tax purposes. Stamp duty at 1% would still arise, but this cost will outweigh the benefits of qualifying for business relief.

- *Assets* – In order to qualify for business relief, the business must be wholly or mainly a trading business, as opposed to certain other types of non-qualifying investment activities. If a company's assets comprise both business activities and non-business investment activities, it may be appropriate to re-designate share rights so that certain shares derive their value from the business assets and certain shares derive their value from the non business assets. You could then consider gifting the shares deriving their value from the business assets to family members, thus crystallising the event qualifying for business relief. The class of shares relating to the investment assets could be capped to minimise future exposures, with a growth class of share relating to the investment assets granted to family members.

- *Assets* – Since to qualify for relief, a company must wholly or mainly be carrying on business activities, if the company's investment activities start to exceed the activities of the business, the entire company may not qualify for business relief. In such a case, it may be appropriate to hive off either the business assets or the investment assets to a separate company. Hiving off one of the businesses can be done tax efficiently. The effect of such a spin-off is to have the business activities in one company and the investment activities in another company. The shares in the company with the business activities are then ring-fenced and qualify for business relief. Alternative planning can be carried out in respect of the company holding the investment business.

- *Debt* – The relief only applies in respect of business assets, and not non-qualifying assets such as investment assets. Where non-qualifying assets are held by a subsidiary that has borrowed to acquire those assets, the value of that subsidiary in determining the overall assets of the group must take account of a deduction in respect of its debt. Where debt is ring-fenced against non-qualifying assets, it may be advantageous to maximise the overall potential business relief claim.

Retirement relief for CGT

Retirement relief applies for capital gains tax when an individual aged 55 or over disposes of business assets which have been their business assets for more than ten years. The relief applies either:

- For a transfer to a family member, in which case it is a total relief or exemption from CGT.

- On a disposal to a third party, any disposal of less than €750,000 in value is not liable to CGT. This is a lifetime limit. Tax will apply once the consideration for a disposal to a third party exceeds €750,000.

Certain conditions apply if availing of the relief on shareholdings in companies. In addition to the 55 years of age threshold, the company must be either:

1. An individual's "family company," with over 75% of the company controlled by the individual and their family.

2. They must hold at least 25% of the voting shares in the company.

When an individual disposes of shares in a company, they must have been a working director of the company for a period of not less than ten years, including being a full-time working director for a period of at least five years. The relief will also extend to assets used by the company that are owned by the individual outside of the company, when these assets are disposed of at the same time and to the same person to whom the shares in the company are transferred.

Where the disposal of the business assets is to a child or a niece/nephew who has worked substantially on a full-time basis in the business, a total relief applies. If the child or niece/nephew disposes of the business assets gifted to them within six years, there will be a claw-back of the retirement relief previously claimed. The liability for the tax arising on the claw-back is the child who is disposing of the assets. In other words, the tax liability follows the asset, and is assessable in the child's hands on their onward sale of the asset.

Structuring your affairs for retirement relief

To ensure that the disposal of business assets satisfies the conditions of retirement relief from CGT, you should consider the following:

1. *Age requirement* – The individual making the disposal must have reached age 55. If they have not themselves reached 55, but their spouse has fulfilled the age requirement, (as well as the remaining conditions of the relief), they should consider transferring the assets

to the spouse prior to making the disposal, thus availing of the relief. This transfer between spouses is tax neutral.

2. *Working director requirement* – Even if someone has been a director of the family business for ten years or more, they need to be sure that they were a fulltime working director during five of the previous ten years. Where possible, they should defer any disposal to family members until the five year working director requirement has been fulfilled. Alternatively, if their spouse has been a fulltime working director for five of the last ten years, and satisfies the other requirements of the relief, it is worth transferring their interest in the business assets to the spouse prior to the ultimate disposal, in order to avail of the relief.

3. *Ten-year ownership requirement* – Not all business assets may have been acquired at the same time. You should consider the ownership period for each chargeable asset separately. A piecemeal disposal of business assets to family members may be appropriate to ensure all assets have been held for the requisite ten year period.

Interaction of CGT Retirement Relief with CAT Business Relief

Transfer of business assets during an individual's lifetime if they are over 55 is usually structured on the basis that:

– Retirement relief for CGT applies on the transfer to a child, so that no CGT arises.

– Business relief for CAT applies, so that the effective rate of tax for CAT purposes is 2.5%.

In such a situation, the tax liability on a transfer of a business can be kept to a relatively low level.

Commission on Taxation Report

The report of the Commission on Taxation released in September 2009 recommended a scaling back of the level of relief available for both CAT business relief and CGT retirement relief. The report recommended that a 75% level of relief should apply for CAT business relief purposes, with relief capped at €3m. No relief would then apply in excess of that amount. CGT retirement relief would also have a cap on transfers to family members of €3m. Changes to the current levels of relief will clearly place a significant financial burden on the transfer of business assets between generations, and there is concern that some change to the level of relief may be introduced in the future.

CGT/CAT Offset

Where the gift of an asset gives rise to a CGT liability as well as a CAT liability, the former can be offset against the latter, resulting in only one tax charge. If an asset used in connection with a business is transferred to a beneficiary, and neither CGT retirement relief nor CAT business relief apply, the CGT can be offset against the CAT liability. The net effect is that the overall taxes arising will be the higher of the two liabilities. Even where reliefs apply, some CAT/CGT may still arise. In such situations, the offset may also be claimed. There is a requirement that the beneficiary retain the assets for two years to preserve their entitlement to the relief. This, however, is a worst-case result. With appropriate structuring, both CAT business relief and CGT retirement relief should substantially reduce the tax arising.

Tax based structuring alternatives

Although business relief for CAT purposes and retirement relief for CGT purposes are both valuable reliefs, it cannot be assumed that these reliefs will automatically protect all family business assets. There are several potential pitfalls in the various conditions that must be satisfied to ensure entitlement to both reliefs. For assets that do not qualify for any relief, other alternatives include allowing value in the business to shift gradually over a long period of time to selected beneficiaries, thus avoiding up-front charges to tax, or availing of other structuring which will enhance the tax reliefs provided for under the tax code. These alternatives might include:

– Share structures

– Partitioning shareholdings

– De-mergers of family businesses

Share structures

Depending on your requirements, it may be possible to divide the rights to your shares in your family company or shareholdings in any other companies, to facilitate your wishes while passing value to family members. Alternatives include capping the value of your shares at their current market value, and passing shares to family members, that will attract all future growth over and above the current value of your shares. As the shares given to family members have little to no value, gift or inheritance tax does not apply.

If, for example, your company is currently worth €30m, ambitious projections and potential future growth plans could give the company a value of €50m in five years time. If you reconfigure the ordinary shares in your company, your 'A' ordinary shares are entitled to the first €30m in value of the assets of the company, and your 'B' ordinary shares are entitled to any value in the company/business exceeding the €30m attributable to the 'A' shares. If you allocate the 'B' shares to your children, and if the company is indeed worth €50m in five years time, your 'B' shares will have a value of €20m. In effect, €20m will have passed to those shareholders without any immediate tax charge arising. The only potential disadvantage is that if the children sell those shares in the future, they will have little or no cost base for CGT purposes. Should they dispose of the shares in the future, from a cash flow perspective, they should generate funds to discharge any liability arising. In a family business where those shares may be held long-term, any subsequent disposal by the children to other family members may potentially avail of CGT retirement relief, or may pass under their will so that no CGT arises. In that context, no tax may potentially arise on allocating 'B' shares to family members.

In this example, capping one class of shares and providing for a second class of shares facilitates value passing over time to the individuals who hold the second class of shares. Each class of shares has equal voting rights, but if you wish to retain control, the new class shares may have no voting rights. Alternatively, you can create a third class of voting shares which you would retain initially, before allocating them to appropriate family members. In this situation, Revenue uses a 'rule of thumb' allocation of 15% of the value of the company to those shares with voting rights. When you allocate value between family members, and deal with different classes of shares, bear in mind the value attaching to voting rights, as those shares with voting rights have a value, and will incur tax liabilities when allocated to family members.

Other classes of shares with deferred rights may be allocated to family members, so that those shares only have a value attributed to them when certain events happen. The initial allocation of those shares to family members results in little or no taxes. In the future, however, events such as the death of a family member or the company reaching certain targets or other commercial criteria, may move value out of existing ordinary shares to these new shares. The transfer of value on this basis may not result in a tax liability.

Partitioning

Shares can be divided into separate classes of shares with different rights, where the shareholders all agree to take such action. If there is no transfer of value between shareholders on such segregation, no tax liabilities arise. Such structuring may however facilitate shareholders in earmarking certain parts of the business or assets of the company for their benefit.

For example, Joe and Mary are a brother and sister who operate two businesses through the family company. Joe is primarily involved in business A, Mary in business B. They decide that the future value attributable to each of them from the company/business should be directly attributable to their involvement in their respective businesses. Accordingly, Joe's shares are re-designated as 'A' shares which will derive their value from the profits, assets and activities of the A business. Mary's shares are re-designated as 'B' ordinary shares which will derive their value from the profits, assets and activities of the B business. Shareholders of each class of shares would have total control in respect of the operation of their separate businesses, and would financially enjoy the benefits of their businesses. The only potential downside is in the event of commercial difficulties. Both businesses are operated through the one company. If one business performs badly, the creditors of that enterprise have the right to pursue the company (and consequently the second business) for any debts due to them. However, if the A and B business are operated through two separate subsidiary companies which are held by a holding company, and the share rights in that holding company are separated, and the shareholdings in the holding company derive their values from the respective underlying trading subsidiaries, both businesses are effectively 'ring-fenced' from each other. The family can continue a business together, but are separately rewarded based on their own individual efforts.

De-mergers

Where a company is involved in a number of businesses, it may be possible to tax effectively segregate one or more of those businesses from the existing company into a second, separate company. This is particularly effective where the founder of the business wishes to pass different businesses to different family members. For example, Joe owns a hotel chain consisting of five different hotels operated in different locations. Joe has a child employed in each hotel. He decides that rather than allocating shares in his existing company to all five children, with them continuing to carry on a business together, it would be more effective to package the businesses such that one hotel is retained by the existing company, while the other four hotels are transferred to four separate new companies. Joe would then have five companies, each owning a separate hotel. He could transfer the shares in each company on the basis of one company per child. Various reliefs from CGT, stamp duty and income tax are available for corporate reorganisations of this nature. It should be possible to effect the restructuring on a tax neutral basis. Joe can then separately transfer the shares in each company to one of the children. When Joe reaches 55, and has been operating the business for more than ten years, it should be possible to claim business relief for CAT purposes and retirement relief for CGT purposes.

The only tax cost in this example would be the 1% stamp duty on the transfers of the shares in the companies to the children. Once the businesses/companies are under separate ownership, they will no longer be part of a group of companies for corporation tax purposes. They will no longer surrender losses from one to the other from a tax perspective. They will also not be a group of companies from a company law perspective. This will limit any funding arrangements or financial assistance they might otherwise provide each other, unless specific mechanisms are put in place to facilitate crossover of debt arrangements, loans or the provision of financial assistance between the companies.

DIFFERENT CAT/CGT VALUATION RULES

Shareholdings in family businesses are valued differently from a capital acquisitions tax perspective than the general valuation rules, which would apply a market value basis of valuation. When valuing shares in a private company, after obtaining an overall valuation of the business, discounts may be applied to minority shareholdings. This is because a 75% shareholder can carry a special resolution, but with less than 75% of the shares, the shareholder does not have absolute control in respect of the company's affairs. Over 50% of the company may give de facto control, except on issues that require a special resolution. Less than 50% does not give day-to-day or operational control. Less than 25% does not even block a special resolution. Minority shareholdings, particularly less than 50% and less than 25%, may be discounted significantly in arriving at the market value of those shares. The commercial rationale as to who would purchase a minority shareholding in a private company is recognised in determining the market value of the shares. In other words, what would a willing purchaser pay for those shares? This is the basis of valuation that applies for both capital gains tax and stamp duty purposes.

For capital acquisitions tax, where the business is controlled by family members, no such discount is available in valuing a minority shareholding. The shares are valued as if they were a proportional part of a larger shareholding that gave control over the entire company. For example, on a gift of a 20% shareholding in a company to a child, one value will apply for CAT purposes in determining any CAT liability, while a different value will apply for both CGT and stamp duty purposes in determining the liabilities to those taxes. From a CAT perspective, this may not be an issue where business relief applies. Similarly, for a capital gains tax perspective, if the parent transfers shares in their company to a child who benefits from retirement relief, stamp duty may well be the only tax cost. In some cases, the reliefs may not be available. If the CAT/CGT offset is being claimed, there may be consequential differences in how the valuation and consequential tax liabilities are arrived at for both taxes.

FOREIGN ASSETS AND DOUBLE TAXATION

Where you have assets overseas, you may be liable to potential inheritance or gift tax liability in Ireland. The assets may also be subject to foreign gift/inheritance tax in the country where your assets are located. Ireland has double tax agreements relating to inheritance tax with the UK and the US. The effect of the treaty is to give either country sole taxing rights, or provides for a credit for the tax suffered in one country against the tax suffered in another.

In all other instances, relief from double taxation is afforded under Irish basic legislation, where a credit is available in respect of the foreign tax suffered. If you hold foreign assets, seek advice about the likely impact of the foreign inheritance taxes on your overall tax position.

Business assets may also qualify for a relief similar to business relief under the tax laws of the foreign jurisdiction. Foreign business assets will also qualify for business relief in Ireland.

OTHER RELIEFS AND PLANNING ALTERNATIVES

Although the focus on this book is on business succession, other planning alternatives may minimise your overall wealth transition to family members. Consideration should be given to some of the following:

- *Gift splitting*: To fully utilise CAT thresholds, assets may be passed among a wider range of family members. For example, rather than making a gift to your child, you could include their spouse and their children (your grandchildren).

–   *Skipping generations*: Similar to the above. Instead of passing an asset to a child and incurring a tax liability, and then incurring a second liability if they pass the asset on to their child, skip a generation, and eliminate one charge to tax. This should be considered in making appointments from family trusts.

–   *Gift assets that are likely to appreciate significantly in value.*

–   *Agricultural assets*: A similar relief to CAT business property relief applies to agricultural assets, reducing their value by 90% for tax purposes. If the family business is a farm, it may be possible to choose either agricultural relief or business relief. This is important as you may qualify under the terms of one relief but not under the terms of the other.

–   *Dwelling-house relief*: In certain circumstances, the gift or inheritance of a house can be exempt if the beneficiary has lived in it for three years, and does not own any other residential property.

–   *Small gift exemption*: You can gift €3,000 a year tax free to any number of beneficiaries. For a husband and wife, this is a combined amount of €6,000. If you have five grandchildren, you can make them tax free annual gifts up to €30,000. Over a number of years, the amount will build up.

–   *Family partnerships*: These structures are particularly favoured for investment assets. The partnerships are configured so that the greater part of the future appreciation in the assets accrues to the next generation.

TAXATION ISSUES WITH TRUSTS

Trusts can often be used as a mechanism to hold assets on behalf of a group of beneficiaries. Trusts usually fall into one of the following categories:

1.   A bare trust – Legal title is held by the trustee, but the beneficial or economic ownership over the asset is held by someone else. Bare

trusts are commonplace where assets are held for minors who cannot legally hold the assets in their own right.

2.   A fixed trust. The entitlements of parties under the trusts are fixed. Fixed trusts tend to be rather inflexible.

3.   Discretionary trusts. The trustees have discretion as to who among the class of beneficiaries they may appoint assets of the trust. Since there are no fixed entitlements, these trusts offer a significant amount of flexibility. The trustees can take into account the different circumstances of different beneficiaries, how they mature, which of them are involved in the business, and to whom it would be more appropriate to appoint shares in the business as part of a business succession planning exercise.

Where business assets are held in trust, they are usually held under a discretionary trust arrangement by virtue of the flexibility it affords. Particular rules apply to the taxation treatment of discretionary trusts.

Since nobody is automatically entitled to the assets retained by a discretionary trust until the assets are transferred by the trustees to them as a beneficiary, these trusts are a useful method of delaying payment of gift/inheritance tax. A significant drawback is that discretionary trust tax applies to a discretionary trust. This discretionary trust tax recognises the fact that gift or inheritance tax (CAT) may be delayed until such time as assets are appointed to a beneficiary. Discretionary trusts are liable to discretionary trust tax where:

A.   The person who set up the trust has died.

B.   The spouse and children of the person who set up the trust are over 21 years of age.

There are two tax charges to discretionary trust tax: an initial one-off charge at 6% (reduced to 3% in certain circumstances); and an annual 1% charge applies thereafter. Such trusts can be very useful if the assets held by the estate are illiquid, such as property and unquoted shares.

This could impact on realisable values if the assets need to be sold to meet inheritance tax liabilities.

When business assets are appointed from a discretionary trust, they may qualify for business relief for CAT purposes. Retirement relief for capital gains tax will not be available. No stamp duty arises where assets are appointed from the discretionary trust to a beneficiary. In income tax terms, such trusts incur income tax at the standard rate of 20%. Where the income is not distributed to the beneficiaries within 18 months, the trusts suffer a second 20% income tax surcharge. The effective rate of income tax is 40%, which is favourable when benchmarked against the top marginal rates of taxation where the income would be received personally. Such trust structures allow income to accumulate relatively tax efficiently, while providing flexibility around future distribution of assets to family members. They also provide a protection mechanism in allowing the trustees the flexibility to appoint shares in the business to the more appropriate family members, based on their potential business knowledge, business acumen, and marital position.

BUYING OUT FAMILY MEMBERS TAX EFFICIENTLY

When all of the members of a family have received shares in the family business, they may not all wish to be involved, and some may wish to realise the value of their investment. Where that investment is illiquid, it is a source of potential conflict, since they cannot realise any value in respect of it. If the company and/or other shareholders have the financial wherewithal to purchase the shareholding of the family member who wishes to exit, consideration needs to be given as to how this can be effected as tax efficiently as possible.

The most significant tax differential here is where the shareholders have to fund the purchase of the exiting shareholder individually, as opposed to being funded by the company. Individuals will have earned or generated their capital or funds to effect such a purchase out of income, after paying income tax, PRSI and the universal social charge at their top marginal rates of taxation. The company will usually have a 12.5% corporation tax cost in generating funds, so as to either accumulate the capital to buy out an exiting shareholder, or in repayment of any loan incurred for the purposes of funding the buyout of an exiting share-holder. It is significantly more tax efficient for the company to fund the buyout of a family member who wishes to exit from the business. There are two alternatives:

1. A new holding company is put in place to effect the buyout of the exiting family member.

2. The company itself buys back or redeems the shares of the exiting family member.

In this holding company alternative, the holding company simply offers shares in itself to all those shareholders remaining in the business, and borrows from a bank and pays cash to the exiting shareholder. Stamp duty costs will arise, capital gains tax will be payable by the exiting share-holder, but it should be neutral from a capital gains tax perspective for all the remaining shareholders. The existing company would then lend funds to the new holding company to assist it in repaying any debt ob-ligation it had incurred in buying out the family member who had wished to depart.

The second alternative is where the company has sufficient distributable profits. The shares of the family member who wishes to exit can simply be bought back. From a taxation perspective, a buyback of shares is treated as a distribution that is liable to income tax. If it can be estab-lished that the buyback of shares in an unquoted trading company is for the purpose of benefiting the company's trade, once certain other conditions are satisfied, capital gains tax treatment will be afforded to the exiting shareholder. It is usual in the context of a family business that where one shareholder is disgruntled and wishes to exit, that it is to the benefit of the trade that the shareholder exits. In such a situation, if their shares are acquired by the company, their tax liability would be payable at the capital gains tax rates. A buyback or redemption of the shares can be structured so that no stamp duty applies when the com-pany buys out the exiting family member.

Take these alternatives into account when structuring shareholdings be-tween family members. A family member wishing to exit should be considered in conjunction with the terms of any shareholders agreement and liquidity plan. Provision should be made for changes at shareholder level and release of funds/value to shareholders.

FUNDING PAYMENT OF CAT

The person providing the benefit will usually discharge the capital acquisitions tax liability on behalf of the beneficiary, or the beneficiary will discharge payment out of the proceeds of the gift/inheritance they received. The beneficiary may even have their own resources to discharge payment of the CAT liability on their own account.

Two other considerations may arise:

1. Certain insurance policies can be used to fund CAT.

2. Shares can sometimes be repurchased by the company to fund the beneficiary's CAT liability.

Insurance may be ideally suited to the provision of cash resources to allow beneficiaries to discharge CAT liabilities. The illiquid nature of many estates may incline them to make provision for future payment of the tax in whole or in part by way of an insurance policy. That is why favourable tax treatment is afforded to particular types of insurance policies which are taken out specifically to discharge gift or inheritance tax. If the proceeds of the insurance policy are used to pay gift or inheritance tax, it will be exempt and not be a taxable benefit. However, where the proceeds of this type of policy are not fully used to pay inheritance or gift tax, the part of the policy that is not so used becomes a gift/inheritance, and tax is payable on the policy or that part not used. Having a policy of this nature can sometimes merit consideration for funding part of a future potential inheritance tax liability.

Another alternative is to fund some or part of the inheritance tax liability on an inheritance of shares by way of a buyback of some of the shares. Under general principles, a buyback of shares from a shareholder is usually treated as a distribution for income tax purposes. But where a buyback of shares occurs and the person to whom the payment is made applies substantially the whole of the payment made to them on the buyback in discharging their inheritance tax liability, capital gains tax treatment will be afforded to them on the buyback of those shares. In most instances, where the buyback occurs shortly after inheritance of shares in a business, there should be little or no uplift in value, and thus no capital gains tax. Any buyback of shares will be subject to the usual company law requirements, such as the need for sufficient profits for distribution equivalent to or greater than the level of funds moving to the shareholder on the buyback. Where an individual succeeds to and inherits a relatively illiquid estate, the buyback of part of their shares in the family company may provide a mechanism whereby cash can be released to fund some or part of their inheritance tax liability.

REWARDING AND INCENTIVISING MANAGEMENT

There are many means of remunerating management, some more tax efficient than others. These include:

- Basic salary (subject to PAYE).

- Performance related cash bonuses (subject to PAYE).

- Pension provision via an employer sponsored occupational pension scheme.

- Provision of a car as a benefit in kind (subject to PAYE).

- Revenue-recognised allowances or reimbursement of expenses which are tax neutral for the employee.

The most common alternative form of incentivising and aligning shareholder and management/employee interests is stock awards. Since 2011, however, these awards have been taxable under the PAYE system. Employers should factor the tax cost of the withholding obligation into the overall equation. However, employer PRSI will not apply to share based remuneration. The tax implications attached to the various types of awards include:

- *Free shares:* This is taxable as a benefit in kind, with the employee taxed at their marginal rate of taxation on the market value of the shares. This is only advantageous for shares that have an initial low value that is likely to appreciate significantly in value.

– *Stock options:* Where options are granted at market value (or less than market value if they are no longer than seven years in duration), income tax will only arise when the stock option is exercised, and then on the difference between the price payable for the share and its then market value. If the options are granted for an amount of less than market value, and can be exercised outside of a seven-year period, there is an upfront tax charge on the discount/difference between the exercise price and market value. They are usually granted at market value. In terms of the executive's cash flow, they are only ever exercised prior to a liquidity event.

– *Restricted shares:* Where free shares are given, but there is a restriction on their disposal and certain other conditions are met, the level of benefit in kind is reduced, with a reduction in the income tax on their allocation. The greatest level of abatement of the benefit in kind is 60% where the restriction on the disposal is for a minimum period of five years and one day. Lesser discounts apply for shorter periods. It does serve to significantly reduce the tax otherwise payable.

– *Stock option over restricted shares:* When the option is exercised, a restriction will apply to the disposal of the shares acquired under the option. Assuming all other conditions are satisfied, the restriction will reduce the level of benefit taxable on exercise of the stock option. The reduction will be similar to an award of restricted shares.

– *Forfeitable shares:* These are liable to income tax upfront. The amount subject to tax depends on whether they are free or restricted shares. The fact that the shares are forfeitable should not be taken into account on any valuation. But tax legislation provides that if the shares are forfeited, the employee will obtain a refund on the income tax originally paid.

– *Convertible shares:* These are shares allocated, with a low value due to having minimal rights or entitlements which convert into shares with full rights and entitlements, either when certain events occur, or over time. In some instances, this uplift may only be liable to capital gains tax when the shares are sold. Income tax anti-avoidance provisions often make the uplift in value liable to income tax.

–   *Growth shares:* These have a low or nominal value on allocation to the executive resulting in little or no income tax. Any growth in value of the shares is liable to capital gains tax.

–   *Phantom share scheme:* This is a bonus scheme linked to the value of a notional allocation of shares in the company to the executive. As a bonus, it is taxable in the normal manner.

Subject to cash-flow considerations, the optimum position is to crystallise any income tax liability on the shares early. This minimises the overall level of income tax, and allows any increase in value of the shares into the future to be taxable as a capital gain on their eventual disposal. There may be a number of niche arrangements which will afford an uplift at the lower capital gains tax rate, rather than the executive being liable to income tax.

Liquidity is a key concern for executive participants. Another concern is minority discounts from a valuation perspective, as this may reduce not only the amount subject to tax on award, but also the amount received on disposal.

CHAPTER 10 – ACTIONS

– Taxation is one of the more complicated areas of estate and succession planning. You should:

– Seek advice specific to your situation.

– Ascertain how tax liabilities will interact with your overall commercial objectives.

– See whether different structuring alternatives may improve your position.

– Consider tax position of any family trusts.

CHAPTER 11

IRISH SUCCESSION STORIES

This chapter presents some practical examples of Irish succession stories, in the hope that these case studies will provide some guidance or insight into the steps certain families have or have not taken. The case studies may help you identify issues in your own business, and provide food for thought about potential outcomes.

The case studies are composites drawn from actual examples, but bear no relation to any one client. The facts and circumstances have been changed to preserve confidentiality.

Case study 1 – Refer to next page

Case study 1

A client business is currently in the third generational stage of its transition at both an ownership and a management level. The business originated when the founder joined his parent's family business together with two siblings. Due to a dispute between the founder and his two siblings, he left his parent's family business and went off on his own to establish a business which he co-owned with his wife.

They subsequently had three children. Illness forced the founder to remove himself from the business, which was then run by his wife. Of their three children, the eldest joined the business, but he had no real business acumen. He was not viewed as a candidate for ultimate succession at a management level. Meanwhile, a second child joined the business. At this stage, the financial controller was the most likely person to succeed at a management level, but following various misdemeanours, the controller left the business. The second child who joined the business married someone working outside the business, and this spouse became involved in the family business, eventually taking over as managing director. The second child, now married to the managing director, remained quite involved in the business.

The third child never worked in the business, and established a business funded by the parents. When this business venture was unsuccessful, the third child broached the question of entering the family business, but the parents decided it was not suitable.

The family business did well throughout the 1980s, generating huge value. By then, the founder had passed away. His wife, the controlling shareholder, decided it did not make sense to continue to grow the value in the existing companies, increasing future inheritance tax exposures for the second generation. The business established a parallel trading structure, and it acquired and initiated any new ventures that the family entered into. From an asset protection perspective, some of the shareholding in the new parallel structure was retained in trust. Some shareholdings went to the three children. In respect of the child who had married, some shares were also allocated to their children. In respect of the original group of companies, the ownership had always been in trust, so as to avoid potential wealth taxes that everyone thought would be introduced in the 1970s. The shareholdings in the parallel structure were the first shares to be held personally. Around the same time, other parallel companies were also incorporated, and placed in the hands of the second and third generations. The intention was to give a certain amount of value to individual family members at second and third generational level.

It became apparent to the founder's wife that the child who was actively involved in the business, and who was married to the managing director, was the family member who should continue with the business. The founder's wife wished to ensure that the business passed ultimately for their benefit. But the two other second-generation children needed to be provided for. There was a concern that family difficulties may arise from a relationship perspective, since ultimately a share in the business was not passing to them. These two children were ultimately bought out, and their shareholdings in some of the parallel companies were acquired in return for liquid assets and cash. In addition to being removed at shareholder level, they were also restricted from being employees or directors of any of the family companies. Separately, cash was placed in trust for these two siblings, neither of whom had children of their own. They were provided for in such a way that they could enjoy a very good standard of living. The business was protected so that it would pass to the third generation, the children of the third sibling.

Although the two second-generation siblings who exited were also provided for with non business assets under the founder's spouse's will, there was family dissension for some time due to the arrangements. The third sibling and her managing director spouse had been running the business for 15-20 years by then, and were responsible for building up a lot of the value in the business. It was difficult to manage the expectations of the two siblings who received no interest in the business. They unrealistically felt they had entitlement to one third of the business interests, ignoring the efforts of the third sibling and her managing director spouse. The overriding concern of the founder's spouse was that the business continued after she passed away. In light of the age of members of the third generation, it was decided to put some of the value aside for them with certain projects. Individual vehicles were put in their names so that some value would accrue to them. At this stage, the third generation was in their early 20s. As they progressed to their 30s, some of them had college degrees appropriate to the type of business. They had also worked elsewhere, obtaining outside experience. One third generation family member had joined the business at this stage. Another third generation family member also showed interest in a family business career.

Takeaway 1

This case study shows the difficulties in ensuring suitable candidates at a management level to run the business, and how it may be better to look to individuals outside of the family, or to in-laws, when looking for appropriate management talent. It shows the types of decisions that need to be made from an overall control perspective in ensuring the transition of the business from one generation to the next, and ensuring it remains within both family ownership and control. Some family members are clearly more suited to running the business than others. It also illustrates the difficulties of having to choose among children in a business context. The decision that is best for the business will usually facilitate a successful transition and its future continued operation. A family oriented decision to leave the business equally among members of the second generation could have had detrimental consequences.

Case study 2 – Refer to next page

Case study 2

A first generation business was originally wholly owned by the founder, who became heavily reliant on one of his key employees who became a key member of management, and to whom he awarded some equity in the company. As time progressed, the founder realised that his two children were not yet ready to run the business. One child had no involvement in the business and no interest in becoming involved. A certain part of the family's wealth was derived from the business, and because the founder wanted to maintain equality between both children, he decided to allocate some equity in the business to the child who was not working in the business.

When it came to finalising arrangements, it was decided to gift shares to the child in the business and the child outside the business, leaving the child involved in the business with a 51% shareholding. A 24% shareholding would be left for the child not involved in the business. The founder's remaining shares were to be bought out, providing him with capital gains tax treatment on the payment, and facilitating him to have wealth outside of the business in retirement. By now, the key employee had been made managing director, and was also allocated additional equity. His shareholding increased to 25%.

The business now operates with family member employed in the business, shadowing the managing director, who is in his early 50s. When the managing director retires in about ten years' time, it is anticipated that the family member employed in the business will be ready to take over.

A shareholders agreement governs the relationship among the shareholders in the business. There are different issues arising for all of them. The shareholders are:

– One family member employed in the business, majority shareholder (51%)

– One family member not employed in the business, minority shareholder (24%)

– One non-family member, managing director of the business who is also a shareholder (25%)

The shareholders agreement protects the interests of all concerned. In certain circumstances, the non-family member executive's shareholding can be reacquired by the company or by family. If any of the shareholders become ill or suffer ill health, the company can reacquire their shares to facilitate them being removed at shareholder level. All three individuals are directors of the company. There are set salary and bonus guidelines for those employed in the business. Any excess of profits not reinvested in the business is payable as dividends to the three shareholders pro rata to their shareholding.

Takeaway 2

A carefully thought out succession plan can accomplish a number of goals. It gives the founder an opportunity to realise value for their equity, to engage appropriate management to ensure future continued operation of the business, putting in place a management transition plan for the next generation, and establishing an overall governance structure to facilitate arrangements between the different interests of shareholders.

Case study 3 – Refer to next page

Case study 3

A business is currently held by the second generation of family members, having diversified from the activities originally commenced by the founders. The founders were four siblings who owned the business equally. One sibling died without family, leaving their share to the three surviving siblings. Of the three remaining founders' families, only one third-generation child was interested in joining the business. All the others pursued their own careers. This child started at the bottom, worked her way up, learned the business, and worked in various departments. When the three surviving founding members started to take less active roles, the one family member of the second generation involved in the business became the main family director or representative in the business. The business always had outside non-family managing directors who were the main operating officers for the group of companies. The family member from the second generation was heavily involved at a strategic direction level.

At some stage, some of the family of one of the three founder shareholders wished to receive value from the business, and was bought out. Two of the original founders remained at shareholder level. The one family member involved in the business was given some value or shares in certain subsidiary companies, but not in the holding company. The rewards were primarily by virtue of their role as an executive in the business.

The two founder shareholders subsequently decided to transfer all their equity in the main holding companies to their children. Each founder shareholder transferred their 50% equally between their respective children. There were now two groups of first cousins, a dozen in all, owning the business. Each individual had an 8-12% shareholding. Given the nature of the business and potential competitive risks, it was decided over a number of years to engage in a divestment and diversification strategy. This was implemented throughout the 1990s. Certain parts of the business were sold to third parties. The family retained a large share of the property interests held by the family companies. The divestment and diversification strategy involved a number of challenges, including persuading the family to sever ties with a business with which they had a long-term association, and finding purchasers for different parts of the business. Now that the business has been sold, the value retained has been invested. The family companies and the families have stayed together to maximise investment opportunities. Over time, certain assets have been put into the names of the individuals and/or into the names of the separate families. Not everything is trapped in the companies. The shareholders have had value pass out to them.

There has been occasional agitation at shareholder level as to how the business has been operated. Family meetings, called to explain the rationale as to why certain decisions were taken, have served to alleviate concerns. Shareholdings had historically been held by family trusts, but all the shares have now been appointed from the trusts to family members to avoid discretionary trust taxes. There are shares with a dividend value entitlement, and a separate class of voting shares. It was decided to unify the control issue around the separate class of voting shares by holding all the shares through a nominee company. The shareholders all signed a nominee agreement governing what decisions the directors of the nominee company can make, and what decisions must go back to the shareholders. The nominee agreement replicates a shareholder agreement. Most of the decisions are left with the nominee company, so that any family dispute will not alter or impact the day-to-day running of the business. There are four directors of the nominee company, two from each side of the family. Each family member can discuss their preferences indirectly with their own family directors. There is also a mechanism to deal with disputes at director level, providing for independent mediation to resolve any issues that arise. The basis for the nominee arrangement is to try and achieve the same protection from a control perspective that a trust might provide. In effect, the nominee company acts as a family forum/family board of directors to oversee the family issues at shareholder level. There are strict transfer provisions under the overall arrangement, to ensure that shareholdings do not pass out of the family to third parties.

Of the current second generation, only one individual from the two families is actively involved in running the business. Another individual from the other family is also a company executive, but peripherally. There is no apparent family successor to continue to run the family's investment and business interests, but this could change in the future. Of interest is the fact that when shareholdings pass down to the next generation, there could conceivably be 30 or 40 shareholders. It remains to be seen whether various investment assets will be sold and the value distributed to shareholders, or whether at a governance level appropriate structures can be implemented to ensure that the business continues as an ongoing family investment business.

Takeaway 3

Diversification is a real option if you want to preserve the wealth that has accumulated in a family business. What may have worked in the past may not work in the future. Even after a family has disposed of a business, it may still be advantageous to retain overall interests together from a wealth maximisation perspective, due to the leverage afforded a family investment vehicle. This is better than breaking up a corporate structure after the sale of core business assets, and the distribution of the accumulated value in its entirety to the wider family.

Governance structures for family can take many forms, depending on circumstances. The incorporation of a specific shareholder/family representative forum through a nominee company or otherwise, can be tailored to suit individual family needs.

Case study 4 – Refer to next page

Case study 4

Historically, a business currently in the fifth generation which is in transition to the sixth generation, has been operated as a partnership. The family has taken care to ensure that the business transitioned successfully from generation to generation, with family members in each succeeding generation obtaining appropriate qualifications and experience to continue operating the business. The business can be separated between its core activities and its investment assets, with the latter very much supporting the former. The investment assets are to transition to the sixth generation of family members in the form of a partnership structure. The core business will transition to corporate ownership to ensure its continued operation and the success of the succession to the sixth generation.

At an operational level, two members of the sixth generation have the necessary technical qualifications to be involved in the technical side of the core business. Another member of the sixth generation has engaged in a management transition plan, whereby they obtained appropriate college qualification, gained experience overseas for a number of years in similar businesses, and shadowing the fifth generation CEO for a year, ultimately succeeding to the post of managing director, with the previous incumbent becoming chairman of the business. The management transition has all been part of a long-term strategic plan for the business. The family has successfully managed the transition process through five generations.

Over time, some branches of the family exited when they no longer wished to remain involved in the business. This necessitated the occasional sale of investment assets to facilitate their exit. Currently, the core business is undergoing a redevelopment. At a governance level, financial institutions that are funding the redevelopment have sought the addition of a non-family board member with relevant industry experience, to provide support from an overall governance perspective, but also to counter-balance the family.

This family clearly have a successful history of transitioning between generations. The most notable factor is the significant effort and time invested in communication and planning to ensure not just the smooth business transition to the next generation, but that the transition ensures the company's continued viability in the hands of future generations.

Takeaway 4

This case study illustrates that the continued successful transition of a business requires effort and, appropriate focus. It also requires access to resources, in order to accommodate family members who may wish to exit.

Case study 5 – Refer to next page

Case study 5

A business founded by a single individual in the 1970s branched out from its original core activities and developed an associate investment group. None of the founder's four children wished to be directly involved in the business, which always had professional management. The founder was very marketing oriented, and had brought in strong financial management. He also recruited strong and well-paid professional management as the need arose in various sectors of the business. The founder also wisely engaged non-executive directors who were actively involved individuals with appropriate financial and legal skill sets. The business operated with a number of divisional CEOs who were appointed to the board, and board had a strong external chairman.

The value in the business passed to the family in the 1990s through a separation of the shareholdings between those with rights to the profits and those with rights to the voting. The founder shareholder and spouse retained control of the business through a separate class of voting shares. Only modest dividends were paid out to the children as equity shareholders.

The founder got sick and was no longer able to attend to the business. The structure carried the group forward under the strong divisional CEOs, strong board committees, and strong chairman, all of whom reported informally to the four equity shareholders. The founder died before the implementation of the final phase of the plan, with the voting shares passing to the surviving spouse, who became engaged in the final transition arrangements.

The shareholders agreed to a family constitution, which covered

– Dividend levels.

– The salary positions for any shareholder should they ever become involved in the business.

– The employment position of grandchildren if they ever wished to work in the business.

– Board membership for shareholders.

– Audit committees and rotating membership of these committees among director shareholders.

– Access to services within the business (i.e. a family office).

– Access to some of the facilities within the business by family members.

They also had a separate shareholders agreement governing ownership issues such as a wish to sell shares, or procedures after the death of a shareholder. Regarding the latter situation, there was an automatic transfer notice under the shareholders agreement, offering the shares to the other shareholders. This meant in effect that in-laws could be bought out where required. The buyout provisions were at market value. If a deceased shareholder left shares in their will to their children, the buyout provisions would not apply. If any grandchildren came into the business, they would be obliged to sign adherence agreements in connection with the shareholders agreement and the family constitution. Because the founder shareholder died during the transition process, the children were appointed as directors after his death, but all the external directors were retained. One of the children became more actively involved in the business. This drove the need for a family constitution governing involvement of shareholders in the business. The surviving spouse, as part of the overall arrangements, subsequently transferred the voting shares equally between the four children, but only after she was made a director of the group of companies for life. This ensured she retained a casting vote should any disputes arise at director level. For the first time, a group CEO was appointed by the shareholders. This CEO was the shareholder's person, and also replaced the founder at an operational level. The family also actively utilised non-executive directors, including a solicitor, two former partners of Big 4 accountancy firms, and someone who had previously been the financial director of a publicly quoted company. Now that the existing non-executive directors have been in place for some time, the family are now looking to reinvigorate the non-executive directors by making some new appointments.

Takeaway 5

This case study shows the importance of good governance, and reliance on professional management and non-executive directors where the family wishes to secure the future operation of the business without being directly involved at an operational level. It also outlines appropriate governance at a family level, with shareholders agreements and a family constitution providing a framework for protecting future transition of the business to the next generation.

Case study 6 – Refer to next page

Case study 6

A very successful individual had a number of businesses in the leisure and entertainment industry, and was separately involved in a number of property activities. The founder, aged almost 50 and unmarried, made a will, leaving various assets and businesses to siblings and a number of nephews and nieces. Under this will, shareholdings in the various companies were to be split among siblings and nephews and nieces. It was an extremely complex will.

The founder's girlfriend managed some of the businesses. She became pregnant, had twins, but the founder died shortly after marrying his girlfriend, and before he could make any substantial changes to his will. He left a number of notes as to how he intended to change the will in favour of the girlfriend and the twins.

After his death, a dispute arose over who would get what assets under the founder's estate, with his siblings and nephews and nieces disputing the entitlement of his new wife and their children. His wife was running the business together with a professional manager, to whom the founder had left a 10% shareholding in the business. While the dispute was ongoing, the wife agreed to a compromise whereby the siblings would run one side of the business, while she and the professional manager ran the other side, pending an agreement. The litigation dragged on. Up to one quarter of the very large estate was dissipated in legal fees, before a settlement was eventually imposed by the court.

Takeaway 6

This is a very important lesson about how to plan to leave your assets. In particular, it shows that leaving minority shareholdings in private companies does not work. You should ideally package your assets, leaving separate assets to individual family members. It is also a lesson that shows how essential it is to keep your will current, keep it simple and straightforward, and updated following significant changes in circumstances. You cannot keep all of the people happy all of the time. Try and avoid splitting assets and creating multiple ownership situations. If that is the case, you are better off leaving an asset such as an office block to six beneficiaries, so they can all enjoy a one-sixth share of any rental stream, or a one-sixth share of the proceeds of sale of the property. The property can be independently managed by an agent, rather than leaving six individuals equal shareholdings in a company. This has the potential to lead to chaos.

Case study 7 – Refer to next page

Case study 7

Two cousins went into business together, with everything on a 50/50 basis. Both were actively involved in the business. When they reached retirement age, they realised that it would be difficult for their two sets of children to continue on in the business together, due to the number of family members involved. Accordingly, the cousins split the business between their two sets of children. They had no cash resources to allocate to family members, so each family member of both families received shares in the business. Some family members of both families were involved in the business. Others were not. The nature of the business demanded that both families had to co-operate in certain activities. After the two cousins split the business, they gave some but not all of the shares in the respective businesses to their families. The families subsequently borrowed monies in the business to buy out their parents, and continued with two separate businesses that were still linked in relation to some activities. In one family, two siblings were involved in the business and two were not. In the other family, three siblings were involved in the business and three were not. Each family had to agree on processes governing decision making, and directors and shareholders' meetings. When the businesses were split, one family independently sought advice from outside advisors, with the other family retaining the existing advisors.

On one side, there was always tension over what the family member who was managing director of the business could make decisions on, and what the shareholders should make decisions on. This was eventually resolved by a shareholders' agreement, which specified job roles and salary levels. As time progressed, this family started to consider alternatives for the business being transitioned to the third generation. One family member decided they wished to exit the business, and their shares were bought out by the other three siblings, two of whom had children and wished to pass their shareholding to their children. The shares were transitioned to the next generation, with a new shareholders agreement entered into by one sibling from the second generation and the children of the third generation. The three members of the second generation were all made directors for life in the family companies, to ensure their continued involvement after they had transitioned their shareholdings.

Takeaway 7

As this case study shows, businesses do not automatically have to transition in their entirety from one generation to the next. The two founders decided to split the business to protect their respective family interests and ensure continuity of the overall business, but as separate entities. The second generation recognised that different issues that may arise at shareholder level. They facilitated the exit of one shareholder; two shareholders transitioned their shares to the third generation; and one shareholder continued to retain shares.

Case study 8 – Refer to next page

Case study 8

A group of companies has passed down through three generations. The ultimate holding company is held by three separate discretionary trusts established in the 1970s on behalf of different branches of the family. Since then, no assets have been transferred across to the family members by way of direct equity interests in the holding company. A number of family members are involved in the board of directors, but the business operates totally independent of the shareholders. When the business is doing well, dividends are paid to the trusts which pay the dividends to family members. The dividend policy is very much ad hoc, and based on business needs.

The structure was primarily set up before business relief was prcvided for gift and inheritance tax purposes. At the time, the top rate of gift/inheritance tax was 40%. Discharging the inheritance tax liability would have placed the business under a significant burden. By the time business relief was introduced in the 1990s, much of the business no longer qualified for business relief, as funds generated from the trading activities had been reinvested into activities that would no longer have qualified for business relief. So even though a gift/inheritance tax relief for family businesses was available, it provided no advantage due to how the business had developed. Discretionary trust tax arose within the family trusts as they continued to retain the shareholdings in the family holding company, instead of appointing the shares out to beneficiaries. The family trusts discharge the discretionary trust tax liability annually.

Takeaway 8

This is a good example of how discretionary trusts might apply to avoid placing a huge burden on the next generation and on the business in discharging a significant CAT liability. It was easier for the business to facilitate paying the annual 1% discretionary trust tax charge, than to suffer the burden of paying CAT at 40% (or now at 25%) where the shares in the holding company are appointed out to family members.

Case study 9 – Refer to next page

Case study 9

A highly successful family business was in its first generation stage, but the family recognised that to take it forward they would probably need to sell it to a third party, given the high level of reinvestment required and the fact that the next generation may have difficulty in bringing the business forward. Some of the next generation were involved in the business, others were not. The first generation decided to transfer shares to the second generation, whereby the first generation availed of capital gains tax retirement relief, and the second generation claimed business relief for CAT purposes. Those second generation family members involved in the business were charged with continuing to run the business successfully.

The second generation held onto their shareholding in the business for the claw-back period for both reliefs of six years, before the business was sold outright to a purchaser. The second generation had the benefit of a high base cost on a tax effective basis, having benefited from the CGT and CAT reliefs on the transfer six years earlier from the first generation. If the first generation had sold the business, significant CGT would have arisen for them, and significant CAT would have arisen in leaving the cash value generated to family members under their wills.

Takeaway 9

If a business is going to be sold, sometimes it is worth transferring the business early to the next generation, so as to benefit from an uplift in the cost base. In this instance, the reliefs were used to tax effectively re-base the value of the assets in advance of a future sale. It shows the advantage of planning well ahead of future events – in this case allowing for a six year lead in period to any eventual sale.

Case study 10 – Refer to next page

Case study 10

A first generation business still relies hugely on its entrepreneurial founder. The three children of the founder are involved in the business, but the founder is exceptionally commercial, and has a keen understanding of the marketplace in which the business operates, its customers and the overall business dynamic. The founder is in his mid-60s and has a very solid progressive business. A big question mark hangs over what will happen next. The family members involved have different roles, and there are also several non-family individuals involved. No single individual is being groomed for the top role, and there is no formal board structure or management structure that can assess potential candidates, and educate them to make strategic decisions around the business's future. The entrepreneurial founder still makes all decisions. There is a significant risk that without any formal programme to bring people along, if anything happens to the founder in the short term, there is no one ready to step in.

Takeaway 10

This highlights the importance of ensuring an appropriate succession or transition programme at a management level, with appropriate training and educational support or mentoring arrangements. This would ensure that family and non-family managers could become the best and most capable employees possible, while providing an assessment system for choosing the most appropriate candidate for the top job. Even though this was raised specifically to the entrepreneurial founder, he continued to dither. Like so many owner managers, he did nothing, even though he knew that this was not in the best interests of the business.

These case studies highlight the diverse situations that can materialise when family issues, business issues and broader financial considerations are taken into account in a succession planning context. They demonstrate the importance of decisive action, of putting into place appropriate structures, and of getting professional advice. They also illustrate that there is no one-size-fits-all solution. Any planning undertaken needs to be specific to the needs of your business and your own family circumstances.

CHAPTER 11 – ACTIONS

– Consider the requirements in your own situation.

– Can you identify with any of the issues raised in the case studies?

– Can you leverage off any of the steps taken in the case studies in your own situation?

– How is your situation different from the case studies?

– Identify what you need to do because it is different.

– Seek appropriate assistance.

CHAPTER 12

SUCCESSION – AN INTERNATIONAL PERSPECTIVE

In larger markets with a tradition of larger family business enterprises, the need for greater sophistication in finding appropriate strategies for planning succession to the business emerged earlier than in countries such as Ireland. This can be seen by the large number of large-scale family businesses in certain countries, and the level of academic research in those countries in the family business area.

Internationally, there are many large-scale family businesses that are wholly privately owned. It is also interesting to observe that in certain countries, ultimate ownership and control of publicly quoted companies are substantially also in family hands. A 2002 study of 13 European economies found that families were the most common type of controlling shareholders in many listed companies. 44.3% of western European corporations were family controlled. Family control of publicly quoted companies was the lowest in the UK and Ireland, at about 24%. In continental Europe, family-controlled firms were in the majority.

Given the size and wealth historically generated in its economy, most academic research, business theories and analysis of family firms emanates from the United States. The rest of the world is catching up. An analysis of family firms that have transitioned successfully through a number of generations across jurisdictions demonstrates many of the principles outlined in earlier chapters.

The failure of many family firms to prevail beyond the second or third generations is by no means a uniquely Irish phenomenon. Similar statistics also emerging in most other economies.

National differences in approach to succession planning are based on several factors:

– Culture.

– Legal requirements such as succession laws.

– Different governance practices.

– Different tax regimes.

– Educational support available: through professional bodies, universities, other third parties in the wider business community, or specific support through government sponsored programmes.

CULTURE

Western, Asian and Islamic cultures have different criteria and customs for family involvement and transition of a business:

– The degree to which family members are utilised in the business.

– Level of planning for succession.

– Preferences for succession.

– Expectations for succession.

One study showed that Eastern Asian parents start early in influencing the career direction of the child. Because of the emphasis on respect for family, children feel terribly guilty if they do not follow the direction of the parents. It can be difficult for someone raised in a Western culture to understand this dynamic. Children from an Asian background who are raised in a Western culture can still feel this dynamic, and often feel conflicted between honouring the family (a more Eastern concept) and following their own dreams (a more Western concept).

In societies that are strongly patriarchal, the "pater" exercises complete control over the family. His decisions are unquestioned and family members must conform. In the absence of the father, the eldest son normally assumes the role of head of the family. In cultures where such an attitude dominates, the opportunities for female family members to join and participate in the family business are somewhat limited. In some societies, to maintain harmony, the good of the family takes precedence over the goal of any individual. To support this value, family members are morally obligated to support each other, so that the family is normally consulted in matters of career and marriage.

Asian families place a high value on harmony and smooth personal relationships. This encourages dependence and deference, traits that can be dismissed by western societies that uphold a person's individuality. This will impact on the dynamic, interpersonal dealings and communication required to successfully transition a family business from one generation to the next. Western society has transitioned more to a stage where business owners realise that the future successful continued operation of the family enterprise is best secured by entrusting its management to those most capable, whether they happen to be family or not. The inability of some societies (particularly in South and East Asian) to trust non-family results in a business environment composed of many small businesses unable or unwilling to make the leap to more progressive enterprises. Countries like the United States, Germany and Japan have fostered outside talent to grow businesses that can propel the global economy. These countries are considered "high trust" societies, because people are able to bestow their trust to others outside their family unit, allowing their business to grow faster and larger. In some cultures, the general reluctance to trust outsiders can be stimulated by a desire for confidentiality, but it also means that there is less willingness to seek professional advice. In these countries, there are very few shareholder agreements or exit plans in place.

Differences in ethnic background may influence the expectation of family business members in a succession process. There may be differences in the basic philosophy and underlying assumptions of the family members of different ethnic backgrounds in relation to how a succession is planned for and implemented. For example, Japanese family businesses often have one male heir who is the successor and receives all the shares in the business. A Chinese family enterprise is usually divided equally among the male successors. Other issues that may vary across cultures are the modes of conflict resolution (direct or indirect), value given to education, patterns of communication (e.g. face saving/confrontation) and the position of women in the culture.

LEGAL REQUIREMENTS

In common law countries, we are used to the principles of freedom of attestation, by which a business owner's will constitutes the final determination as to who the business will pass to when it has not been gifted to family members during the business owner's lifetime. In countries like France, there are protected heirship rules. Each child gets a fixed share of a parent's estate, and it is not possible to disinherit children. Unless there are substantial private assets, a shareholding in a business will normally be split among several children. Under Islamic inheritance laws, male descendants are generally preferred to female descendants in respect of business assets at a ratio of 2:1. However, there is no preclusion on them making gifts to whichever family members they see fit during their lifetime, despite the generally accepted principle that it should be in accordance with fixed shares that pertain in an inheritance situation. Such constraints will generally drive the nature of family involvement in the business in the future. That is why in Middle Eastern countries and Arab states, it is usually the eldest son who succeeds to the business, regardless of his abilities.

In countries where children receive fixed shares to a parent's estate, appropriate structures must be put in place to manage their involvement in the business. Ireland has a significant advantage in this respect, as such problems do not arise unless someone dies intestate. When someone makes gifts during their lifetime or carefully considers their will, such difficulties should not arise where appropriate and correct decisions are made.

CORPORATE GOVERNANCE PRACTICES

Prevailing governance structures will vary in different jurisdictions. For example, the German system of corporate governance has three core characteristics which distinguish it from the Anglo-Saxon model: concentrated ownership, a dual board structure (supervisory board and management board), and extensive worker representation on the supervisory board. Governance structures generally permeate downward from what is expected of the listed plcs in a particular jurisdiction. Germany has a concentrated system of share ownership. Even large companies like Bertelsmann are owned by founding families or by a small number of private investors. Comparatively few companies are listed on the stock market. A study in the 1990s showed that Germany has only one-sixth as many listed companies as the US and one-seventh as many as the UK on a per capita basis. Ownership of companies listed on the stock market is much more concentrated. Over half of German public companies have a major shareholder that controls at least 50% of voting rights, such as BMW. Germany is typical of several continental European countries, and is substantially different from Ireland, the UK and the USA.

Unlike the single board system predominant in the Anglo-Saxon world, large German companies are required by law to have a dual board structure. No individual can simultaneously serve on both boards of the same company. The top managers responsible for day-to-day operations are represented on the management board, often referred to as the executive board. Stakeholders in the company, whether shareholders, creditors or employees, are represented on the supervisory board which is responsible for appointing and overseeing members of the management board and for approving key policies and strategic decisions. This contrasts strongly with the strong CEO model of many US companies. Under the German structure, the dual board system supports a consensus approach to corporate governance. A distinguishing feature of the German corporate governance system is the mandatory inclusion of worker representatives on the supervisory boards of large companies.

From a cultural perspective, some countries have a stakeholder corporate governance system where a second board or group of individuals supervises the management board. In these countries, the concept of a family council is not as alien as it might appear in countries that adopt the Anglo Saxon method of governance. Another interesting cultural contrast is seen in the Middle East. In addition to family councils, the family governance structures in many family businesses include an extra body, a council of elders or seniors. Because of the deep-seated respect for the senior generation that underpins many aspects of Middle Eastern life and culture, such an entity will be at the top of the family governance hierarchy, while the family council acts as its executive committee.

The Anglo-Saxon method of counterbalancing the views of family is usually provided by independent directors. There is a clear culture and history of independent directorships in an Anglo Saxon environment, compared to that in other countries where other systems of governance prevail. Clearly a combination of a systematic corporate governance structure, such as the dual board structure in Germany, combined with independent directors as provided for under the Anglo-Saxon model, is one way of obtaining the best of both worlds. At a practical level, this could be achieved by having the family council as the supervisory board overseeing the activities of the board of management, with the board of management comprising both family and non-family members (internal professional managers and/or external non-executive directors).

TAX SYSTEMS

When it comes to government assistance in facilitating successful transition or succession to a family business, it is the provisions of the country's tax system that most directly impact on the future continued success of an enterprise. In some countries, there are no gift or inheritance taxes. In other countries, valuable reliefs apply for the gift or inheritance of business assets. The chart below compares the level of relief on business assets in Ireland from a tax perspective, with the tax regimes prevailing in several European and other Western economies.

Country	Tax regime for passing business assets	Effective Tax Rate on Business Succession
Austria	**Inheritance/ gift tax:** None **Other relevant taxes:** Real estate transfer tax may arise in limited situations. Full/partial exemption available*	Nil Nil
Canada	**Inheritance/gift tax:** None **Other relevant taxes:** CGT – deemed disposal of assets on death – various reliefs available Sales tax – may arise on assets being transferred. Transfer tax – may arise on transfer of real property	Nil 50% of gain taxed at marginal rates Progressive rate depending on province.
Cyprus	**No inheritance/gift taxes**	Nil
Finland	**Inheritance/ gift tax:** Relief for business assets* **Other relevant taxes:** Transfer tax – None where no consideration given CGT – None if relief applies*	0%-12.8% Nil Nil
France	**Inheritance/gift tax:** Relief for business assets* Further reduction in rates for gifts. **Other relevant taxes: CGT** – deferred exemption*	1.25%-10% Nil (deferred)
Germany	**Inheritance/gift tax:** Relief for business assets*	0%-15%
Holland	**Inheritance/gift tax:** Relief for business assets* **Other relevant taxes:** CGT – rollover relief*.	Value of assets <€1m – Nil Value of assets >€1m –0-40% Nil (deferred)
India	**Inheritance/ gift tax:** Full exemption for gifts and inheritances between relatives **Other relevant taxes:** Stamp duty on the gift	Nil Dependent on amount of consideration & state
Ireland	**Inheritance/gift tax:** Relief for business assets* **Other relevant taxes:** CGT – relief applies* Stamp duty –some relief for blood relations	2.5% Nil 1–3%

Country	Tax regime for passing business assets	Effective Tax Rate on Business Succession
Luxembourg	**Inheritance/ gift tax:** No inheritance tax between direct line relations and spouses/partners where there are common children. A progressive rate applies to non direct line relatives.	Nil 1.8%-4.8%
Portugal	**Inheritance/ gift tax:** No inheritance/ gift tax between direct line relatives. **Other relevant taxes:** CGT on transfer or assets between non direct line relatives.	Nil Others – 10% Direct line relative: Nil Non direct line relative: 20% Small companies: 10%
Spain	**Inheritance/gift tax:** Relief for business assets* **Other relevant taxes:** Capital gains tax arises on gifts	0.38%-1.7% 19% on first €6,000 gain, 21% on excess.
Sweden	**No inheritance/gift taxes**	Nil
UK	**Inheritance/ gift tax:** Relief for business assets* on inheritance. No gift tax. **Other relevant taxes:** CGT (on gifts) – rollover relief* Entrepreneurial relief: Reduction of the rate of CGT*	Nil Nil (deferred) Gains <£5m – 10% (lifetime limit) Gains >£5m full CGT rate
USA	**Inheritance/gift tax:** Individuals may gift/leave estate up to $5million tax free. State taxes and generation skipping taxes may also apply.	Value of assets <$5m – Nil Value of assets >$5 million – 35% federal tax.

Reliefs subject to conditions being satisfied

This comparison is of particular importance in the context of suggested dilution of the reliefs available for business assets in Ireland, both capital gains tax retirement relief and business relief for capital acquisitions tax, under both the Commission on Taxation report in 2009 and the Four Year Plan published by the Government in December 2010. Increases in the effective rates of capital gains tax or capital acquisitions tax on the transition of family business would not be positive in ensuring their continued viability and protecting the employment they currently provide.

At a time when many charities and voluntary organisations are struggling with funding, it may be possible to change tax reliefs to encourage donations for philanthropic purposes. In the US, when someone sells their business, they can transfer the shares to a charitable trust. There is no tax on the transfer to the trust, and the trust pays no tax on the disposal of the business. However, under the trust, a schedule of annual payments can be made to the vendor and their spouse. Thus the vendor is encouraged to give the funds to charity because of the tax efficiencies on disposal, and because they are still allowed to retain an income for life from the charity post disposal of their business.

EDUCATIONAL

The results of a questionnaire sent to all of Deloitte's international network of offices showed that the one area where a lack of support or services appears to arise for family businesses contemplating succession, is the access to publicly available information, or appropriate educational support. This support includes direct government intervention, provision of such information by the wider business community, professional organisations, and other bodies. In some countries, the Family Business Network or affiliated enterprises of the Family Firm Institute, provides some educational support. Various business organisations also supply information on an ad hoc basis. See the Useful Contacts section below for a list of contacts in an Irish context.

Here in Ireland, a lot more could be done to assist business owners in preparing family members for joining the business in the future, and in providing them with support of family business specific issues such as succession planning. Dr Naomi Birdthistle is course leader of the MBS in International Entrepreneurship in University of Limerick which has a twelve week family business module. She has confirmed our view that we here in Ireland are way behind best practice overseas, outlining that nearly all US universities would have some form of family business module. At the time of writing University College Cork and University of Limerick are insofar as we are aware the only third level institutions providing a family business module as part of courses in their business faculties.

PLANNING STRUCTURES

The general legal structures associated with passing a family business vary from country to country, based on the tax regime and the likely impact that tax will have on the next generation or the business, where they have no choice but to seek recourse to the business to fund their liabilities.

In some countries, different classes of shares, or trusts and foundations, are used to facilitate succession. In other countries, ownership just transitions directly from one generation to the next, sometimes accompanied by appropriate agreements at shareholder level to govern relationships between family shareholders.

The prevalence of marital breakdown in some countries is more of a concern than in others. Concerns over the political system in some jurisdictions are also a factor in how families with businesses structure their affairs, often diversifying business interests significantly outside their domestic economy. With planning, there is no one-size-fits-all solution.

COMMON DIFFERENTIATOR

Family firms will continue to be the dominant economic force worldwide. They will continue to be the largest category of employers and make the largest contribution to economies. The greatest single factor in the continued success and successful transition of a family business is preparing the next generation to take over. Regardless of the culture, legal requirements and governing tax regimes that apply across the world, this factor alone is the single biggest differentiator between those businesses that transition through a number of generations and those that do not. It is people that make the difference, provided they are prepared and adequately supported.

CONCLUSION

Succession planning is not a single issue in isolation. It is a combination of issues that need to be addressed in order to ensure a successful transition from one generation to the next. Planning is the critical activity in managing any succession. Planning challenges the status quo. It assesses the existing situation and focuses attention on the future. It looks at the factors impacting on ownership and management transition.

Planning can be reactive, adaptive or strategic. When succession planning is carried out on a reactive or adaptive basis, it tends not to succeed, while strategic succession planning can assist in achieving a number of goals:

– Continuity of ownership.

– Talent management and development.

– Wealth creation to facilitate retirement.

– Family harmony – by having no ambiguity surrounding the criteria for entering the family business, or surrounding the identity of whom ownership ultimately devolves to.

The complexity of business succession and the strategy devised to facilitate depends on the complexity of your overall business structure. They say that failure to plan is planning to fail. This is very much the case with succession planning. Failure to plan can see even the most simply structured family businesses fail to pass successfully from one generation to the next. Planning succession can put a family business, emotions and relationships to unprecedented test and strain. The willingness of family business owners to plan for their succession is often the single most decisive factor in determining the survival of their business.

A systematic, well-structured approach to succession planning is required in order to overcome the inclination to do nothing. Another major factor is the preparedness, or lack of, of the next generation to successfully manage and operate the family business once it transitions to them. Mentoring the successor generation is a priority. It is critical to utilise the full intellectual capital of the successor generation so that they become the best family managers they can be. The recognition that management of the business may sometimes be best suited to professional managers rather than to family is also important.

You should establish a retirement date regarding your own reduced involvement in the business. Stick to that date. To facilitate your stepping down, make sure you have set aside financial resources to provide you with a nest egg in retirement. If the business is transitioning to a number of family members, put in place appropriate governance structures to minimise the potential for dispute. Failure to plan appropriately can have detrimental effects on your family business. The rewards for undertaking a successful succession plan are huge, not just for the continued financial viability of the business, but also for managing family expectations and maintaining family harmony. It is never easy or straightforward if disputes arise, but good planning should provide the means for resolving difficulties at an earlier stage. Without planning, it may be much more difficult to resolve problems.

The aim of this book is to help you appreciate the significance of having a comprehensive and appropriate succession planning structure for your business. Hopefully, some of the processes have been de-mystified in these chapters, and you are motivated to get started. Starting early is paramount in the succession planning process. Once you have started planning, you can always update your plan and adapt it in light of changing circumstances. Don't keep putting it off.

Now that you have read the book, you should do more than consider the issues as they impact on you and on your family business. You should also share the ideas and principles with the key family members or stake-holders who are likely to be impacted in any succession planning process. Help them understand what is involved, so that they provide you with the support you need in making critical decisions.

Get advice from someone completely removed from the business, some-one who can look at all issues objectively, without emotional baggage. Advice from a third party can be critical as you face decisions that will not only impact on you in your retirement, but will impact on your family for years to come.

Every family business is different. Every family business is shaped by its business or industry sector, the personalities within the family, their con-cerns and relationships, the future objectives of the business, the family's values, and the sense of family history/legacy in transitioning the busi-ness from one generation to the next. As you determine what is right for your business, hopefully some of the principles and structures out-lined in this book will prove useful. Above all, don't dither.

GLOSSARY

A

ARF

Approved Retirement Fund – an investment account into which certain pension funds can be transferred into on retirement.

B

Buy/sell agreement

An agreement between the shareholders of a company which details the procedures if one or more shareholders wish to exit the business. This may also be addressed by put/call options or more specifically under a shareholder agreement.

C

The Code

The UK Corporate Governance Code sets out standards of good practice in relation to board leadership and effectiveness, remuneration, accountability and relations with shareholders.

CAT

Capital Acquisitions Tax, including both gift and inheritance tax.

CGT

Capital Gains Tax

Closely held business

A company with a small group of controlling shareholders.

Core competencies

The skills and behaviours that a candidate needs to perform a job.

D

Demerger

The process by which part or parts of a company split to become independent companies.

Discretionary trust

Where a trustee holds assets on trust for specified or non-specified beneficiaries of the trust – also called a family trust.

E

Enduring power of attorney

A binding agreement under which you choose someone to manage your affairs and property in the event that you become mentally incapable of doing so.

EPP

Executive pension plan – an occupational pension scheme established by your employer company specifically for you.

F

Family council

Functions like a board of directors in family-run business. The family council structure assists the family to distinguish family issues from business issues.

Family office

The professionally managed financial component of a family-owned business, often employing a management team and staff of accountants and administrative assistants.

Fixed trust

A trust in which the beneficiaries are said to have a vested and indefeasible interest in a share of the income and capital of the trust.

H

Higgs report

A UK report into the role and effectiveness of non-executive directors.

Hive off

Also referred to a spin off. A demerger or splitting of a business into two or more entities.

I

Inter vivos trust

A trust that can be created during a lifetime.

IPO

Initial public offering, when a company first issues shares to the public, usually through a stock exchange listing.

L

Lead consultant

An external advisor who offers advice to the business owner (or other stakeholders) throughout the succession-planning process, sometimes as lead consultant in a team of specialist consultants.

P

Parallel companies

Companies run side by side or in conjunction with one another, but which are not in a group relationship. They may often have common shareholders.

PRSA

Personal Retirement Savings Account – one of the pension funding alternatives available.

R

RAC

Retirement Annuity Contract – a pension funding alternative.

S

Senior debt

Debt with priority over others for repayment.

Shareholder agreement

An agreement between shareholders that dictates the terms and conditions on which the shareholders interact with one another on a day-to-day basis or in the event of a future exit.

Sinking fund

A sum set aside periodically from the income of a business and allowed to accumulate for a specific purpose.
Stakeholders
Parties having an interest in a particular company, project or outcome.

Subordinated debt

Debts repayable after other loans have been paid – also called mezzanine debt.

SWOT analysis

An examination of a business designed to identify its strengths, weaknesses, opportunities and threats.

T

TCA

Taxes Consolidation Act 1997

Testamentary trust

A trust created through a will, coming into force only when the individual dies.

W

Walker report

A UK report on corporate governance of banks and other financial institutions.

SOURCE MATERIALS –
FURTHER READING

BOOKS:

- Aronoff, Craig, Joseph Astrachan, John Ward, *Family Business Sourcebook*, 3rd edn (Family Enterprise Publishers, 2002)

- Astrachan, Joseph and Kristi S McMillan, *Conflict and Communication in the Family Business* (Family Enterprise Publishers, 2003)

- Bishop, Matthew and Michael Green, *Philanthrocapitalism: How Giving Can Save the World*, (A & C Black Publishers 2008)

- Bork, David, Dennis Jaffe, Sam Lane, Leslie Dashew, Quentin Heisler, *Working with Family Businesses, A Guide for Professionals* (John Wiley & Sons/Jossey Bass Publishers, 2003)

- Carlock, Randel and John Ward, *Strategic Planning for the Family Business* (Macmillan, 2001)

- Carlock, Randel and John Ward, *When Family Businesses are Best* (Palgrave Macmillan 2010)

- Crosbie, Alan, *Don't Leave it to the Children* (Marino Books, 2000)

- Gersick, Kelin, *The Succession Workbook: Continuity planning for family foundations* (Council on Foundations, 2000)

- Gersick, Kelin (ed), *The Best of FBR II* (Family Firm Institute, 2006)

- Gersick, Kelin, John David, Marion McCollom Hampton, Ivan Lansberg, *Generation to Generation: Life cycles of the family business* (Harvard Business School Press, 1997)

- Hillburt-Davis, Jane and W Gibb Dyer, *Consulting to Family Businesses: A practical guide to contracting, assessment and implementation* (Jossey Bass/Pfeiffer, division of Wiley, 2003)

- Holland Craig, *The Art of Business Succession: who will fill your shoes?* (John Wiley & Sons, 2008)

- Hughes, James E. Jr, *Family Wealth, Keeping it in the Family* (Bloomberg, 2004)

- Kenyon-Rouvinez, Denise and John Ward, *Family Business Key Issues* (Palgrave Macmillan, 2005)

- Kaslow, Florence, *Handbook of Family Business and Family Business Consultation: A global perspective* (Haworth Press, 2006)

- Kets de Vries, Manfred, Carlock, Randal and Elizabeth Florent-Treacy, *Family Business on the Couch:A psychological perspective* (John Wiley & Sons, 2008)

- Lansberg, Ivan, *Succeeding Generations: Realising the dream of families in business* (Harvard Business School Press, 1999)

- Leach, Peter, *Family Businesses: The essentials* (Profile Books, 2007)

- Mackenzie, Susan (ed), *A Guide to Giving* 3rd edition (Association of Charitable Foundations, 2008)

- McDonald Ian and Jonathan Sutton (ed), *Business Families and Family Businesses – the STEP Handbook for Advisors* (Globe Business Publishing Limited, 2009)

- McGoldrick, M, R Gerson and S Shellenberger, *Genograms: Assessment and interventions* (Norton Publishers, 1999)

- Miller D and I Le Breton Miller, *Managing for the Long Run: Lessons in competitive advantage from great family businesses* (Harvard Business School, 2005)

- Montemerlo, Daniela and John Ward, *The Family Constitution* (Palgrave Macmillan, 2011)

- Neubauer F. and Lank A.G. *The Family Business: Its Governance for Sustainability* (Macmillan, 1998)

- O'Hara, William, *Centuries of Success: Lessons from the world's most enduring family businesses* (Family Business Consulting Group, 2004)

- Ward, John, *Perpetuating the Family Business: 50 lessons learned from long lasting, successful families in business* (Palgrave Macmillan, 2004).

– Ward, John, *Creating Effective Boards for Private Enterprises: Meeting the Challenges of Continuity and Competition* (Jossey Bass, 1991).

ARTICLES/JOURNALS:

– Naomi Birdthistle (2007) 'Family Business Education: A Myth or Reality?', *Irish Business Journal*, 3(1), 64-73

– Naomi Birdthistle (2008) 'Family SMEs in Ireland as Learning Organisations, *The Learning Organisation: The International Journal of Knowledge and Organisational Learning Management*, 15(5), 421-436

– Naomi Birdthistle (2009) 'Splitting heirs – Divorce planning and pre-nuptial agreements for family businesses in Ireland', *Electronic Journal of Family Business Studies*, 2(3), 97-117

– Tom Davidow (2006) 'Reshaping – not Retiring', *Families in Business*, September-October

– Peter Davis (1990) 'Three types of founders – and their dark sides', *Family Business Magazine*, February

– Elaine Doyle, Naomi Birdthistle and Adrian Godwin (2009) 'Examining succession and tax planning in family businesses in Ireland', *Irish Taxation Institute*, April

– Andrew Drake (2004) 'Keeping It In the Family: The Fear of Outsiders', *Families in Business*, September-October

– Dennis T Jaffe (2003) 'Resolving Family Feuds', *Families in Business*, January

– Dennis T Jaffe (2003) 'Creating Effective Management Teams', *Families in Business*, April-May

– Dennis T Jaffe (2003) 'The Burdens of Wealth', *Families in Business*, June

– Harry Levinson 'Conflicts that plague family businesses', *Harvard Business Review*, March-April 1971.

– Harry Levinson (1974) 'Don't Choose Your Own Successor', *Harvard Business Review*, November-December

– Harry Levinson (1983) 'Consulting with family businesses: What to look for, what to look out for', *Organisational Dynamics*, Summer, American Management Association, New York

– Barbara Murray (2005) 'From My Hands to Yours: Retirement as Self-Renewal', *Families in Business*, November-December

–   Randall J.Ottinger and Philip F. Strassler (2009) 'In pursuit of generational gold', *Journal of Practical Estate Planning,* December 2008-January 2009

–   Judith Ross (1999) 'A taste of tradition: Kenzaburo Mogi and Kikkoman', *Harvard Business School Bulletin Online,* February, www.alumni.hbs.edu/bulletin

–   Melanie Stern (2004) 'Sell In, Not Out', *Families in Business,* July-August

–   Renato Tagiuri and John A Davis (1982) 'Bivalent attitudes of the family firm', *Family Business Review,* Volume IX, No.2

–   Jane Zalman (2005) 'Expanding the vision', *Families in Business,* November/December

–   François de Visscher (2005) 'Family Offices: An Old Yet Emerging Model', *Families in Business,* January-February

USEFUL CONTACTS

C

Chambers Ireland

The country's largest business organisation, with 60 member chambers representing over 13,000 businesses throughout Ireland. Each member chamber, comprised of local business representatives, works to promote the economic and social development of their community.

Visit the website at: **www.chambers.ie**

Chartered Accountants Ireland

The largest and longest established accountancy body in Ireland. It is the leading voice for the accountancy profession in Ireland and provides a range of useful information for all members of the Institute of Chartered Accountants.

Visit the website at: **www.charteredaccountants.ie**

Companies Registration Office

Visit **www.cro.ie** for a wealth of general information on company filing requirements, business incorporation and business termination.

County/City Enterprise Boards

County and City Enterprise Boards (CEBs) that provide support for the micro-enterprise sector in Ireland. The statutory function of CEBs is to stimulate economic and entrepreneurial activity at city and county level and to develop local indigenous enterprise potential in the micro-business sector.

Visit the website at: **www.enterpriseboards.ie**

D

Deloitte

Deloitte offers invaluable advice on all areas of succession planning.

Visit the website at: **www.deloitte.com/ie/succession**

E

Enterprise Ireland
A state body responsible for the development and growth of Irish enterprises in world markets. Enterprise Ireland assists Irish enterprises in the initial start-up phases and supports them as they grow, ensuring sustainable economic growth, regional development and secure employment.

Visit the website at: **www.enterprise-ireland.ie**

European Group of Family Enterprises (GEEF)
A European network devoted to lobbying and the promotion of family businesses within the European Union. The goal of GEEFI is to promote a full understanding of the key role of family-owned enterprises in Europe's economy, to press for policies that will support the creation of a level playing field for family businesses compared to all other types of companies, and to ensure recognition of their contribution to the entrepreneurial culture and social cohesion in Europe. GEEF also represents and supports the next generation of entrepreneurs.

Visit the website at: **www.efb-geef.eu**

F

Family Business Network (FBN)
A not-for-profit international network for families in business. With chapters in many countries, FBN is run by family businesses, for family businesses, with the aim of strengthening success over generations.

Visit the website at: **www.fbn-i.org**

Family Firm Institute
The leading international membership association for professionals serving the family enterprise field. Through its international journal, certificate programme, educational endeavours, and preeminent international conference, FFI upholds the highest standards in family enterprise best practices.

Visit the website at: **www.ffi.org**

Financial Reporting Council
The UK's independent regulator responsible for promoting high quality corporate governance and reporting to foster investment. It promotes high standards of corporate governance through the UK Corporate Governance Code. Copies of the Code and other corporate governance guidance are available from their website.

Visit the website at: **www.frc.org.uk**

I

Institute of Directors
The representative body for senior, strategic business professionals in Ireland. Its members include chief executives, chairpersons, board members, senior executives and partners of large national and international entities in Ireland. The Institute also runs courses, some specifically aimed at family operated businesses.

Visit the website at: **www.iodireland.ie**

Irish Business and Employers Confederation (IBEC)
The national umbrella organisation for business and employers in Ireland. IBEC provides its members with knowledge, influence and connections.

Visit the website at: **www.ibec.ie**

Irish Financial Services
The role of the Financial Regulator is to ensure proper and effective regulation of financial institutions and markets in Ireland.

Visit the website at: **www.ifsra.ie**

Irish Management Institute (IMI)
Ireland's Executive Management Centre provides a range of development programmes for management tailored around their clients' specific needs with a view to building smarter organisations through management learning.

Visit the website at: **www.imi.ie**

Irish Small and Medium Enterprises Association (ISME)
An independent organisation for the Irish small and medium business sector. ISME offers a comprehensive range of Advisory Services and Publication, Independent Lobbying and Representation, Cost Saving Schemes, Training and Development Programmes, and Regional Networking Events designed to enhance the day-to-day running of members' businesses.

Visit the website at: **www.isme.ie**

Irish Taxation Institute
Ireland's leading professional body for taxation affairs. The Institute works to support an efficient, fair and competitive tax system that encourages economic and social progress.

Visit the website at: **www.taxireland.ie**

L

Law Society of Ireland
The educational, representative and regulatory body of the solicitors' profession in Ireland.

Visit the website at: **www.lawsociety.ie**

P

Pensions Board
A statutory body set up to regulate occupational pension schemes, trust RACs and personal retirement savings accounts in Ireland.

Visit the website at: **www.pensionsboard.ie**

Plato Ireland
A business network that offers a programme for individuals who wish to pass on the family wealth to the next generation. The programme consists of a series of

modules delivered through workshops and presentations. Participants are also given the opportunity to receive individual advice and guidance on issues which are unique to their particular circumstances.

Visit the website at: **www.plato.ie**

R

Revenue Commissioners

Visit Revenue online at **www.revenue.ie** for any general taxation queries you may have both in a personal context and business context.

S

SmallBusinessCan

Provides a one-stop resource to small and medium enterprises who face challenges in the establishment and growth of their ventures. The site provides advice on various stages of the life cycle of the business, including succession planning and passing on family wealth.

Visit the website at: **www.smallbusinesscan.com**

Small Firms Association (SFA)

Acts as the «Voice of Small Business» in Ireland. The aim of the Association is to assist small firms in managing their business, as well as allowing members to interact with fellow members through a members directory, on-line advertising and discussion forum.

Visit the website at: **www.sfa.ie**

Social Welfare

Visit **www.welfare.ie** for information on the Department of Social Protection. The Department formulates appropriate social protection policies and administers and manages the delivery of statutory and non-statutory schemes and services.

T

The Society of Trust and Estate Practitioners (STEP) is the leading worldwide professional body for practitioners in the fields of trusts, estates and related issues. STEP members help families plan their long-term financial future, facilitating good stewardship and financial planning across future generations. STEP members also help families comply with the often complex law and tax rules surrounding trusts, estates and inheritance.

Visit the website at: **www.step.org**

Deloitte offices in ireland

Dublin

Deloitte & Touche House

Earlsfort Terrace

Dublin 2

Telephone: 353 (0)1 4172200

Fax: 353 (0)1 4172300

Cork

City Chambers

No. 6 Lapps Quay

Cork

Telephone: 353 (21) 4907000

Fax: 353 (21) 4907001

Limerick

Charlotte Quay

Limerick

Telephone: 353 (61) 418577

Fax: 353 (61) 418310

Deloitte.

INDEX

Q

R

S

Designed and typeset in Ireland by The Book Producers
Printed and bound in Ireland by The Varsity Press Group

www.thevarsitypress.com